Say's Law and the Keynesian Revolution

Say's Law and the Keynesian Revolution

How Macroeconomic Theory Lost its Way

Steven Kates

Chief Economist, Australian Chamber of Commerce and Industry

Edward Elgar

Cheltenham, UK • Northampton, MA, USA

Published by
Edward Elgar Publishing Limited
The Lypiatts
15 Lansdown Road
Cheltenham
Glos GL50 2JA
UK

Edward Elgar Publishing, Inc.
William Pratt House
9 Dewey Court
Northampton
Massachusetts 01060
USA

Paperback edition 2009

A catalogue record for this book
is available from the British Library

Library of Congress Cataloguing in Publication Data

Kates, Steven, 1948–
    Say's Law and the Keynesian revolution : how macroeconomic theory
lost its way / Steven Kates.
    Includes bibliographical references.
    1. Say, Jean Baptiste, 1767–1832. 2. Keynes, John Maynard,
1883–1946. 3. Markets. 4. Demand. 5. Keynesian economics.
6. Macroeconomic—History. I. Title.
HB105.S25K37   1998
330.15'3—dc21   97–44511
                                                              CIP

ISBN 978 1 85898 748 4 (cased)
ISBN 978 1 84844 826 1 (paperback)

Contents

Acknowledgements

I have incurred many debts in researching and writing this work on Say's Law.

I owe, first of all, an immense debt of gratitude to my PhD supervisor, Mr John King. It was he who first guided me into the issue of Say's Law and the Keynesian Revolution, and for this alone I will remain forever grateful. But he has also provided me with encouragement and guidance during the many years it has taken to bring this to completion. His patience, diligence and good humour, but also his strategic direction, have been invaluable.

I owe a debt almost as great to Professor Mark Blaug of the University of Exeter and Emeritus Professor at the London School of Economics. Over a number of years of correspondence, he has asked the difficult questions which have required the most detailed analytical thought. There are many passages in this final work which are far better than they would have been had it not been for his interest and assistance. A critical eye with a measure of sympathy is a rare combination. I feel myself very fortunate that Professor Blaug took the trouble to reply to my requests for guidance on what were, I fear, the all too frequent occasions that I asked.

I owe an extensive debt of gratitude to Michael Schneider of La Trobe University and Ray Petridis of Murdoch University, whose wise counsel and kind friendship have helped me through many difficult periods. Their time freely given in providing me with assistance and advice is deeply appreciated.

I would also like to express my deepest appreciation to Professor Willie Brown of Cambridge University for his instrumental role in providing me with the opportunity to come to Cambridge as a Visiting Scholar. It was only through his kind and generous assistance that I was able to undertake my researches in the Modern Archive at King's College. I would also like to express my appreciation to Jackie Cox, the archivist at the Modern Archive, for her invaluable assistance.

I also owe a special debt of gratitude to my employer, Mr Ian Spicer, the former Chief Executive of the Australian Chamber of Commerce and Industry, who not only provided the opportunity for me to complete this work, but insisted that I take the time needed to get it done. His kindness and consideration have been invaluable. Without his generous support this work could never have been finished.

But the greatest debt of all is owed to my wife, Susie, whose support has been total. I am too aware of the time I have taken in completing this work, but her willingness to put up with my long hours of involvement has been absolute. My children, Benjamin and Joshua, have also had to endure these long periods of work and their patient willingness to make allowances for my time away is deeply appreciated.

Lastly, however, this book is dedicated in love and gratitude to my parents, Ben and Eva Kates, as the smallest possible measure of thanks for all they have done.

List of Abbreviations

The following abbreviations are used for the collected works and papers of John Maynard Keynes. The volume number in the *Collected Writings* is shown in the text as part of the bibliographic reference.

CW: J.M. Keynes, *The Collected Writings of John Maynard Keynes*, ed. Donald Moggridge, London: Macmillan.

KP: Keynes's Papers, Modern Archive, King's College Library, Cambridge, UK.

Introduction

So that there can be no doubt about the intent of this work, it should be understood from the start that the central argument in what follows is that, because John Maynard Keynes in his *General Theory of Employment, Interest and Money* misunderstood and misrepresented Say's Law, an analytical framework, which pre-Keynesian economists had rightly understood as a fallacy, was placed at the very centre of macroeconomic analysis. This is Keynes's most enduring legacy and it is a legacy which has disfigured economic theory to this day.

Say's Law is the proposition that failure of effective demand does not cause recession. While a number of paths to this conclusion were adopted by economists throughout the nineteenth and early twentieth centuries, it was to demonstrate this one conclusion that the arguments were marshalled. The *General Theory*, being a book about the importance of effective demand failure in determining the level of output and employment, is therefore a book-length attempt to refute Say's Law. That this was the issue was made clear by Joan Robinson, who wrote:

> The old orthodoxy, against which the Keynesian revolution was raised, was based on Say's Law – there cannot be a deficiency of demand. (1976: 121)

John Stuart Mill states the terms of the original debate in Book III Chapter XIV of his *Principles*. This is the chapter containing Mill's discussion of Say's Law. There Mill wrote:

> Because this phenomenon of over-supply, and consequent inconvenience of loss to the producer or dealer, may exist in the case of any one commodity whatever, many persons, including some distinguished political economists, have thought that it may exist with regard to all commodities; that there may be a general over-production of wealth; a supply of commodities in the aggregate surpassing the demand; and a consequent depressed condition of all classes of producers. ([1871] 1921: 556–7)

The central issue in the debates over Say's Law was thus whether recessions might be due to 'a supply of commodities in the aggregate surpassing the demand', that is, whether recessions are caused by deficient effective demand. The answer, according to Say's Law, was no. Moreover, as the quotation from Mill also shows, Say's Law also denies the possibility of 'a general over-

1

production of wealth', which is the same phenomenon as a deficiency of demand. Demand deficiency and over-production are two ways of describing the same phenomenon: too much production relative to the demand for it. It was this possibility which Say's Law was formulated to deny.

Say's Law was based on a particular way of understanding how economies work. It was based on the appreciation that the creation of value added is the basis for demand. The sale of goods and services to the market is the source of the income from which purchases are financed. It is, of course, also possible to finance purchases through borrowing from others who have earned incomes, or for a government to tax income and spend the proceeds. But the fundamental point was that it is sales proceeds from production which enable one to buy from others.[1] For an individual in an exchange economy, only by selling to the market will one be able to buy from the market. To buy one must first sell. This is what Mill means in the passage cited in the *General Theory* (*CW* VII: 18):[2]

> What [is it] which constitutes the means of payment for commodities. It is simply commodities. Each person's means of paying for the productions of other people consists of those which he himself possesses. All sellers are inevitably and *ex vi termini* buyers. (Ibid.: 557–8)

There are thus two aspects of Say's Law: the conclusion that recessions are not due to failure of effective demand and the profound observation, upon which that conclusion is based, that demand is constituted by supply. The conclusion is reached because, if demand is constituted by supply, then what might superficially appear to be demand failure is in fact due to problems on the side of supply. The apparent failure of demand, which is how recession is perceived by sellers, is in fact due to factors which have caused the production process to break down. Demand failure is a symptom, not a cause.

Keynes, in the *General Theory*, did not put matters in quite this way. The principle of effective demand is discussed at length while Say's Law is mentioned briefly. In a short exposition, they are related in terms of the aggregate demand and supply curves (*CW* VII: 25–6). There the classical proposition, that demand is

---

[1] Or to state the same thing in reverse, it is only if one's potential buyers have themselves been able to earn incomes from selling what they have produced that they are able to buy what is presented for sale.

[2] The quotation as found in the *General Theory* is not quite exact and is in fact as found in the Marshalls' *Economics of Industry* ([1879] 1881: 154) and in a form slightly altered from the Marshalls, in Hobson and Mummery's *Physiology of Industry* (1889: 102n). Hobson and Mummery acknowledge that they had taken the quotation from the Marshalls, but Keynes cites J.S. Mill's *Principles* as the source (*CW* VII: 18n). This raises a number of issues, not least of which is the question of whether Keynes actually ever read Mill, which is doubtful. That the quotation was taken from either Marshall or Hobson and Mummery was recognised by Davis and Casey (1977: 329). Patinkin (1978: 341n) argues that, even so, there is no reason to believe that Keynes did not read the original, but of course, there is equally no reason to believe he did. Kahn (1984: 11) takes it for granted that Keynes took the quotation from Hobson and Mummery.

constituted by supply, is turned into the phrase 'supply creates its own demand', and the conclusion that recessions are not due to demand failure is turned into the proposition that total sales are always equal to the total cost of production,[3] which, in effect, states that everything produced is bought. Keynes then makes his judgement on Say's Law, which was to become almost universally accepted and which follows naturally from his interpretation, namely that 'Say's Law...is equivalent to the proposition that there is no obstacle to full employment' (ibid.: 26). Much of the subsequent discussion of the accuracy of Keynes's understanding of Say's Law has tended to revolve around the issue of whether unemployment and recession are consistent with a belief in Say's Law.[4] Say's Law was made to seem the very foundation for a policy of *laissez-faire*.

Where we find Keynes dealing with the fundamental meaning of Say's Law, no mention of Say or his law of markets is found. The key sentences to understanding the *General Theory* as an attempt to refute Say's Law are these:

> The idea that we can safely neglect the aggregate demand function is fundamental to the Ricardian economics, which underlie what we have been taught for more than a century. Malthus, indeed, had vehemently opposed Ricardo's doctrine that it was impossible for effective demand to be deficient; but vainly. For, since Malthus was unable to explain clearly (apart from an appeal to the facts of common observation) how and why effective demand could be deficient or excessive, he failed to furnish an alternative construction; and Ricardo conquered England as completely as the Holy Inquisition conquered Spain. Not only was his theory accepted by the city, by statesmen and by the academic world. But controversy ceased; the other point of view completely disappeared; it ceased to be discussed. The great puzzle of Effective Demand with which Malthus had wrestled vanished from the economic literature. (Ibid.: 32)

Thus, in the passage where Keynes explains that he is attempting to refute the belief that it is 'impossible for effective demand to be deficient', he makes no mention of Say's Law. He instead describes this belief as 'Ricardo's doctrine'. Yet it is 'Ricardo's doctrine', as Keynes calls it, which is the closest parallel to a proper interpretation of Say's Law found in the *General Theory*.

---

[3] The exact words are: 'the aggregate demand price of output as a whole is equal to its aggregate supply price for all volumes of output' (*CW* VII: 26).

[4] For example, more than half a century after the publication of the *General Theory*, Blaug (1991a: ix), in his introduction to a collection of readings on J.-B. Say, feels it necessary to point out that Say's Law 'never implied any denial that depressions would occur and that when they did, they might last for several years'. Kates (1997a: 239), in summing up areas of agreement in the *Eastern Economic Journal* symposium on Say's Law, also felt it necessary to point out that 'classical economists understood perfectly well that prolonged recessions and involuntary unemployment are a fact of economic life'. Each participant in the symposium had dealt with what is an extraordinarily enduring myth.

FUNDAMENTAL ISSUES

What will be shown in the following chapters is that, prior to the publication of the *General Theory*, the law of markets was a statement which denied that demand deficiency/over-production was a valid explanation of recession. It was not, however, a denial that recessions could occur. With the publication of the *General Theory*, what became accepted was that a belief in the validity of Say's Law entailed an assumption of full employment, in the sense that there was no obstacle to full employment. Supply created its own demand, which was translated by Keynes to mean that total production costs are always covered by total revenues earned. According to Keynes, classical economists assumed that all savings would always be invested, implying that variations in the demand for money never occurred and therefore never affected the demand for goods. In short, acceptance of Say's Law meant that one assumed that 'the economic system was always operating up to its full capacity' (*CW* VII: xxxv). Say's Law thus ruled out the possibility of recession.

What therefore remains the greatest irony is that Say's Law, far from assuming full employment, was instead the basis for the classical theory of the cycle. Rather than Say's Law being a denial of the possibility of recession, it was actually part of the explanation for it. Recessions were not caused by a failure of demand, but rather were due to problems associated with the structure of demand relative to the structure of supply. Demand, according to Say's Law, was constituted by supply, that is, by the sale receipts received from selling one's production. If one could not sell then one could not buy. The reason for a failure to sell was that one had miscalculated about what others wished to buy. If production miscalculations occurred in one part of the economy during the expansion phase of the cycle, then excess stocks of unsold goods would be the result, and incomes lower than anticipated would be earned. In consequence, demand for other products would be lower than was originally anticipated, and the economy would contract.

Only two books devoted exclusively to Say's Law have been written since the publication of the *General Theory*. The first of these is Thomas Sowell's, *Say's Law: An Historical Analysis* (1972). Although Sowell is critical of Keynes, in the first line of the first chapter, Say's Law is related to 'supply creates its own demand' (1972: 3), correctly indicating that Sowell does not intend to challenge the Keynesian explanation. While there are many crucially important points made by Sowell in regard to the surrounding issues, as will be shown, he failed to understand the core meaning of Say's Law.

The second book was by W.H. Hutt (1974). Its title, *A Rehabilitation of Say's Law*, clearly indicates that a different agenda from Sowell's is intended. It is Hutt's view that, because of the understanding provided by Say's Law, 'the non-Keynesians of the inter-war period had a deeper insight into the origins of chronic unemployment and depression than the overwhelming majority of today's professional economists' (1974: 2). As will be shown, while Hutt had a correct understanding of the processes involved in Say's Law, he does not properly relate his theoretical understanding to the causes of recession.

In the professional journals, the single most influential article has been Becker's and Baumol's 'The Classical Economic Theory: The Outcome of the Discussion' (1952), which was a summing up of a journal debate conducted during the late 1940s and early 1950s. The importance of this article lies in its introduction into economic theory of the three-part division of Say's Law into 'Walras' Law', 'Say's Identity' and 'Say's Equality'. It is these terms which have become the basis for the modern interpretation of Say's Law. While these terms will be more fully explained as part of the evolution of the modern interpretation of Say's Law, it is important to have some familiarity with them as modern discussion of classical theory often conceives of the issues in their terms.

'Walras' Law' generally means that total demand, including the demand for money, is equal to total supply, including money. This is merely a definition and has no economic implications. 'Say's Identity' refers to the proposition that the total demand for goods is always equal to the total supply of goods. Therefore, variations in the demand for money do not affect the level of economic activity. It is this proposition which is generally seen as the meaning of Say's Law contained in the *General Theory*. Finally, 'Say's Equality' means that while the demand for goods may move out of equilibrium with the supply of goods, the processes of the economy will rapidly bring the two back into equilibrium. This proposition is generally seen as the meaning of Say's Law held by classical economists.[5]

The significant point is that the classical meaning of Say's Law and the modern are very different. And in this it is important to recognise that, although there is a modern meaning to Say's Law, if it is not what classical economists meant by it, then it has no intrinsic value as a means to understand pre-Keynesian economic theory. Say's Law should have only the meaning attached to it by economists who believed it was a valid principle of economic analysis. Sowell (1972: 5, 37), for example, argues that the modern interpretation is as valid as any other. Modern interpretations, which do not explain what classical economists actually meant, may have value in their own terms, but they should not be confused with the classical meaning of the law of markets.

In summary, the law of markets, as understood by classical economists, denied the relevance of variations in effective demand as an explanation for variations in economic activity. Since the publication of the *General Theory*, the law of markets has been supplanted in the mainstream literature by what is now referred to as Say's Law, the practical significance of which, Keynes argued, was that it assumed that involuntary unemployment was theoretically impossible and that the major cause of recessions was variations in effective demand.

---

[5] Aside from the original Becker and Baumol article, a very thorough discussion of these concepts may be found in Blaug (1985: 149–60). Sowell (1972: 34–6) and Baumol (1977) also provide good overviews of these issues.

CHAPTER OUTLINE

The following chapter outline provides an overview of the argument developed in the text.

Chapter 1: Say's Law in the Structure of the *General Theory*

This chapter discusses Keynes's interpretation of Say's Law as found primarily in the *General Theory*. Keynes described Say's Law as the classical 'axiom of parallels', whose acceptance meant classical economists were unable to recognise an entity called 'involuntary unemployment'. Because of their acceptance of Say's Law, Keynes wrote, classical economists always assumed the existence of full employment. They were therefore incapable of explaining the existence of involuntary unemployment because they always assumed none existed.

Chapter 2: J.-B. Say, James Mill and Robert Torrens

This chapter discusses the development of the law of markets, focusing on J.-B. Say, James Mill and Robert Torrens. The fundamental question is, what was the issue at hand which led to their writing as they did? For Say it was the complaint often heard during recessions that lack of money was the cause of poor sales. For James Mill, the issue was to refute William Spence, who had argued that demand failure was the cause of recession. Torrens, stimulated by the writings of Sismondi and Malthus, completed the development of the concepts underlying the law of markets. It was Torrens who first employed Say's Law to explain how a downturn in one part of the economy due to business miscalculation could lead to an economy-wide recession.

Chapter 3: David Ricardo

Ricardo's importance is due to his refutation of Malthus, who had put forward an over-saving argument. Ricardo's position made no advance on that of James Mill, but his significance today lies in his long-running debate with Malthus on the possibility of general gluts. Understanding Ricardo's debate with Malthus provides a key to understanding the major issues involved. It also provides an important link between the Keynesian refutation of Say's Law and the original general glut debate, because, as will be shown, it was the influence of Malthus which led Keynes to focus on the issue of Say's Law and effective demand.

Chapter 4: John Stuart Mill

This chapter provides an overview of what many commentators consider the best classical explanation of the law of markets. There are two main sources of Mill's view: his second essay in *Some Unsettled Questions of Political Economy* and his *Principles of Political Economy*. Mill's aim in both works was to demonstrate that demand deficiency was an invalid explanation of recession. Mill also bent over backwards to demonstrate that the issue was not whether recessions might or might not occur, but only whether demand deficiency was a valid explanation of recessions when they did occur.

Chapter 5: Say's Law in English Classical Theory

The chapter commences with a discussion of the matrix of ideas which constituted the law of markets as understood by classical economists. From these principles, the theories of major late nineteenth-century and early twentieth-century economists are provided, showing that their theories of the business cycle are not only consistent with the law of markets but in fact based on it. The aim of this chapter is to provide examples of the extent to which Say's Law permeated the thinking of classical economists yet did not prevent their recognising the fact of unemployment and the problems of the business cycle.

Chapter 6: Say's Law in the Classical Theory of the Business Cycle

This chapter discusses specific works by Henry Clay, Frederick Lavington, Wilhelm Röpke and Gottfried Haberler to show in greater detail how Say's Law was embedded in the classical theory of the business cycle. Clay's widely used text, *Economics: An Introduction for the General Reader*, provides a clear exposition of an economy based on reciprocal demand where demand is constituted by supply. But while the theory presented is based on Say's Law, Clay also shows how an economy can and does go into recession due to the manner in which it operates.

Lavington's *The Trade Cycle* provides a concise statement of the theory of the business cycle which is shown to be embedded in a proper understanding of Say's Law. What makes this work more significant is that Robert Clower cites it as presenting what Keynes really meant (1989: 26). Lavington's theory of the cycle thus provides a link with Clower's reinterpretation of Keynes and with his formulation of what he has termed 'Say's Principle'.

Röpke's *Crises and Cycles* was the last major work published in the English language on business cycle theory before the publication of the *General Theory*. In this work, Röpke explicitly refers to the insights of Say and Ricardo in providing the first understanding of the nature of the business cycle. He then shows how an understanding of Say's Law prevents one from making the error of believing that depressions can be due to over-production or over-saving.

Haberler's *Prosperity and Depression* was a compendium of the theories of the cycle held by economists in the 1930s. It is a remarkable document in that it was for the most part written during the same period that Keynes was writing his *General Theory* and thus provides an in-depth account of the theory of the cycle which was about to be abandoned. Examination of *Prosperity and Depression* will show that pre-Keynesian theories of the cycle were based on the law of markets and were similar in character to the theories developed by the early classical writers.

Chapter 7: Keynes's Discovery of Say's Law

This chapter reviews the sequence of events which led Keynes to attack Say's Law. The major reason for this focus was his discovery, in 1932, of Say's Law through his reading of Malthus's correspondence with Ricardo. It was this which led Keynes to develop three concepts which, at least in principle, would mean that demand would not necessarily be equal to supply. These concepts were: the marginal propensity to consume, the liquidity preference theory of interest, and the marginal efficiency of capital.

Chapter 8: Influences Deepening Keynes's Understanding of Say's Law

After Keynes received the germ of his idea on Say's Law he did additional research on these issues. From citations in the *General Theory*, we know that Keynes read both Malthus and Hobson. Two other possible influences on the development of his concept are undocumented. They were Fred Taylor, who had coined the term 'Say's Law', and Harlan McCracken, who had written a book on the then-neglected Malthus and the law of markets.

Chapter 9: Development of Post-*General Theory* Interpretations of Say's Law

This chapter looks at the progress of the concept underlying Say's Law following the publication of the *General Theory*. There are two streams to this development. The first stream follows from Keynes's definition of Say's Law, which was that supply creates its own demand. The second is from the publication of Lange's 1942 article which ultimately resulted in the development of the concepts 'Walras' Law', 'Say's Equality' and 'Say's Identity' by Becker and Baumol in 1952.

Chapter 10: Modern Interpretations of Say's Law

Following Becker's and Baumol's landmark article on Say's Law, there was a convergence of the Keynes and Lange streams. This chapter deals with major statements on the meaning of Say's Law from the early 1950s until Thomas Sowell's statement in the *New Palgrave* in 1987. The aim is to demonstrate that the modern concept of Say's Law has little relationship to the original concept of the law of markets, which was one of the most important theoretical constructs within classical economic theory.

Chapter 11: Critics of the Modern Interpretation

While there have been differences of view on the meaning of Say's Law since the publication of the *General Theory*, the interpretations originating from Keynes on the one hand and Becker and Baumol on the other have come to dominate the modern understanding. This chapter outlines the views of a number of critics of the modern interpretation which provide a genuine link with the classical meaning of the law of markets.

POINTS TO NOTE

There are a number of points which should be borne in mind.

Firstly, and perhaps perpetuating a solecism, the term 'classical economists' will be used, generally speaking, to refer to those economists who were educated prior to the publication of the *General Theory* and who for the most part understood and were disciplined by adherence to the law of markets. The term 'modern economists' will refer to economists who have learned their trade since the publication of the *General Theory*.

Secondly, 'supply creates its own demand' was a form of words formulated by Keynes, but there are echoes of these words found within the writings of various classical writers. A number of possible sources of Keynes's form of words will be noted as part of the text.

Lastly, all passages containing italicised words are as in the original unless otherwise stated.

1. Say's Law in the Structure of the *General Theory*

Say's Law stands in an odd position in the *General Theory*. The discussion of Say's Law was unmistakably an important part of what Keynes wanted to say. Yet, as important to Keynes as it obviously was, it is, to all appearances, merely an incident in the history of economics. In terms of the economic theory which Keynes outlined in the remainder of the *General Theory*, his reference to Say's Law could have been omitted with no loss of continuity: one can make every point without mentioning Say's Law.[1] But in the context of the *General Theory*, and as part of the process in generating a revolution in economic thought, the citation of Say's Law did have a crucial rhetorical role. Keynes used Say's Law to distinguish his own economic theory from those of others, arguing that, because most of his contemporaries had tacitly accepted Say's Law, they were prevented from fully understanding the actual circumstances of the economy around them.

What Keynes argued was that involuntary unemployment was a formal impossibility in the economic theories of his 'classical' contemporaries, precisely because they had tacitly accepted Say's Law as valid. This represented a quite extraordinary attack on the economics profession.[2] Nor was this a criticism from someone who could be ignored. This was an attack from within the citadel, from the most famous and influential economist of his time. If his accusation were true, there could be no more devastating criticism made against economists and economics as a science. A discipline which purported to deal with economic matters, but which did not accept the reality of economic fluctuations, or acknowledge and explain the existence of involuntary unemployment, would undoubtedly have been of little use. No criticism of it would have been too harsh.

It is thus important to be clear that this was precisely what Keynes meant when he stated that classical economists assumed the validity of Say's Law. It was not

---

[1] Indeed, macroeconomic textbooks written today, even the most Keynesian in orientation, generally omit reference to Say's Law.

[2] Dennis Robertson was clearly baffled by this implication. After reading through a draft section of the *General Theory* in March 1935, he wrote to Keynes in some dismay, 'But what puzzles me now is that you now seem to me to be saying that Marshall, Pigou etc....deny that general industrial depression can exist. I don't think you *can* be saying this, and I must have somehow misunderstood you again' (*CW* XIII: 520).

just rhetorical window dressing. It was an attack meant to be taken literally; it provided the linchpin for Keynes's entire attack on classical economics. According to Keynes, it was precisely because of its tacit acceptance of Say's Law that classical economic theory was incapable of explaining the existence of prolonged large-scale involuntary unemployment. Keynes argued that, because of their acceptance of Say's Law, classical economists could not make sense of unemployment which occurred for any reason other than excessive wage rates. Even while they were observers of the mass unemployment of the 1930s, it was Keynes's contention that his classical contemporaries could not encompass within their theories what it was they were observing. Keynes concluded that the mass unemployment which existed during the Great Depression was an impossibility according to the theories employed by his contemporaries.[3]

STRUCTURE OF KEYNES'S ARGUMENT

Keynes constructs his argument as follows. He first states that the classical economists had omitted the notion of involuntary unemployment. This is of itself a most peculiar charge since Pigou, for one, had been using the very phrase 'involuntary unemployment' for two decades by the time of the publication of the *General Theory*.[4] Nevertheless, Keynes believes himself able to argue that classical economists had not recognised the existence of this type of unemployment.[5] He writes: 'We must now define the third category of unemployment, namely "involuntary" unemployment in the strict sense, the

---

[3] It is interesting to contrast the approach adopted by Harrod ([1951] 1972), Skidelsky (1992) and Moggridge (1992) in their biographies of Keynes. There is no mention of Say's Law in Moggridge's work, despite his having discussed the succession between the *Treatise* and the *General Theory* (see Chapter 21). Harrod similarly makes no mention of Say's Law. On the other hand, Skidelsky (1992: 550) understands just how important Say's Law is, writing: 'The attack on Say's Law starts on p. 18; and the rest of the *General Theory* is devoted to showing that Say's Law is false'.

[4] See Pigou (1914: 14) for an early statement on the involuntariness of unemployment. In 1921, Pigou ([1921] 1923: 36) was even more emphatic, writing 'unemployment is not voluntary, but notoriously involuntary. Workpeople in periods of industrial depression do not *choose* to be out of work. They are compelled by circumstances wholly outside their control'. Kahn (1984: 192–3) discusses Pigou's use of 'involuntary unemployment' and even suggests that he may have coined the term. Pigou's close associate, Dennis Robertson (1915: 210), had also mentioned involuntary unemployment prior to the publication of the *General Theory*.

[5] See Hutchison (1978: 129) for a discussion of involuntary unemployment in pre-Keynesian theory. Coddington (1983: 27) further points out that the pre-Keynesian literature already included four classifications of unemployment: frictional, seasonal, cyclical and structural, noting that 'cyclical' was replaced by 'demand-deficient' unemployment following publication of the *General Theory*.

possibility of which the classical theory does not admit' (*CW* VII: 15). Keynes then provides his own convoluted definition of 'involuntary unemployment':[6]

> Men are involuntarily unemployed if, in the event of a small rise in the price of wage-goods relatively to the money-wage, both the aggregate supply of labour willing to work for the current money-wage and the aggregate demand for it at that wage would be greater than the existing volume of employment. (Ibid.: 15)

Keynes states that the classical theory of unemployment if 'realistically interpreted, corresponds to the absence of "involuntary" unemployment' as he has defined it (ibid.). Classical economic theory, he says, is of no use in dealing with involuntary unemployment because it tends to deal with the allocation of resources under conditions of full employment (ibid.: 16). With full employment built in from the start, involuntary unemployment cannot be incorporated into classical theory. As he wrote:

> classical theory...is best regarded as a theory of distribution in conditions of full employment. So long as the classical postulates hold good, unemployment, which is in the above sense involuntary, cannot occur.... Obviously...if the classical theory is only applicable to the case of full employment, it is fallacious to apply it to the problems of involuntary unemployment – if there be such a thing (and who will deny it?). The classical theorists resemble Euclidean geometers in a non-Euclidean world who, discovering that in experience straight lines apparently parallel often meet, rebuke the lines for not keeping straight – as the only remedy for the unfortunate collisions which are occurring. Yet, in truth, there is no remedy except to throw over the *axiom of parallels* and to work out a non-Euclidean geometry. (Ibid.: 16, italics added)

It is the phrase 'axiom of parallels' which links Say's Law structurally with Keynes's argument that classical economists had ignored the existence of involuntary unemployment. After he had explained involuntary unemployment, Keynes turned to deal with Say's Law. In summing up this discussion, Keynes specifies what that 'axiom of parallels' is:

> It is...the assumption of equality between the demand price of output as a whole and its supply price which is to be regarded as the classical theory's 'axiom of parallels'. Granted this, all the rest follows. (Ibid.: 21)

It is not, however, until five pages later that Keynes formally ties this statement to his definition of Say's Law. Here Keynes writes that Say's Law means 'that the

---

[6] In his 1937 article, 'The General Theory of Employment' Keynes, in replying to Jacob Viner's review of the *General Theory* (Viner 1936) and his criticisms of involuntary unemployment, wrote: 'in regard to his criticisms of my definition and treatment of involuntary unemployment, I am ready to agree that this part of my book is particularly open to criticism. I already feel myself in a position to make improvements' (*CW* XIV: 110).

aggregate demand price of output as a whole is equal to its aggregate supply price for all volumes of output' (ibid.: 26).

What makes this argument somewhat confusing is that it is in fact written backwards. If one reverses the order of the argument, it becomes immediately apparent what Keynes is trying to say:

- Say's Law (A) means that the aggregate demand price is equal to the aggregate supply price for all volumes of output (B).
- The assumption of equality between the aggregate demand price of output and its supply price (B) is the classical economists' 'axiom of parallels' (C).
- Because of tacit acceptance of this 'axiom of parallels' (C) by classical economists, involuntary unemployment could not, at least according to their theories, occur (D).

That is, Say's Law (A) implies that involuntary unemployment cannot occur (D). And it was to demonstrate that classical theory is totally impotent in dealing with involuntary unemployment, because full employment is always assumed, that Keynes invoked Say's Law. As he saw it, only frictional and voluntary unemployment were given theoretical recognition (ibid.: 16). Involuntary unemployment, the kind of unemployment associated with cyclical downturns, was, according to Keynes, formally impossible. In Keynes's view, classical theory 'is best regarded as a theory of distribution in conditions of full employment' (ibid.). Or, as he stated in his discussion of Marshall's theory of interest, 'the assumption required is *the usual classical assumption,* that there is *always* full employment' (ibid.: 191, italics added).

Keynes makes this same point in other places. In his 1937 reply to critics, he states that the 'orthodox system' assumes that income is always at the full-employment level (*CW* XIV: 123). Involuntary unemployment is assumed away because the theories employed by classical economists are incapable of dealing with fluctuating levels of employment. Analytically speaking, involuntary unemployment is an impossibility, and Keynes explicitly states this to be due to the acceptance of Say's Law:

> In a system in which the level of money-income is capable of fluctuating, the orthodox theory is one equation short of what is required to give a solution. Undoubtedly the reason why the orthodox system has failed to discover this discrepancy is because it has always tacitly assumed that income *is* given, namely, at the level corresponding to the employment of all the available resources. In other words, it is tacitly assuming that the monetary policy is such as to maintain the rate of interest at that level which is compatible with full employment. It is, therefore, incapable of dealing with the general case where employment is liable to fluctuate....
>
> The orthodox theory would by now have discovered the above defect, if it had not ignored the need for a theory of the supply and demand of output as a whole. I doubt if many modern economists really accept Say's Law that supply creates its own demand. But they have not been aware that they were tacitly assuming it. (Ibid.: 122–3)

In the introduction to the French edition, written in 1939, Keynes states that virtually all economic theory since the time of J.-B. Say has depended on the assumption of full employment. Economists, he notes, could see well enough that there was indeed unemployment, but the theories they used denied the possibility of the very events which they were witnessing. This was again ascribed to their tacit acceptance of Say's Law:

> I believe that economics everywhere up to recent times has been dominated, much more than has been understood, by the doctrines associated with the name of J.-B. Say. It is true that his 'law of markets' has been long abandoned by most economists; but they have not extricated themselves from his basic assumptions and particularly from his fallacy that demand is created by supply. Say was implicitly assuming that the economic system was always operating up to its full capacity, so that a new activity was always in substitution for, and never in addition to, some other activity. Nearly all subsequent economic theory has depended on, in the sense that it has required, this same assumption. Yet a theory so based is clearly incompetent to tackle the problems of unemployment and of the trade cycle. (*CW* VII, xxxv)

Keynes's message was understood and gained acceptance. Sweezy ([1947] 1960: 105), for example, deals comprehensively with Say's Law. He notes that the 'Keynesian attacks, though they appear to be directed against a variety of specific theories, all fall to the ground if the validity of Say's Law is assumed'. Sweezy states that Keynes was attacking economic theorists who, in being guided by their formal theories, and in particular by Say's Law, argued that high and prolonged rates of involuntary unemployment were an 'impossibility':

> [Keynes] was able to demonstrate that his fellow economists, by their unthinking acceptance of Say's Law, were in effect asserting the impossibility of the kind of economic catastrophe through which the world was indubitably passing. (Ibid.: 105)

Hansen, in his *Guide to Keynes*, states that the key issue surrounding Say's Law was the possibility of long-term unemployment. In discussing the background to the *General Theory* he writes:

> As part of this widespread dissatisfaction with the state of economic theory, Say's law in particular was subjected to serious question. But despite numerous attempts, no one [before Keynes] succeeded in making a strong theoretical case against the basic premise that the price system tended automatically to produce full employment. (Hansen 1953: 6)

Dillard ([1948] 1960: 19), in his outline of the *General Theory*, describes the implications of Say's Law in the following terms: 'in an exchange economy, Say's Law means there will always be a sufficient rate of spending to maintain full employment'. Dillard then relates this to the basic theoretical perspective of the classical economists. If there is no involuntary unemployment then, according to Dillard, by definition full employment exists. The classical economists had not acknowledged the existence of involuntary unemployment; therefore unemployment could not exist. As he wrote, 'full employment exists in the absence of involuntary unemployment. In the classical theory, this type of unemployment does not exist' (ibid.: 21).

Pigou (1951: 65), in his retrospective on the *General Theory*, in which he is supposed to have recanted his earlier criticisms of the *General Theory*,[7] finishes with a criticism of Keynes on this very point:

> Nobody before [Keynes], so far as I know, had brought all the relevant factors, real and monetary at once, together in a single formal scheme, through which their interplay could be coherently investigated. His doing so does *not*, to my mind, constitute a revolution. Only if we accept the myth – as I regard it – that earlier economists ignored the part played by money, and, even when discussing fluctuations in employment, tacitly assumed that there weren't any, would that word be appropriate.

In his *The Age of Keynes*, Robert Lekachman (1967: 72) is explicit on the meaning of Say's Law and the role it played in classical economic analysis. He leaves no doubt that, to classical economists, general unemployment was theoretically impossible:

> The older theory which Keynes attacked was founded on an old generalisation, the nineteenth-century French economist Jean-Baptiste Say's Law of Markets. Often summarised in the aphorism...'Supply creates its own demand', Say's Law affirmed the impossibility of general over-production of goods, or general 'glut', in Say's words. Equally impossible therefore was general unemployment.

In his *Keynes and After*, Michael Stewart (1972: 49) similarly leaves no room for doubt as to the implications of acceptance of Say's Law for classical economists. In stating the theory of employment in the 1920s and 1930s, he wrote:

> First, and most basically, full employment was assumed to be part of the natural order of things. This assumption derived from Say's Law. Say's Law stated that supply created its own demand – that the process of creating an article also resulted in the creation of just enough purchasing power to buy that article. Therefore there could be no general surplus of articles, or of the labour employed in making the articles.

Victoria Chick (1983: 6) repeats the same argument: 'Keynes was anxious to refute a particular manifestation of orthodox theory, namely Say's Law and the theorem which derives from it: that involuntary unemployment is impossible'.

And as recently as 1991, Paul Davidson (1991: 7) includes in his *Controversies in Post-Keynesian Economics* a discussion of Say's Law which could have been taken directly from the *General Theory*:[8]

---

[7] Collard (1983: 127) and Littleboy (1990: 107) believe Pigou was far from capitulating.

The neoclassical belief that a free enterprise system inevitably generates full employment and prosperity was grounded in an old economic proposition known as Say's Law. In 1803, a French economist, Jean-Baptiste Say, wrote that 'products always exchange for products'. In 1808, the English economist, James Mill, translated Say's dictum as 'supply creates its own demand' – and this phraseology has since been established in economics as Say's Law. It was this economic law which Keynes railed against in his *General Theory*.

In plain terms we can explain what 'supply creates its own demand' means as follows. People produce – that is, supply – things to the market in order to earn income to buy (demand) other things from the market. Accordingly, Mill's interpretation of Say's Law implied that there could never be a depression, for the very act of production created sufficient income to purchase everything that was produced. Equally, there could never be unemployment since businessmen seeking profits would always be able to find a sufficient demand to sell any output produced by workers.

The implication that an acceptance of the validity of Say's Law implied the belief that involuntary unemployment was impossible is one of the most enduring legacies of the Keynesian Revolution.

SAY'S LAW AND *LAISSEZ-FAIRE*

The issue in regard to Say's Law is not *laissez-faire*. *Laissez-faire* is about policy, and Keynes was dealing with economic theory. Keynes believed he was moving to a higher level of theoretical abstraction in raising the issue of Say's Law. The question raised by Keynes was not whether *laissez-faire* is the best approach to dealing with economic matters but why economists thought this was so. He was, in effect, asking this question: what is it that economists believe that makes them accept *laissez-faire* as the optimal approach to the formation of economic policy? And the answer he gave was that, because economists believed Say's Law to be valid, they were always assuming the existence of full employment, even during periods of mass unemployment. In a fully employed economy, Keynes found *laissez-faire* policies perfectly acceptable (*CW* VII: 21).

Keynes's attack on Say's Law must therefore be understood as other than just an attack on *laissez-faire*. Had Keynes meant to criticise a hands-off attitude to economic management, he could have focused on *laissez-faire* specifically and left it at that. But Keynes meant something more. He meant to attack the very theories of his contemporaries which, he argued, left involuntary unemployment a theoretical impossibility. He wished to show that the conceptual apparatus of his contemporaries meant that it was impossible to explain the existence of persistent periods of mass unemployment, and that they were therefore incapable of providing solutions to this problem. Keynes believed that economists were prevented from understanding the causes and nature of unemployment because they accepted the validity of Say's Law. The point behind Keynes's invocation of

---

[8] Cf. Davidson (1994: 14–17).

Say's Law was to attack the economic theories of his contemporaries, not just to attack the notion of *laissez-faire*.

If Keynes had merely stated that his contemporaries had ignored the possibility of insufficient demand as a cause of economic downturn, he would have been saying something far less momentous. This would have been one more possible explanation for the Great Depression, which could have been assessed against other possible explanations.[9] But Keynes went well beyond this. His allegation was that the economic theories developed by his contemporaries always assumed full employment, and therefore that mainstream economics did not even have a theory of unemployment. Keynes's allegation was that the economists of his time had no explanation for the breadth and depth of the unemployment which the world had so recently experienced. Keynes was therefore saying that he was not just bringing forward another explanation for depressions, but was in fact introducing into mainstream economic theory the *first* such explanation.[10]

The implication was that Keynes was providing mainstream economics with what it did not previously have: a theoretical structure capable of recognising and explaining the existence of unemployment which was neither frictional nor voluntary. It was this allegation which gave the *General Theory* its revolutionary tone. Once this claim was accepted as a valid statement of fact, it led, within the matter of a decade, to the abandonment of an economic tradition of business cycle analysis which had been patiently developed over a period of a century and a half.

To refute Say's Law, Keynes had to explain how demand failure could, of itself, lead to a fall in economic activity and an increase in unemployment. Classical theory was in no doubt that variations in the demand for money could lead to variations in economic activity (Becker and Baumol 1952: 373–4; O'Brien 1975: 161–2). Since there was general acceptance that the purchasing power to buy what had been produced was in the hands of potential buyers, a theory of demand failure had to show that what was missing was a willingness to buy what had been produced. This is what Keynes set out to do. A full discussion of Keynes's reasoning in the *General Theory* is found in Appendix A.

CLASSICAL AND KEYNESIAN INTERPRETATIONS CONTRASTED

Say's Law, as understood by classical economists, was the proposition that recessions and unemployment are never due to demand failure but could be due to any number of other factors. Keynes recognised that Say's Law meant demand failure could not occur, but interpreted that to mean that therefore recession and unemployment could not occur, at least not in theory. Yet *only* if one assumes that

---

[9] This is what Haberler's *Prosperity and Depression* (1937) attempted to do.

[10] Keynes did acknowledge that there had been others who had had similar ideas to his own, but none of these were part of the mainstream.

demand failure is the only possible cause of unemployment would the Keynesian proposition be equivalent to the classical.

However faulty Keynes's explanation of Say's Law might have been, he did direct his criticisms at its correct meaning: the *General Theory* is an attempt to prove that demand failure can cause recession and unemployment. But Keynes wished to do more than just introduce one further possible cause of recession. To add to the apparent urgency of his message he made the impossibility of involuntary unemployment a direct implication of the acceptance of Say's Law. Keynes therefore dealt with two intertwined propositions. The first he called 'Say's Law', which he defined as the proposition that total demand always equals total supply, with the direct implication that involuntary unemployment is theoretically impossible. The second proposition he referred to as 'Ricardo's doctrine', which was 'the idea that we can safely neglect the aggregate demand function' (*CW* VII: 32). 'Ricardo's doctrine' is implied by Keynes's definition of Say's Law, but Say's Law, as understood by classical economists, did not imply that involuntary unemployment was impossible. The classical position was that involuntary unemployment was not only possible, but occurred often, and with serious consequences for the unemployed. There was no implication in classical theory that recessions could not endure for extended periods of time or that those who were unemployed chose to be so. What Say's Law affirmed was that, when recession and unemployment did occur, it was due not to a failure of demand, but to other factors. This position was succinctly put by Baumol (1997: 227):

> It is clear that [classical economists] did not use the Law of Markets to deny the occurrence of unemployment, and that the notion of a theory of unemployment would have been anathema to them only if it were based on a model requiring the occurrence of a universal glut of commodities.

Keynes's distinction between Say's Law and Ricardo's doctrine did, however, serve the useful purpose of permitting him to argue the possibility of demand failure while also giving this possibility more importance than it would otherwise have had. The consequence was the 'Keynesian Revolution', which captured economic theory more firmly than the theories of Ricardo ever did. Indeed, the ultimate effect of Keynes's attack on Say's Law was virtually to obliterate the classical theory of the business cycle which had developed over the course of more than a century and to establish, in its place, fluctuations in demand as the single most important consideration in the new field of macroeconomics.[11] Yet the issues surrounding Say's Law go to the very heart of a proper understanding of how an economy operates[12] and the measures which might successfully be taken to reduce the level of unemployment and shorten the length of recession.

---

[11] Haberler (1941: 248n) credits Frisch with coining the term 'macroeconomics' in an article published in 1933.

[12] Cf. Hutt (1974: 10) and Clower ([1973] 1984c: 146).

THE POINT AT ISSUE

The next five chapters deal with the classical understanding of Say's Law through to the publication of the *General Theory*; that is, from its initial development by Say and James Mill to its final discussion just as the *General Theory* was being published. The aim is to show that Say's Law was an integral part of pre-Keynesian economic thinking, and that the modern interpretation that has become entrenched is far different from the concept which was thrashed out in intense discussion at the start of the nineteenth century.

Importantly, what will be shown is that the theory as it emerged was fundamentally different from the theory as it was interpreted by Keynes. It will be shown that every one of the statements made by Keynes on Say's Law is untrue. Classical economists did not always assume full employment or the absence of obstacles to full employment. They did not assume, either implicitly or explicitly, that involuntary unemployment was impossible. They did not argue that everything produced would be sold at prices which cover all costs of production. There was no assumption that the total costs of production would inevitably be covered by total revenue. There was no assumption that variations in the demand for money never affect the demand for goods. There was no assumption that all savings would be invested. Nevertheless, as Thweatt (1979: 80) has correctly observed: 'because of the ecumenic influence of the *General Theory* the idea that a competitive market system has a built-in tendency towards an equilibrium exhibiting stable prices and full employment has been associated ever since with the name of Say'.

What will also be shown in these five chapters is that classical economists had a different and far more penetrating understanding of the nature of recession and the business cycle than Keynes, or indeed most modern interpreters of classical theory, give them credit for. And, in what may be the greatest irony of all, it will be shown that the theory of the cycle held by classical economists was based on an understanding of Say's Law. That is, far from being an impediment to understanding the causes of recession and unemployment, Say's Law was a fundamental part of the theory which explained their occurrence.

What will be shown is that the basis of the classical theory of the cycle was the structure of demand rather than the level of demand. Classical economists argued, on the basis of the law of markets, that no obstacle to growth existed on the demand side, so long as production corresponded to the demands of buyers. Classical theory explained recessions by showing how errors in production might arise during cyclical upturns which would cause some goods to remain unsold at cost-covering prices.

There was an enormous variety of such explanations, but each of them was an attempt to show how individual production decisions could turn out to have been wrong when seen in the context of the entire set of economic relationships. The classical theory of recession was based on trying to understand why mistakes might be made in business decisions, and how such mistakes might be transmitted from one business to the next. Recessions were thus seen to be caused by a breakage in the mechanism of exchange. This is a far different concept from the process proposed by Keynes, who argued that the cause of recession was too little demand. What will be seen is that the pre-Keynesian theory of recession represented a profound understanding of the operation of an economy, providing a highly sophisticated theory of recession and unemployment.

2. J.-B. Say, James Mill and Robert Torrens

This chapter traces the early development of what eventually became known as the law of markets. While the roots of the argument have been traced back to the middle of the eighteenth century, and can be found in *The Wealth of Nations*,[1] the conscious development occurred in the works of J.-B. Say and James Mill. The first edition of Say's *Treatise*, published in 1803, contained an argument which ranged across a number of chapters dealing with the issues of the law of markets.[2] Mill followed with a deeper analysis in his *Commerce Defended*, first published in 1807.[3] Say's second and subsequent editions of the *Treatise* were revised in light of Mill's analysis. The result was an argument which denied that demand failure was the cause of recession. There could be no universal glut, although partial gluts could occur and frequently did. Torrens's contribution was to extend the analysis to demonstrate what had been implicit in earlier arguments, that the disharmonies created by partial gluts were the fundamental cause of recession and unemployment.

The origins of Say's Law commence in the writings of J.-B. Say and James Mill. There has been an extensive and on-going debate over whether Say's Law was first stated by Say or James Mill[4] and in fact it is not certain who did first state the issue clearly.[5] It is argued here that Say came most of the way towards

---

[1] See Spengler (1945a and 1945b) and Thweatt (1979).

[2] The principal argument was contained in a chapter entitled *des Débouchés* from which the classical name, the law of markets, was derived. Its association with J.-B. Say has led to the modern name, Say's Law.

[3] A second edition was published the following year.

[4] The literature is indeed enormous. See, for example, Dobb ([1940] 1980: 41n); Spengler (1945b: 342); Schumpeter ([1954] 1986: 491n); Lambert (1956: 11–13); Chipman (1965: 709n); Winch (1966: 34); Sowell (1972: 17–19); Baumol (1977 146–7, 159–60); Hollander (1979: 95–7); Thweatt (1980: 469).

[5] Baumol is surely right to state that 'any one who seeks to pinpoint its first origins must do so at his peril' (1977: 160). Sowell (1972: 18) also makes the valid point that, given the number of propositions which underlie the argument, 'it is a matter of judgement which of these propositions are the key ones that can be regarded as the essence of Say's Law'.

isolating the proposition which has come down to us as Say's Law[6] but the final crucial refinements were provided by James Mill. Two issues are used here as criteria. While Say prepared the groundwork, it was Mill who first attempted to controvert an argument proposing that the encouragement of unproductive consumption was necessary to the employment of labour.[7] It was also Mill who first put the argument in the form in which it was thereafter almost invariably found, while Say's approach was largely abandoned amongst English economists.[8] The priority between Say and Mill is, however, not the issue of this chapter. The meaning of Say's Law is.

Both Say and James Mill provide more than a single statement of the law of markets. Say's claim to having been its originator comes from interpretations of the first edition of his *Treatise*. The relevant chapters have been reproduced in English by Baumol (1977: 147–8, 149–52, 155–6).[9] But the second and subsequent editions of the *Treatise* included a substantial revision of the relevant sections. Mill read and was influenced by Say's first edition, but Say's more complete statement occurred after Mill had himself written his own first discussion which had an obvious influence on Say. It will therefore be necessary to look at both versions of Say's *Treatise*, but the emphasis will be on the later revised version in its English translation (Say 1821). Mill also produced two discussions of the law of markets, one in *Commerce Defended* and the second in his *Elements of Political Economy* (both reprinted in Winch 1966). With regard to the law of markets, the second was for the most part a repeat of the first and therefore the focus will be on Mill's earlier work.

SAY'S *TREATISE*, FIRST EDITION (1803)

It was Say's discussion in the first edition, though scattered across three separate chapters, which provided the initial impetus to the development of the law of markets amongst classical economists. It was this which opened the discussion on production as the basis for demand and even dealt, in a primitive way, with the impossibility of demand deficiency. It was the Say of the first edition who influenced James Mill and it was Mill who was largely responsible for refining the arguments which became the law of markets.

The first of the three chapters reproduced by Baumol is the chapter 'On Markets' (1977: 147–8). It is a chapter devoted to explaining how each person's own productions create a market for the goods produced by others. Say's aim is to point out that it is not money that creates demand but other products; money, as part of the process of exchange, is only a mechanism to effect the exchange. Goods buy goods through the mediating role of money. The argument was

---

[6] Winch (1966: 34) points out that Mill himself gave Say priority.

[7] Dobb ([1940] 1980: 41n) emphasises this point.

[8] Torrens ([1819] 1984c: 76), for example, noted in 1819 that both Say and Mill had written on this principle but found Mill's treatment 'the most [sic] clear and conclusive'.

[9] Baumol's views on the law of markets are discussed in Chapter 9.

directed towards the Mercantilist doctrine of money as the source of wealth (Thweatt 1979: 80; Dobb [1940] 1980: 41n; Hollander 1987: 243). As Say wrote:

> It is not the abundance of money but the abundance of other products in general that facilitates sales.... Money performs no more than the role of a conduit in this double exchange. When the exchanges have been completed, it will be found that one has paid for products with products. (Say 1803, quoted in Baumol 1977: 148)

Say is explaining the process of exchange along the lines of C–M–C′ where C is an initial set of commodities which have been converted into money, M, and that money has been reconverted into a different set of commodities, C′. He draws from this the conclusion that when some goods fail to sell, the solution is to produce even more goods of another kind to exchange for the goods which cannot be sold, writing that 'when a nation has too large a quantity of one particular type of product, the means of disposing of them is to create goods of another variety' (ibid.).

The second of the chapters of the first edition reproduced by Baumol bore the title, 'Is the Wealth of a State Increased by its Consumption?' (ibid.: 149–52). In this chapter Say argues that consumer demand cannot add to the wealth of a community while saving does. Say emphasises the importance of saving in augmenting the capital of a nation. His aim is to convince his readers that consumption is not a stimulus to wealth and that savings, if invested, do not mean a fall in the level of demand (Spengler 1945b: 344).[10]

The last of the chapters reproduced by Baumol is entitled 'In What Proportions the Value of Productions is Distributed Among the Three Factors of Production'.[11] Say's argument is based on consumption being, by definition, the destruction of utility (Spengler 1945b: 343). Since production is antecedent to consumption, production is therefore the cause of consumption, not its consequence. Demand, being based on the level of production, is 'in general' equal to it. Say 'dismissed as unfounded the fear that frugality might lead to a diminution in expenditure and output' (ibid.). The existence of goods which cannot be sold at cost-covering prices is due to misdirected production, where the wrong assortment of goods has been produced. Production of goods with no market can only be a temporary phenomenon, which must rapidly cease. But while particular goods can be produced to excess, all goods together cannot. In the end, demand is made up of the entire production of the nation. This is why demand for output had doubled or even trebled compared with the time of Charles

---

[10] The third proposition Baumol attributes to Say is that 'a given investment expenditure is *a far more effective stimulant* to wealth than an equal amount of consumption' (1977: 149, italics added). To Say, consumption provided no stimulus to wealth creation, but was its very antithesis, amounting to the destruction of utility, while production represented its creation (see Spengler 1945b: 343). This is part of the foundation on which the law of markets is built.

[11] Baumol (1977: 155) notes that both Spengler (1945b) and Sowell (1972) maintain that this chapter provides the first statement of Say's Law.

VI[12] – the ability to demand had risen in step with production, which had also doubled or trebled since that time.

This chapter, while more suggestive than logically tight, has the power to command assent. It puts, probably too strongly, the argument that goods buy goods because it does not present an explicit role for variations in the demand for money. It also provides the argument that goods open a market to other goods because, once goods have been produced, others can buy them with their own productions. It makes the structure of production the key to demand and notes that goods remain unsold due to the wrong things having been produced, not because there is insufficient purchasing power. Say did not, however, deal with the possibility of a general recession. In dealing with gluts, Say reduces the question to gluts of particular goods rather than all goods together. He does indeed mention that he cannot personally imagine all goods being in excess at one and the same time (in Baumol 1977: 156), but this is more of an aside than the issue at hand.

There were four subsequent editions of Say's *Treatise*, but to understand the development of the law of markets properly it is first necessary to discuss James Mill's *Commerce Defended*, which was published before the second edition of Say's *Treatise* appeared in 1814. Chipman (1965:709n) and Thweatt (1979: 90) have argued that Say was almost certainly influenced by Mill. Chipman further notes that the entire chapter on *débouchés* was rewritten for the second edition, with only a single sentence carried over from the first. According to Chipman (1965: 709n) and Thweatt (1980: 468), this rewriting of the chapter was to carry no developments beyond those provided by Mill. Baumol (1977: 147, 159), on the other hand, argued the novel position that Say's Law was first stated fully by Say but only in the *second* edition of his *Treatise* in 1814, almost a decade after the publication of Mill's *Commerce Defended*.

JAMES MILL (1808)

It was in the writings of James Mill that the issue of over–production is genuinely and unmistakably raised for the first time. It is Mill who specifically replies to an argument in which higher levels of unproductive consumption are sought to maintain the level of effective demand (cf. Spengler 1945b: 341). And it is in Mill that the law of markets is for the first time outlined in a focused and comprehensive fashion.

James Mill's *Commerce Defended* was written during the Napoleonic wars to rebut arguments that commerce was unnecessary to the economic success of England. The basis for this argument was the Physiocratic doctrine that agriculture was the only source of wealth. The doctrine was revived because England was on the point of losing its trade with the Continent. William Cobbett and William Spence had argued that such loss of trade would not adversely affect national prosperity. Mill therefore wrote his own short polemical tract to rebut

---

12 This form of argument had been used by Adam Smith (see [1776] 1976: i. 365, 366).

their arguments. (Winch 1966: 28–30 provides the background to *Commerce Defended*.)

In regard to Say's Law, it was Spence's arguments which drew Mill's focus. Spence had argued that it was demand which was at the heart of the wealth creation process:

> It is clear, then, that expenditure, not parsimony, is the province of the class of land proprietors, and, that it is on the due performance of this duty, by the class in question, that the production of national wealth depends. And not only does the production of national wealth depend upon the expenditure of the class of land proprietors, but, for the due increase of this wealth, and for the constantly progressive maintenance of the prosperity of the community, it is absolutely requisite, that this class should go on progressively increasing its expenditure. (Spence 1807: 33)

In Spence's view, it is spending not saving which causes wealth to grow, as the following passage makes clear:

> The *prosperity* of the country would be as much promoted, if an owner of an estate of 10,000*l.* a year, were to expend this sum in employing 500 men to blow glass bubbles, to be broken as soon as made, as if he employed the same number in building a splendid palace.... The 500 glass blowers would require as much wealth to be brought into existence from the soil, would consume as much food, and would consequently be as prosperous, as the 500 palace builders. (Ibid.: 36)

Spence accepts that it would be better to build palaces since this would add to the capital stock of the nation. But even so, the creation of no value at all would have the same economic effect on the level of prosperity as the building of a palace.[13] It was to this kind of argument that James Mill replied. The subject of Chapter VI of *Commerce Defended* is 'Consumption'. It is here that Mill deals with Spence's support for unproductive consumption as a stimulus to the growth of national

---

[13] There is no difference of substance between this and Keynes in the *General Theory* where he wrote:

> Pyramid-building, earthquakes, even wars may serve to increase wealth, if the education of our statesmen on the principles of the classical economics stands in the way of anything better....
>
> If the Treasury were to fill old bottles with banknotes, bury them at suitable depths in disused coalmines which are then filled up to the surface with town rubbish, and leave it to private enterprise on well-tried principles of *laissez-faire* to dig the notes up again...there need be no more unemployment and, with the help of the repercussions, the real income of the community, and its capital wealth also, would probably become a great deal greater than it actually is. (Op. cit.: 129)

Keynes too stated that it would be better to build something useful, but argued that even completely unproductive spending would add to wealth. And for both Keynes and Spence, it was the restrictions in demand caused by saving which was at the heart of the problem (see Spence 1807: 31–2).

wealth.[14] Mill opens the chapter with an extended quotation from Spence in which the arguments supporting unproductive consumption by the owners of land are provided. Mill draws attention to Spence's argument that it is consumption rather than saving which is the necessary condition for growth and prosperity (cf. Spengler 1945b: 334–7). Mill begins his dissection of Spence's argument by making the same distinction as Say between unproductive and productive consumption (ibid.: 339). The first is the destruction of value pure and simple, while the second is the destruction of value in the process of creating even greater value:

> There are two species of consumption; which are so far from being the same, that the one is more properly the very reverse of the other. The one is an absolute destruction of property, and is consumption properly so called; the other is a consumption for the sake of reproduction, and might perhaps with more propriety be called *employment* than consumption. (Mill [1808] 1966a: 128)

From this Mill concludes:

> It appears from this very explanation of the meaning of the term, that it is of importance to the interests of the country, that as much as possible of its annual produce should be *employed*, but as little as possible of it consumed. (Ibid.)

If one takes the annual produce of a country, writes Mill, and divides it into two parts, that which is consumed is gone. On the other hand, that portion which is used in the production process returns in the following year, and with a profit. The more of the produce of a country that is devoted to productive uses, the faster that country grows. Mill then concludes:

> If by consumption therefore Mr Spence means, what we have termed consumption properly so called, or dead unproductive consumption, and it does appear that this is his meaning, his doctrine is so far from being true, that it is the very reverse of the truth. The interests of the country are the most promoted, not by the greatest, but by the least possible consumption of this description. (Ibid.: 129)

Spence had been putting forward a crude under–consumptionist argument. Buying by the landed classes would ensure a market for the goods produced. In a forthright and justly famous passage (see, for example, Hollander 1985: 10), Mill assures Spence that there is no need to be concerned that any production will go to waste:

> Let not Mr Spence, however, be alarmed. Let him rest in perfect assurance, that the whole annual produce of the country will be always very completely consumed, whether his landlords choose to spend or to accumulate. No portion of it will be left unappropriated to the one species of consumption, or to the other. No man, if he can help it, will let any part of his property lie useless and run to waste. Nothing is more

---

[14] Ambirajan (1959: 148–9) provides a good summary of Spence's position.

clear, than that the self-interest of men, ever has impelled and ever will impel them, with some very trifling exceptions, to use every particle of property which accrues to them, either for the purpose of immediate gratification, or of future profit. That part, however, which is destined for future profits, is just as completely consumed, as that which is destined for immediate gratification. (Ibid.: 129)

Mill compares the effects of consumption by a soldier and by a ploughman. At the end of the year, the soldier has consumed but left nothing of value behind. In contrast, the ploughman will have more than produced the value of what he has consumed during the year. A country is therefore benefited by productive consumption, but no benefit is provided by those who merely consume but do not produce. The question still left open is what would happen if individuals who had received incomes failed to spend those incomes. And in one of the curiosities of this particular facet of the general glut debate, it is Spence who rejects this as an issue.[15] It is important to Spence that he does so, since his proposal is that higher money incomes be retained by land-owners. Since they were, as a class, the most wealthy individuals in the country, there was an obvious concern that the additional money would be hoarded and not spent.

In dealing with Spence, Mill is replying to the argument that an increasing demand for consumption goods is needed to maintain the level of employment: too much saving will reduce the demand for consumer items and therefore leave an economy operating well below its potential. Mill is trying to demonstrate that it is not consumption that needs encouragement, but production (cf. Winch 1966: 30). Whatever is produced will be put to use by whomever has produced or purchased it. Mill's conclusion is that consumption is not needed to encourage production.[16] But, Mill wrote ([1808] 1966a: 134), 'there is another idea' which he reluctantly feels the need to deal with. And with this, Mill enters deeper still into the issues surrounding the law of markets, which are that output in general, and capital in particular, may increase more rapidly than demand. Mill explains the issue this way:

> The Economistes and their disciples [i.e. Spence] express great apprehension lest capital should increase too fast, lest the production of commodities should be too rapid. There is only, say they, a market for a given quantity of commodities, and if you increase the supply beyond that quantity you will be unable to dispose of the surplus. (Ibid.: 134–5)

---

[15] Cf. Malthus in his *Definitions in Political Economy*, where he defined saving as: 'In modern times [1827], implies the accumulation of capital, as few people now lock their money up in a box' (Malthus 1986: VIII. 109). Winch (1987a: 465) in effect criticises Mill for casting his argument in the same form as it was structured by Spence.

[16] Like Say, Mill argues that the direction of causation is from production to consumption, either productive or unproductive: but there is no suggestion by Mill that the level of production will remain at its maximum level. 'Consumption in the necessary order of things is the effect of production, not production the effect of consumption' ([1808] 1966a: 134).

That is, there is a problem that demand will be unable to keep pace with the growing level of production. Thus Mill, unlike Say, specifically confronts the problem of demand deficiency. But while the question is raised for the first time by Mill, the answer has J.-B. Say written all over it. To what extent Mill would anyway have attacked Spence's writings on consumption is unknowable, although it is probable that he would have done so. It is also unknowable how he would have approached the issues had he not previously read Say on the same topic. But the fact is that, when Mill came to deal with the issue of demand deficiency, it was Say's own arguments which clearly influenced the structure of Mill's. Mill is, as usual, forthright in setting out the issue (cf. Chipman 1965: 709n; Hutchison 1978: 31; Hollander 1985: 12; Winch 1987a: 465, who see Mill's statement as overly dogmatic):

> No proposition however in political economy seems to be more certain than this which I am going to announce, how paradoxical soever it may at first sight appear; and if it be true, none undoubtedly can be deemed of more importance. The production of commodities creates, and is the one and universal cause which creates a market for the commodities produced. (Mill [1808] 1966a: 135)

His argument is that the means to pay for an increased flow of goods is provided by those goods themselves. Therefore, the power to purchase is always available and is constituted by the very goods which have been brought to market. As Mill wrote (ibid.: 137), in providing a phrase reminiscent of 'supply creates its own demand': 'How great soever that annual produce may be it always creates a market to itself'.

But Mill also provides the central qualification to goods exchanging against other goods. It is not just any goods that will exchange themselves for other goods; they must be precisely those goods which are demanded by other sellers.[17] One set of goods will only purchase a second set if the sellers of the first set of goods wish to buy what the second group has to offer. Or, to be more precise, only if producers are willing to use the sales proceeds received from selling their own goods to buy just those goods which have been put up for sale, will 'the demand of the nation be equal to the produce of the nation' (ibid.: 136). Mill puts the qualification in this way:

> All that here can ever be requisite is that the goods should be adapted to one another; that is to say, that every man who has goods to dispose of should always find all those different sorts of goods with which he wishes to supply himself in return. (Ibid.)

On the central issues as to whether a nation can use too much of its annual output in production rather than 'mere consumption', and whether more can be produced in total than the community would be both willing and able to purchase, Mill

---

[17] Hollander (1979: 96) notes that Mill emphasised that 'the composition of output must be adapted to the tastes of consumers and investors and in this vital respect his statement stands far and away above that of Say'.

replies that such views are an 'absurdity'. As he wrote in the concluding lines of the chapter:

> Little obligation then has society to those doctrines by which this consumption is recommended. Obstacles enow [sic] exist to the augmentation of capital without the operation of ridiculous speculations. Were the doctrine that it can increase too fast, as great a truth as it is an absurdity, the experience of all the nations on earth proves to us, that of all possible calamities this would be the least to be feared. Slow has been its progress every where; and low the degree of prosperity which has in any place been given to the mass of the people to enjoy. (Ibid.: 139)

Winch (1966: 32–3) has pointed out that *Commerce Defended* represents an important link between Adam Smith and Ricardo, and that Mill versus Spence gives a foretaste of Ricardo versus Malthus. A number of conclusions were reached which constitute what is usually referred to as the law of markets; a country cannot have too much capital; investment is the basis for economic growth; consumption not only provides no stimulus to wealth creation but is actually contrary to it; demand is constituted by production; and, most importantly, demand deficiency (i.e. over–production) is never the cause of economic disturbance. Economic disturbance arises only if goods are not produced in the correct proportions to each other.

SAY'S *TREATISE*, FOURTH EDITION 1821

In the fourth edition[18] and as in the first, Say makes the issue of the chapter on *débouchés* the question of whether there is sufficient money available to purchase everything that is produced. Say frames his discussion as a refutation of those who 'pronounce money to be scarce' (1821: 162) as the explanation for poor sales.[19] His aim is to show that slow trade is due not to a scarcity of money but rather to a failure of other producers to produce.[20] He uses an analogy to make his point:

> Should a tradesman say, 'I do not want other products for my woollens, I want money,' there could be little difficulty in convincing him, that his customers cannot pay him in money, without having first procured it by the sale of some other commodities of their own.... 'You say, you want only money; I say, you want other commodities, and not money.'... To say that sales are dull, owing to the scarcity of money, is to mistake the means for the cause; an error that proceeds from the

---

[18] It is only the fourth edition which has ever been translated in its entirety into English.

[19] In the first edition, Say's conclusion was: 'I trust this shows that it is not the abundance of money but the abundance of other products in general that facilitates sales' (Say 1803, quoted in Baumol 1977: 148).

[20] In this, Say is repeating what is found in the *Wealth of Nations*: 'No complaint...is more common than that of a scarcity of money' (Smith [1776] 1976: i. 458; also i. 362).

circumstance, that almost all produce is in the first instance exchanged for money, before it is ultimately converted into other produce. (Ibid.: 163–5)

The dynamic is the dynamic of the law of markets (goods buying goods), but the issue is whether a shortage of money is the reason for the slowness of demand. Say's aim is to show that 'sales cannot be said to be dull because money is scarce, but because other products are so' (ibid.: 165). In Say's view, no one need fear that a shortage of money will cause recession since 'there is always money enough to conduct the circulation and mutual interchange of other values, when those values exist' (ibid.). Say's argument is thus not an argument dealing with the possibility of demand failure in a more general sense, but only in the more restricted sense of poor sales due to there being insufficient money in circulation.

Say's own means of conceiving the law which a century later would take his name was that the production of a product by one person opened up an opportunity for a second person to sell whatever it was that the second person had produced. This is what was meant when he wrote that production 'opens a vent' for other products. The conception Say had was that goods failed to find a market because other goods had not been produced. Since sales were in reality an exchange of one product against another, for sales to occur it was essential that other products also be produced.

This was a clumsy way of making his point. Rather than arguing that the production of one good enables its producer to sell that good for money and then buy something else, Say looks at the process from the opposite direction. Say argued that the production of one good permits others to exchange what they have produced for money which can then be used to buy that first good. His point is that unless there are other goods produced, it is useless for anyone to produce goods of their own for sale. He is trying to show that the more producers there are, the better off all producers become. His aim is to demonstrate the benefits of free trade and the importance of encouraging production.

Say is looking at the process of exchange from the point of view of a seller and asking: what must occur if I am to sell what I have produced? And his answer is that others must also produce and sell to earn the income with which to pay for my goods. That is why *débouchés* is often translated as 'outlets', which provides a closer meaning than 'market' or 'demand'.[21] It provides a more precise understanding of what Say had in mind, that a good once produced becomes an object to be purchased. As he put it, 'a product is no sooner created, than it, from that instant, affords a market for other products to the full extent of its own value' (ibid.: 167).

It is from this clumsy approach that Say conceives of his solution to dull sales. If goods cannot find a market, then it is because there are not enough products being produced by others to provide a market. This is by no means an empty approach. A bookseller, for example, may find it difficult to sell books because

---

21 See, for example, the translation of *théorie des débouchés* in Blanqui, where the translator wrote: 'literally, *theory of outlets, i.e.,* openings for sales of products; generally translated, *theory of markets*' (Blanqui [1880] 1968: 444).

those who would like to buy them do not have incomes large enough to pay cost-covering prices. If these potential buyers increased their productions and earned higher incomes, they could buy more books. Thus Say is right that the failure to sell can arise because of the failure of others to produce more and sell more. Nor does Say entirely ignore the possibility that some commodities may have been produced in excess of market demand; it is just that he seems to see this as a secondary issue:[22]

> I would not be understood to maintain in this chapter, that one product cannot be raised in too great abundance, in relation to all others; but merely that nothing is more favourable to the demand of one product, than the supply of another. (Ibid.: 170n)

His approach leads him into further problems. Say is clearly wrong where he writes that 'it is observable, moreover, that at the same time that one commodity makes a loss, another commodity is making excessive profit' (ibid.: 168). It is his approach which pushes him in this direction and leads him to observe phenomena which are not in reality there. It is his search for the phantom goods which were not produced which undermines his perceptions of the nature of recession. His approach remained part of the canon of Say's Law throughout the classical period, but it was married to the more logical approach adopted by James Mill, which ultimately came to dominate.

But, in its wake, Say's depiction has created a misunderstanding of the nature of the law of markets which has led to confusion about the central issues involved. The belief that Say's Law was addressed to the issue of secular stagnation (Baumol 1977: 152–3; Patinkin 1965: 647–9; Blaug 1985: 157) arises to some extent from a famous passage in Say (1821: 165):

> How could it be possible, that there should now be bought and sold in France five or six times as many commodities, as in the miserable reign of Charles VI? Is it not obvious, that five or six times as many commodities must have been produced, and that they must have served to purchase one another?

This quite striking passage seems to say that, over long stretches of time, demand will keep pace with supply, while leaving shorter periods as an open question.[23]

---

[22] Ricardo (1951–73: VIII. 227) criticises Say for his approach, arguing that Say 'appear[s] to think that stagnation in commerce arises from a counter set of commodities not being produced with which the commodities on sale are to be purchased, and...seem[s] to infer that the evil will not be removed till such other commodities are in the market. But surely the true remedy is in regulating future production, – if there is a glut of one commodity produce less of that and more of another'.

[23] This is how it is interpreted by Baumol (1977: 152–3). To his credit, Baumol ends up puzzled by the absence of any real discussion of long-run demand and supply, writing that 'it must be admitted that Say seems never to have devoted much space to a discussion of the very long-run correspondence of demand with supply, and I have not found any place where [James] Mill dealt with it at all' (ibid.: 153). It does not occur to

But the actual point Say is making is not that demand and supply will match, but that the size of the stock of money is irrelevant to whether everything produced will be sold. This is the same point and the same argument that is made in the first edition.[24] Since it is goods buying goods, the amount of money available is of no importance. The conclusion Say takes from making his comparison with the time of Charles VI is this:

> Thus, to say that sales are dull, owing to the scarcity of money, is to mistake the means for the cause.... There is always money enough to conduct the circulation and mutual interchange of other values, when those values really exist. (Ibid.)

Say also argued in a manner that has been taken as evidence that classical monetary theory assumed no one ever held money for speculative or precautionary purposes but instead 'immediately' spent all of the proceeds received:

> A product is no sooner created, than it, from that instant, affords a market for other products to the full extent of its own value. When the producer has put the finishing hand to his product, he is most anxious to sell it immediately, lest its value should vanish in his hands. Nor is he less anxious to dispose of the money he may get for it; for the value of money is also perishable. (Ibid.: 167)

It is again Say's way of stating his law which causes the meaning to be obscured. A market is instantaneously created for other goods because there is immediately something available that someone with money can buy. Moreover, the implication that someone receiving money must be better off spending receipts as soon as possible certainly overstates Say's position. Money can fall in value if prices are rising, and money held as cash balances loses interest.[25] Say's notoriously imprecise language leaves him open to attack and misinterpretation.[26] And because it is 'Say's' Law, it has been assumed that Say must know what that law is. The closest Say comes to the law of markets in his fourth edition is where he wrote:

Baumol that he may have misunderstood the point Say is making. The issues surrounding the law of markets had nothing to do with secular stagnation. Cf. Sowell (1972: 5, 13) who is also adamant that secular stagnation was not the issue surrounding the law of markets.

[24] In the first edition, however, the difference in the level of production was only a factor of two or three.

[25] That did not stop Say from recognising that money might be held rather than spent if there were insufficient outlets for productive investment. There is, in fact, no interpretation of Say's 1821 reply to Ricardo that 'capitals are quietly sleeping in the coffers of their proprietors' ([1821] 1967: 49n) consistent with Say's Identity.

[26] For example, Schumpeter ([1954] 1986: 618) wrote that Say's chapter on *débouchés* 'abounds in reckless statements, which were precisely the ones to attract attention', and later on the same page describes Say's writing as 'careless'. Ricardo was equally scathing, writing that 'in Say's works, generally, there is a great mixture of profound thinking and egregious blundering' (Ricardo 1951–73: VIII. 302).

The encouragement of mere consumption is no benefit to commerce; for the difficulty lies in supplying the means, not in stimulating the desire of consumption; and we have seen, that production alone, furnishes those means. Thus it is the aim of good government to stimulate production, of bad government to encourage consumption. (Ibid.: 177)

Consumption cannot and does not stimulate production; it is production which stimulates consumption. Demand is a rising function of production, or in Say's words, 'the general demand for produce is brisk in proportion to the activity of production' (ibid.: 180). This leads Say to take note of the unemployment and worse which can occur in an economy which has not been appropriately managed. Mistakes, not only by the government but by the 'nation', can lead to extraordinarily grim results:[27]

Wherever, by reason of the blunders of the nation or its government, production is stationary, or does not keep pace with consumption, the demand gradually declines; the value of the products is less than the charges of their production; no productive exertion is properly rewarded; profits and wages decrease; the employment of capital becomes less advantageous and more hazardous; it is consumed piece-meal, not through extravagance, but through necessity, and because the sources of profit are dried up. The labouring classes experience a want of work; families before in tolerable circumstances are more cramped and confined; and those before in difficulties, are left altogether destitute. Depopulation, misery, and returning barbarism, occupy the place of abundance and happiness. (Ibid.: 181–2)

What is quite extraordinary is that the disastrous outcome described occurs where production 'does not keep pace with consumption'; that is, where demand is greater than supply. This is a reversal of the logic of Keynesian theory in which an economy would be expected to expand if aggregate demand were greater than aggregate supply.[28] According to Say, however, if more is being consumed than produced, then 'demand gradually declines'. This point is derived directly from Say's conception that consumption, both productive and unproductive, is a using up of output while production is its replacement. Thus, if output is being used up faster than it is being replaced, distributable product must fall and demand – which is constituted by supply – must ultimately contract. Stimulating consumption to promote growth would have been a concept totally foreign to Say.

It is important to bear in mind that, as conceived by Say, the law of markets is in continuous operation irrespective of the level of activity. No matter what the level of unemployment, the basis for each individual's demands are the productions brought to market and sold for money. Production very rapidly ceases for goods which find no market. All capital available, of which there can never be

---

[27] This appears to be paraphrased from Mill ([1808] 1966a: 138–9).

[28] Malthus took the same position as Say, writing in the introduction to the *Principles*: 'If consumption exceed production, the capital of the country must be diminished, and its wealth must be gradually destroyed from its want of power to produce' (Malthus 1986: VI. 9).

too much, is put to use. There is clearly nothing in the operation of Say's Law which means that an economy will always run at its maximum potential, nor is there even a suggestion that there might be an automatic mechanism which returns an economy to full employment of resources after deviations of a short duration. Mistakes by the 'nation' in the above passage include mistakes by business, and the consequences of such mistakes can be exceedingly destructive. Keynes's interpretations of Say's Law, which insisted that full employment is guaranteed by the operation of the law of markets, will not bear comparison with this passage from Say himself. Say clearly understood that economies can and do enter prolonged periods of economic depression. But what he was at pains to argue was that increased levels of unproductive consumption are not a remedy for a depressed level of economic activity, and contribute nothing to the wealth creation process. Consumption, whether productive or unproductive, uses up resources, while only productive consumption is capable of leaving something of an equivalent or even higher value in its place.

Unfortunately, Say's exposition was less coherent than it ought to have been. Schumpeter ([1954] 1986: 625) was right when he wrote that Say 'hardly understood his discovery himself and not only expressed it faultily but also misused it for the things that really mattered to him'.[29] Say's discussion had many gaps in its logic, and has contributed to the misunderstanding of the law of markets.

During the classical period, the law of markets was thought of as the conclusion from a lengthy discourse amongst economists in which the issues were refined through prolonged debate. The question was the possibility of a general glut, and most particularly the possibility of demand deficiency. One has only the slightest indication that these are the issues Say is dealing with, and this arises only towards the end of the chapter where Say denies that encouraging consumption can increase the wealth of the community. Indeed, one must almost be alerted by the translator's extended footnote (almost three pages) that this passage forms part of the general glut debate. Ultimately, the discussion in the fourth edition provides a poor understanding of Say's Law, and in itself would have been unlikely to commence a revolution in economic thought.[30]

---

[29] Niehans (1990: 111) argued that the debate over the law of markets revealed Say as a 'second rate theorist', while Spiegel (1991: 264) said of Say's treatment that it was 'vague and invited a variety of interpretations'.

[30] Interestingly, Blanqui, who succeeded Say in the Chair of Political Economy at the Collège de France, does not mention the general glut debate when describing the significance of the law of markets in his own text on the history of economics. He instead stressed the issue of free trade, writing: 'what assures immortal renown to [J.-B. Say] is his *théorie des débouchés*...which gave the last blow to the exclusive system and hastened the fall of the colonial regime. This fine theory, wholly founded on most careful observation of facts, has proved that nations pay for products only with products, and that all the laws which forbid them to buy, prevent them from selling' (Blanqui [1880] 1968: 444).

DIFFERENCES BETWEEN SAY AND MILL

Two important differences between Say and Mill should be noted. According to Mill, some goods are produced to excess 'but by that very circumstance is implied that some other commodity is not provided in sufficient proportion' (Mill [1808] 1966a: 137). Say's solution was simply to produce more of other goods. Mill's solution was not only to produce more of other goods but also to produce less of the goods which cannot find a market:

> A part of the means of production which had been applied to the preparation of this superabundant commodity, should have been applied to the preparation of those other commodities till the balance between them had been established. (Ibid.: 137)

It is only when this balance has been reached that everything which has been produced will be bought. Where the balance is not properly preserved, some goods will be unable to find purchasers, at least for some time and even then not at cost-covering prices. Mill fully anticipated that some goods will not sell and will remain part of the stock of their producers for a much longer time than originally anticipated. The decision to produce was an *ex ante* decision, while the discovery that demand was lacking would occur *ex post*. When inventories accumulate, producers stop producing what they cannot sell. This is the first part of the adjustment process. How quickly a producer commences producing something else is an open question.

There was a second difference of importance between Mill and Say. Say thought of production as the opening of an outlet for other goods. A good produced offered a market to other producers. Mill, however, conceived of the process as one in which production gives the producer the wherewithal with which to make purchases.[31] Compare Say's statement with Mill's: Say wrote that 'a product is no sooner created, than it, from that instant, affords a market for other products to the full extent of its own value', while Mill, in contrast, wrote: 'whatever be the additional quantity of goods therefore which is at any time created in any country, an additional power of purchasing, exactly equivalent, is at the same time created' (ibid.: 135).

Production provides here an additional power to buy. Mill's conception is that one buys with one's own products, which is profoundly different from Say, who conceived of production as opening opportunities for others to sell. Mill's approach is the more simple to follow and is less likely to end in error. It was his approach which became generally accepted amongst English economists.[32]

---

[31] Hollander (1979: 96) recognises this same distinction. He, however, prefers the approach taken by Say since it appears to him to permit the possibility of excess capacity which will only be corrected after a period of time.

[32] Mill was, however, not fully immune from Say's approach, as for example where he stated that 'the very operation of capital makes a vent for its produce' ([1808] 1966a: 135).

ROBERT TORRENS

Robert Torrens is seldom included amongst the major theorists in the development of the law of markets. Indeed, Thweatt (1974: 437) goes so far as to argue that 'Torrens never made use of the law of markets in any of his writings' and wrote of 'Torrens' continued, lifelong opposition to the Say–Mill Law' (1980: 398).[33] A more balanced approach is provided by Robbins (1958: 177), who points out that Mill's analysis of the possibility of over-production 'was approved in principle by Torrens'. Robbins saw Torrens as having provided what was little more than a standard depiction of the law of markets.

Torrens, however, did say more than had been said before. It was his extension of the concept of miscalculation which, for the first time, constructed a theory of recession from the constituent elements of the law of markets. That the processes of production could lead to goods being produced which would be unable to find markets had already been recognised by the defenders of the law of markets. Particular gluts might lead to dislocations in the production process if the good produced could not be exchanged for money at cost-covering prices. The consequence would be that the particular good in question would not meet sales expectations and would soon stop being produced.

It was Torrens, in his *Essay on the Production of Wealth*, published in 1821, a year after Malthus's *Principles*, who took the next step and showed how particular gluts could lead to a general downturn.[34] He pointed out that if the conversion of one's own productions into money failed to occur, other producers would consequently also fail to sell their own goods. That is, if the first set of producers could not convert their productions into money, then neither would the persons from whom they had intended to buy. A chain reaction from production miscalculations by one group of producers could in consequence place the entire economy in recession. Torrens ([1821] 1965: ix) had no doubt that he was saying something original and profound:

> To M. Say and Mr. Mill belong the merit of having been the first to bring forward the very important doctrine, that as commodities are purchased with commodities, one half will furnish a market for the other half, and increased production will be the occasion of increased demand. But this doctrine, though it embraces the very key-stone of economical science, is not correct in the general and unqualified sense in which these distinguished writers have stated it. Though one half of our commodities should be of the same value as the other half, and though the two halves should freely exchange against each other, it is yet possible that there may be an effectual demand for neither. It is quite obvious that there can exist no reciprocal effectual demand,

---

[33] Thweatt (1974) argues, against the evidence, that Torrens was not the author of the 'Digression on Sismondi' in 'Mr Owen's Plans for Relieving National Distress'. Groenewegen (1984: xix–xx) convincingly shows that Torrens is by far the most likely author. If so, Thweatt's view that Torrens did not accept the law of markets is clearly wrong.

[34] Sowell (1972: 131) notes that 'Torrens was...well in advance of his contemporaries in developing this analysis'.

unless the interchange of two different sets of commodities replaces, with a surplus, the expenditure incurred in the production of both.

Note that Torrens describes the law of markets as embracing 'the very key-stone of economical science'. Torrens seems to believe that he is endorsing the law of markets, yet Sowell (1972: 129) quotes this same passage to demonstrate that Torrens, although having supported the law of markets in 1819, was 'by 1821...beginning to have misgivings'. In fact, Torrens had no fundamental objection to the law of markets; his aim was to extend it, not refute it. It was Torrens's extension which was to embody the theory of recession for the following century. Indeed, Chipman (1965: 713) describes Torrens's statement as 'surely the most detailed formulation of Say's Law to have been attempted up to that time, and indeed, up to the time of [J.S.] Mill'.[35]

Section VI of Torrens's *Essay on the Production of Wealth* is entitled, 'On the Principles of Demand and Supply'. This is, however, more than just a discussion of demand and supply for a single product; it also ranges into the production and sale of the aggregate produce of an economy. The section begins with a discussion of the state of economic relationships before the division of labour. Torrens ([1821] 1965: 339–40) notes that there is a slight compensation for the lower productivity in the fact that goods do not need to find a buyer, so that each improvement in output will necessarily lead to an improvement in welfare.

As the division of labour becomes more extensive, there is a vast increase in the productiveness of the economy, but this brings a series of disadvantages. With the division of labour, breakdowns in one segment of the economy can lead to a breakdown of the economic machinery overall. Thereafter, the welfare of individual workers depends less on their own exertions than on their ability to find people to buy what they have to sell. Moreover, it is not just production which is desired, but the production of precisely those things which will be bought. The need is to ensure that goods are produced in the right proportions relative to each other so that they may be continuously exchanged. Indeed, Torrens notes that 'the great practical problem in economical science is, so to proportion production that supply and demand shall be in the relation of equality' (ibid.: 370). If the proportions are correct, then everything will be sold for cost-covering prices. In Torrens's view, there is not the slightest doubt that, if this were to occur, output could continue to increase without conceivable limit. The question is whether the correct proportions are preserved, not whether aggregate production will outrun the willingness of the community to buy:

So long as this proportion is preserved, every article which the industrious classes have the will and power to produce, will find a ready and a profitable vend. No conceivable increase of production can lead to an overstocking of the market; but, on

---

[35] O'Brien (1988: 205), too, recognises the additional depth, writing that 'Torrens accepted the equality, but certainly not the identity, version of this law, envisioning both the possibility of general over-production and of excess demand for money'. Yet O'Brien seems not to have appreciated that Torrens's aim was to deny the possibility of over-production while simultaneously explaining the cause of recessions.

the contrary, every addition which can be made to this supply of commodities, will immediately and necessarily occasion an increase in the effectual demand for them. Whatever may have been the previous state of the market in regard to abundant supply, *increased production will create a proportionally increased demand.* (Ibid.: 370–1, italics added)

Torrens accepts in full the conclusion that demand failure will never occur; demand will under no circumstances exceed supply. The italicised words also show a striking resemblance to the Keynesian maxim that 'supply creates its own demand'. But Torrens added that all-important qualifier: demand and supply must preserve the appropriate proportions. Supply creates its own demand 'so long as this proportion is preserved'. And, as Torrens makes clear, if the proportions are not preserved, then the result is a market filled with unsold goods:

This happy and prosperous state of things is immediately interrupted when the proportions in which commodities are produced are such as to disturb the equality between effectual demand and supply.... When the ingredients of capital expended in the production of commodities are in excess with respect to the ingredients of capital brought to market to exchange against other commodities, then gluts and regorgements are experienced. (Ibid.: 371–2)

Torrens provides a series of numerical examples to demonstrate the principle that there is no upwards limit to production, so long as supply and demand are properly proportioned. During the course of this exposition, Torrens deals with the specific arguments raised by Malthus, where decisions are made to increase saving rather than to spend (ibid.: 384–5). He concludes:

In every conceivable case, effectual demand is created by and is commensurate with production, rightly proportioned.... Vary our suppositions as we will, increased production, provided it be duly proportioned, is the one and only cause of extended demand, and diminished production the one and only cause of contracted demand. (Ibid.: 397)

But this is clearly not sufficient. As Torrens points out, a theory must conform with the facts of the world as we know it and account for the phenomena which are most familiar. In particular, it is necessary to explain why there are extended periods when goods throughout the whole of industry remain unsold (ibid.: 399). In Torrens's view, not only does his theory explain exchange, it also explains how and why exchange might break down and lead to glutted markets. For an individual commodity, when the price of the article cannot cover the costs of the capital which has gone into its production, then the supply will be in excess of the demand. The reason a glut may occur is either miscalculation on the part of producers or seasonal fluctuations. Torrens provides a further series of numerical examples from which he demonstrates that a particular glut can lead to a general downturn in the economy:

From the foregoing illustrations it will be apparent, that a glut of a particular commodity may occasion a general stagnation, and lead to a suspension of production, not merely of the commodity which first exists in excess, but of all other commodities brought to market. (Ibid.: 414)

Torrens discusses the mechanism by which the inability to achieve profitable sales for one commodity leads to a sequence of reductions in demand for other commodities, which leads, in turn, to a downturn in the economy as a whole. The failure to sell by one group of producers means that they have not received an income to enable them to buy from others (ibid.: 414–15). Torrens shows that this downturn affects all classes of producers, labourers included:

That want of due proportion in the quantities of the several commodities brought to market, which operates thus injuriously upon capitalists, inflicts equal injury upon the other classes of the community.... The ruin of the cultivator involves that of the proprietor of land; and when the motive and the power to employ productive capital are destroyed, the productive labourer is cut off by famine. (Ibid.: 418)

'To be cut off by famine' is hardly a Candide-like view. Torrens has not only used the law of markets to demonstrate that recessions can be and are generated by the operation of a capitalist economy, but he has also provided an explanation for the generation of unemployment which, by any stretch of the imagination, must be reckoned to be involuntary. Moreover, this is not an economy that is effecting exchange by a process of barter. This is a money economy. Goods are exchanged for money and money is exchanged for goods. Money is non-neutral; it affects outcomes. During recessions, Torrens argues, there is an increased demand for money holdings relative to more normal times:

On every occasion of glut or general stagnation, the desire of turning goods into money is rendered more intense than the desire of turning money into goods. (Ibid.: 422)

When Torrens discusses exchange as involving an 'equivalent', it is money which is being referred to. Money is described as the 'universal equivalent' (ibid.). When Torrens states that exchange requires the payment of an equivalent he is not describing barter. It is, instead, the normal processes of an economy where purchase and sale occur, with money (the universal equivalent) as the medium of exchange.

Thus, not only did the law of markets not assume full employment, or the rapid (if not immediate) return to full employment should there be an economic disturbance, but it was in fact employed in explaining the generation of recession and unemployment. 'To be cut off by famine' is involuntary unemployment at its greatest extreme. No one in this position can be said to be voluntarily unemployed. This passage is strongly reminiscent of the passage from Say quoted earlier in which he described the consequences which flow from misdirected production. A situation where 'the labouring classes experience a want of work' leads numerous families into destitution, resulting in 'depopulation, misery and returning barbarism'. In these circumstances wages are in decline. Again, it could not be said that Say is attempting to describe a situation in which wage earners choose in any sense of the word to be unemployed. Their unemployment is utterly involuntary.

The basis of the law of markets is that goods buy goods, but only if the right goods are produced. If the wrong goods are produced, then they cannot be converted into the universal equivalent (i.e. money). If a proportion of goods cannot be sold, then their owners cannot buy. If one set of producers cannot buy, then a second set cannot sell. The result is a general downturn in the economy and warehouses filled with unsold goods. But the cause of recession is not demand deficiency or over-production but the production of the wrong assortment of goods and services. The adjustment process thus required is the redeployment of capital from areas where there is too little demand into areas where there will be demand for the goods produced. There is no reason that the process of readjustment will be rapid, but there is also no reason to believe that the downturn will be permanent. Torrens thus provided, in a primitive form, the theory of recession which was to become the basis for business cycle analysis throughout the remainder of the nineteenth century and well into the twentieth.

3. David Ricardo

Ricardo's discussion would in many ways not form part of an overview of the development of the law of markets. With Ricardo being the dominant figure in economics during his time, his endorsement of the propositions underlying the law of markets is important. But Ricardo did not figure large as the propagator of a new idea nor as a leading public exponent. Indeed Blaug argues that 'the doctrine that supply creates its own demand was never a vital feature of the Ricardian outlook, much less its keystone' (Blaug 1958: 2–3; for the same view, see O'Brien 1975: 41; Meek [1951] 1967a: 183 and 1967b: 64). Peach (1993: 15), however, argues that '"the law of markets"...was anything but an insignificant element in [Ricardo's] analytical system' and that this is the majority opinion (ibid.: 13).[1] Certainly, Keynes argued that Say's Law was an integral and crucially important element in Ricardian economics. Nevertheless, in terms of the actual development of the law of markets, Ricardo could easily be passed over, except that he is one of the critical figures in the Keynesian Revolution. It was Ricardo's correspondence with Malthus which first alerted Keynes to the issue of effective demand and Say's Law.[2] In addition, Ricardo's *Notes on Malthus*, although not published in his lifetime, presents a rich source of early classical criticisms of Malthus and the position he took. Thus, a clearer picture of the issues involved in the debates over the law of markets can be drawn from an examination of Ricardo's commentary on Malthus's *Principles*.

RICARDO'S *PRINCIPLES*

Ricardo's most prominent discussion of the law of markets published during his lifetime occurs in Chapter XXI of his *Principles of Political Economy and Taxation* (Ricardo 1951–73: I. 289–300).[3] There Ricardo argues that the accumulation of capital will never permanently lower profits unless there is a

---

[1] Peach (1993: 15) went so far as to argue that Say's Law was 'central to [Ricardo's] mature theoretical system'.

[2] The critical importance of this correspondence is discussed in Chapter 7.

[3] Other discussions of the law of markets in Ricardo's published works are noted by Hollander (1979: 500–1, 510).

permanent rise in wages (ibid.: 289). He is, in this discussion, rebutting a position held originally by Adam Smith, who had argued the reverse: that falling profits were due to the accumulation of capital. O'Brien (1975: 41), for example, notes that Ricardo made use of Say's Law 'only because it provided a means of establishing that the mechanism of his model which produced declining profits was in fact the *only* mechanism which could produce declining profits, and that over-production theories could not explain a decline in profits'. Similarly, Hollander (1979: 125–6) wrote that 'Ricardo clearly believed that the success of his own theory of profits implied the corresponding failure of the entire Malthusian theory of effective demand'. Ricardo (op. cit.: 290), in raising the law of markets, is thus arguing that demand failure is not a cause of falling profits: 'M. Say has...most satisfactorily shewn, that there is no amount of capital which may not be employed in a country, because demand is only limited by production'.

Ricardo conceives of the issue in the same way as Say and Mill. Production is the means through which purchases of other goods and services are effected. 'By producing,' wrote Ricardo, a producer 'necessarily becomes either the consumer of his own goods, or the purchaser and consumer of the goods of some other person' (ibid.). The desire to consume impels each individual to seek to discover what to sell to others. If goods are produced which fail to find a market, then production of these goods will stop and other goods will be produced instead:

> It is not to be supposed that he should, for any length of time, be ill-informed of the commodities which he can most advantageously produce, to attain the object which he has in view, namely, the possession of other goods; and, therefore, it is not probable that he will continually produce a commodity for which there is no demand. (Ibid.)

Unless wages rise so much that profits disappear, 'there cannot, then, be accumulated in a country any amount of capital which cannot be employed productively' (ibid.). So long as individuals have unmet demands, there will be demand for more goods, 'and it will be an effectual demand while he has any new value to offer in exchange' (ibid.: 291). If a sum of money were given to someone, Ricardo wrote, 'he would not lock it up in a chest' (ibid.). He would either 'increase his expenses...employ it himself productively, or lend it to some other person for that purpose' (ibid.).

The process of exchange is once again presented as commodities first exchanged for money and the money then re-exchanged for a different set of goods: 'Productions are always bought by productions, or by services; money is only the medium by which the exchange is effected' (ibid.: 291–2). And while there may be over-production of individual goods, this cannot happen for all goods together:

> Too much of a particular commodity may be produced, of which there may be such a glut in the market, as not to repay the capital expended on it; but this cannot be the case with respect to all commodities. (Ibid.: 292)

Individuals want more than they have, but to obtain more they must first produce more. As Ricardo wrote, the wish to have more than he already has 'is implanted in every man's breast; nothing is required but the means, and nothing can afford the means, but an increase of production' (ibid.). And individuals clearly do want more than they have, because 'if men ceased to consume, they would cease to produce' (ibid.: 293). This leads to the conclusion that:

> There is no limit to demand – no limit to the employment of capital while it yields any profit, and that however abundant capital may become, there is no other adequate reason for a fall of profit but a rise of wages. (Ibid.: 296)

Ricardo thus repeats what others had said before him: goods buy goods; partial gluts are possible but over-production of all goods taken together is impossible; and, finally, and most importantly, there is no upper limit to demand.

It is these same issues which Ricardo discussed in his correspondence with Malthus. It was this same correspondence which Keynes cited in both the *General Theory* and his essay on Malthus in *Essays in Biography* and which was to have so profound an influence on the course of economic theory.

RICARDO–MALTHUS: FIRST ROUND

Until 1936, it was universally accepted that Ricardo had been in the right in his debate with Malthus over the law of markets. As Ambirajan (1959: 162) rightly states, 'even sympathetic writers and admirers like Dr Bonar considered Malthus's ideas on gluts as fallacious'. Keynes himself, in a speech given on 9 October 1924, contrasted Ricardo with Malthus in the following terms:

> The most important influence of [Malthus's] later years was his intimacy with Ricardo.... Nevertheless they frequently differed on points of economic theory and method. Malthus is the ancestor of the historical, inductive, realist school primarily interested in the applications of their science. *Ricardo will always remain the most powerful abstract intelligence which has found Economics worthy of it.* (KP: PS/2, italics added)

This is a far cry from the attitude which Keynes was to take in his biographical essay on Malthus and then later in the *General Theory*. In 1932, Keynes wrote of the Ricardo–Malthus correspondence:

> One cannot rise from a perusal of this correspondence without a feeling that the almost total obliteration of Malthus's line of approach and the complete domination of Ricardo's for a period of a hundred years has been a disaster to the progress of economics. Time after time in these letters Malthus is talking plain sense, the force of which Ricardo with his head in the clouds wholly fails to comprehend. Time after time a crushing refutation by Malthus is met by a mind so completely closed that Ricardo does not even see what Malthus is saying. (*CW* X: 98)

In 1924, Keynes saw Ricardo as having, 'the most powerful abstract intelligence which has found Economics worthy of it' but by 1932, this same Ricardo has a 'mind so completely closed that [he] does not even see what Malthus is saying'. It is Keynes's later judgement which has come to dominate the modern view of the relative merits of Ricardo and Malthus on the issue of effective demand. For example, St Clair ([1957] 1965: 186) wrote:

> The idea of deficient demand is so foreign to Ricardo's thought that, incredible as it might seem, he entirely misses the point. Ricardo, in fact, was one of those men who, though gifted with keen reasoning powers, nevertheless lack the ability to grasp the meaning of anyone whose mind follows a different train of thought.

Stewart (1972: 30) also accepted that Malthus had had the deeper understanding but had not been able to establish his case, writing, 'although Ricardo had the logic, Malthus had the intuition: there was, or in some circumstances could be, something wrong with Ricardo's argument that wages and profits would all get spent, and that general unemployment was an impossibility'. Stigler also accepted that the deeper truth lay with Malthus but argued that Ricardo had been the more rigorous scholar: 'the triumph of Ricardo over Malthus cannot be regretted by the modern economist: it is more important that good logic win over bad than that good insight win over poor' (Stigler 1965: 324; see also Blaug 1985: 175).

Indeed, whatever misgivings one might have about Malthus's reasoning, to accept that Ricardo was right on the issue of effective demand would require one to embrace the classical meaning of the law of markets. Although it is generally accepted that Malthus and Keynes had entirely different theories, it is also accepted that Malthus had understood the importance of effective demand, the significance of which Ricardo was incapable of appreciating.

Ricardo, in fact, understood Malthus perfectly well, and in his defence of the law of markets he more than held his own against the arguments advanced by Malthus. Their first discussion on the law of markets occurred in the latter half of 1814 in the midst of a correspondence over the effects on profitability of higher imports of foreign grain. The issue turned to the question of the effect of demand on capital accumulation. On 26 June, Ricardo wrote that a rise in the price of corn without an increase in capital would lead to a fall in demand for other things (Ricardo 1951–73: VI. 108). He then added:

> With the same Capital there would be less production and less demand. Demand has no other limits but the want of power of paying for the commodities demanded. Everything which tends to diminish production tends to diminish this power. (Ibid.)

On 25 July, Ricardo, in a similar vein, wrote that 'effective demand...cannot augment or long continue stationary with a diminishing capital' (ibid.: 114). That is, if the capital of a country is falling, so too will the level of demand. In a letter dated 11 August, Ricardo pointed out that both he and Malthus agreed that the ratio of consumption to production is highest where capital accumulation is highest. Therefore, if the level of capital fell by half, profitability would rise while the level of demand relative to production would fall (ibid.: 121). Malthus disagreed, and in disagreeing raised the issue of the willingness of buyers to buy. On 19 August, he wrote:

> I can by no means agree with you in thinking that if the capital of this country were diminished one half 'demand as compared with production would diminish'. Precisely the reverse I think would take place. You do not certainly take sufficiently into your consideration the natural desires of man, which are after all the foundation of all demand. (Ibid.: 123)

Ricardo replied on 30 August. He could not see how it could be denied that demand had fallen if the amount consumed had decreased. He added, 'I sometimes suspect that we do not attach the same meaning to the word demand' (ibid.: 129). This led Malthus, in his reply of 11 September, into a discussion of the meaning of demand. In his reply Malthus accepted, in a qualified way, that demand is constituted by supply, but argued that one could not be sure that those who are able will always exercise the demands they are capable of exercising:

> Effectual demand consists of two elements the *power* and the *will* to purchase. The power to purchase may perhaps be represented correctly by the produce of the country whether small or great; but the will to purchase will always be the greatest, the smaller is the produce compared with the population, and the more scantily the wants of the society are supplied. When capital is abundant it is not easy to find new objects sufficiently in demand.... In a country abundant in capital the value of the whole produce cannot increase with rapidity from the insufficiency of demand. (Ibid.: 131)

This led Malthus to disagree specifically with Mill's views in *Commerce Defended*. According to Malthus, there is no reason to assume that the desire to purchase more will increase as rapidly as incomes:[4]

> I by no means think that the power to purchase necessarily involves a proportionate will to purchase; and I cannot agree with Mr. Mill in an ingenious position which he lays down in his answer to Mr. Spence, that in reference to a nation, supply can never exceed demand. A nation must certainly have the power of purchasing all that it produces, but I can easily conceive it not to have the will: and if we were to grow next year half as much corn again as usual, a great part of it would be wasted, and the same would be true if all commodities of all kinds were increased one half. It would be impossible that they should yield the expense of production. You have never I think taken sufficiently into consideration the wants and tastes of mankind. It is not merely the proportion of commodities to each other but their proportion to the wants and tastes of mankind that determines prices. (Ibid.: 132)

---

[4] This is the issue of satiation of demand, which Black (1967) and Rashid ([1977] 1986) believe to be the central point Malthus was trying to make.

Ricardo replied on 16 September. He agreed that 'effectual demand consists of two elements, the *power* and the *will* to purchase, but', he added, 'I think the will is very seldom wanting where the power exists' (ibid.: 133). Both consumer demand and investment would add to total demand, the only difference being the kinds of goods which would be demanded. If this were not the case, then Malthus would be right to disagree with Mill:

> The desire of accumulation will occasion demand just as effectually as a desire to consume, it will only change the objects on which the demand will exercise itself. If you think that with an increase of capital men will become indifferent both to consumption and accumulation, then you are correct in opposing Mr. Mill's idea, that in reference to a nation, supply can never exceed demand. (Ibid.: 133–4)

Ricardo agreed with Malthus that if the production of any commodity increased by half over the next year, some of it would be wasted, but that, he wrote, is not the real question:

> The real question is this; If money should retain the same value next year, would any man (if he had it) want the will to spend half as much again as he now does, – and if he did want the will, would he feel no inclination to add the increase of his revenue to his capital, and employ it as such. In short I consider the wants and tastes of mankind as unlimited. We all wish to add to our enjoyments or to our power. Consumption adds to our enjoyments, – accumulation to our power, and they equally promote demand. (Ibid.: 134–5)

This is the issue of the law of markets. Is there a need to fear recession and unemployment through failure of effective demand? Of any individual commodity demand may be less than the supply at a price which covers costs. But there is no need to be concerned that the 'wants and tastes of mankind' will not rise rapidly enough to ensure that demand in total keeps pace with production in total. These wants and tastes are unlimited. The desire for consumption and for capital accumulation will ensure that a shortage of demand in aggregate will never occur.

Malthus continued to disagree. In a letter dated 9 October he argued, in effect, that there is a diminishing marginal utility for goods as a whole. The greater the level of production, and therefore consumption, the lower the addition to utility of each additional unit of consumption:

> The true question relative to Mr. Mill's proposition is not whether a man would like to spend half as much again; but whether you can furnish to persons of the same incomes a great additional quantity of commodities without lowering their price so much compared with the price of production as to destroy the effective demand for such a supply, and consequently to check its continuance to the same extent. (Ibid.: 142)

And, interestingly, Malthus appears not to accept that investment is itself a form of demand. Malthus wrote, 'I cannot by any means agree with you in your observation that "the desire of accumulation will occasion demand just as *effectually* as a desire to consume" and that "consumption and accumulation equally promote demand"' (ibid.: 141). Malthus argued instead that 'effectual demand' falls when profits are squeezed, that is, when the 'price of produce falls compared with the expense of production' (ibid.: 142). Since, wrote Malthus, profits are at their highest when the amount of available capital is low, and since effective demand rises when profitability rises, then effective demand is highest when the amount of capital is low. Therefore, an increase in the flow of capital will lower the level of effective demand.

Ricardo would not, of course, agree that effective demand would be highest where the amount of capital was comparatively lowest. In his reply, dated 23 October, he made three points. First, he stated that he had not ignored the wants and tastes of mankind, but had in fact built these into his approach by assuming that they were infinite (Ricardo 1951–73: VI. 148). Secondly, he argued that the accumulation of capital does add to total demand since it leads to an ability to afford more (ibid.). And, thirdly, he pointed out that Malthus was arguing that increased capital would lead not merely to a relative fall in consumption, but to an absolute reduction:

> You seem to infer that [the demand for] commodities will not only be relatively lower but really lower, and this is in fact the foundation of our difference with regard to the theory of Mr. Mill. (Ibid.: 149)

In his reply on 23 November, Malthus, far from denying the accuracy of Ricardo's statement, if anything explicitly accepted it, writing:

> If you were at once to employ all our soldiers sailors and menial servants in productive labour, the price of produce would fall more than ten per cent, and the encouragement to employ the same quantity of capital would cease.... Unless the commodities produced are new and more desirable, or cheaper, the producers will certainly be left to consume what they have produced themselves. Others will have neither the power nor the will to consume more. (Ibid.: 155)

In his reply of 18 December, Ricardo cited the second edition of Say's *Treatise*, which had just been published. According to Say, Ricardo wrote, demand is constituted by supply, but only so long as production is based on an accurate assessment of what buyers wish to buy:

> Mr. Say, in the new edition of his book...supports, I think, very ably the doctrine that demand is regulated by production. Demand is always an exchange of one commodity for another. The shoemaker when he exchanges his shoes for bread has an effective demand for bread.... And if his shoes are not in demand it shews that he has not been governed by the just principles of trade, and that he has not used his capital and his labour in the manufacture of the commodity required by the society, – more caution will enable him to correct his error in his future production. Accumulation necessarily increases production and as necessarily increases consumption. (Ibid.: 163–4)

Finally, on 29 December, Malthus wrote that he had seen the passage in Say's second edition, but did not fully agree with him.[5] And there the discussion came to rest.[6] From Ricardo's point of view, the issue was clear: demand failure could not lead to recession. Both Meek (1967b: 58) and Hollander (1979: 502–3) recognise that the point Ricardo is making is that demand deficiency is not a concern. Yet neither sees this as the central issue of the debate over the law of markets. Meek describes 'Say's Law proper' as the proposition that demand is constituted by the output of the nation, which he considers 'obviously true' (1967b: 61). The other aspects of the logical propositions which deny demand deficiency he calls '[James] Mill's theory'. These are, firstly, that investment creates demand in the same way as consumption, and, secondly, that in the normal course of events, there will be no hoarding (ibid.: 60). Meek thus appears to distinguish Ricardo's conclusions from the law of markets.

Hollander (1979: 506, 507) also sees Ricardo adopting a position closer to that of Mill rather than Say. He accurately summarises Ricardo's position as being 'that there is no limit to the expansion of capacity, however extensive it may be, flowing from a lack of aggregate demand' (ibid.: 507). Yet for all that, in summing up his interpretation of Ricardo, he writes that Ricardo 'adhered to that version of the law of markets labelled "Say's Equality"' (ibid.: 513), which is the version Hollander (1985: 27) associates with Say.[7] Hollander thus focuses on the modern question of whether recessions were possible in a Say's Law world rather than on the point Ricardo was trying to make, which was whether demand deficiency could be the cause of recession. But, having reached his conclusion, Hollander (1979: 513) must then confront the fact that when Ricardo dealt with the post-war depression, he 'failed to recognize the relevance of temporary excess demand for money'. This is a puzzle only because trying to fit Ricardo into the Procrustean bed of Say's Equality loses the point of Ricardo's argument.

RICARDO–MALTHUS: SECOND ROUND

It was the publication of Malthus's *Principles* which caused Malthus and Ricardo to re-commence their correspondence on the law of markets. It was also the

---

[5] The letter is notable for a particular phrase which Malthus uses, 'I think the source of [Say's] error is, that he does not properly distinguish between the necessaries of life and other commodities, – the former *create their own demand* the latter not' (Ricardo 1951–73: VI. 168, italics added). It is possible that Keynes took the phrase 'supply creates its own demand' from this passage.

[6] Meek (1967b: 60) notes that Malthus had 'become very busy writing his pamphlet on rent'.

[7] In his book on Ricardo, Hollander (1979: 510) wrote, 'I conclude that while Ricardo frequently appealed to Say's authority, their positions on detailed analytical matters in fact differed substantially'. In his later work on J.S. Mill (1985: 27) he however wrote, 'the evidence is complex, but on balance I am led to conclude that it is the more qualified version, that of Say, which must be attributed to Ricardo'.

catalyst for a protracted debate amongst English economists on the possibility of demand failure and the need for unproductive consumption to ensure the full employment of resources. And what made Malthus's *Principles* the focus of attention which it became was its argument that unproductive consumption needed to be encouraged to ensure the greatest rate of economic growth and the fullest use of resources.[8]

Malthus's *Principles* was published in April 1820. The first notice that Ricardo had read it is found in a letter to McCulloch dated 2 May 1820 in which the issue of demand deficiency is noted. Ricardo wrote that 'the most objectionable chapter in Mr. Malthus' book is that perhaps on the bad effects from too great accumulation of capital, and the consequent want of demand for the goods produced' (Ricardo 1951–73: VIII. 181). On 4 May Ricardo wrote to Malthus and raised the same objections (ibid.: 185), to which there was no written reply. On 2 August, Ricardo mentioned to McCulloch that he was 'giving a second reading to Mr. Malthus' book' (ibid.: 215), adding: 'I am even less pleased with it than I was at first' (ibid.). In this letter there is a long discussion of Malthus's views (ibid.: 215–17), which Ricardo would later direct at Malthus himself. On 9 October, Ricardo, in agreeing with Malthus on Say's inadequacies in his treatment of Say's Law, restates the issue of the law of markets as clearly and succinctly as possible:

Men err in their productions, there is no deficiency of demand. (Ibid.: 277)

Malthus replied on 26 October, writing that he was 'fortified with new arguments to prove that...if there is not an adequate taste for luxuries and conveniences, or unproductive labour, there must necessarily be a general glut' (ibid.: 285). Ricardo answered on 24 November, saying that there was no need for such arguments, since 'with a very slight alteration I should entirely concur in your proposition' (ibid.: 301). Ricardo also states he has written a series of notes on Malthus's *Principles*, adding:

I can see no soundness in the reasons you give for the usefulness of demand, on the part of unproductive consumers. How their consuming, without reproducing, can be beneficial to a country, in any possible state of it, I confess I cannot discover. (Ibid.)

On 27 November, Malthus provides a perfunctory reply (ibid.: 309), after which their correspondence contains no further discussion on these issues until the middle of the following year. On 25 June 1821, Malthus's question, 'Can There be a Glut of Commodities?', was the subject of discussion at the Political Economy Club (ibid.: IX. 9n) which led to an exchange of letters. The correspondence began with a letter from Malthus on 7 July 1821 and concluded

---

[8] Within five years, other texts on economic principles were written by James Mill, McCulloch and Torrens in which a rebuttal of Malthus formed a large component. In 1821 Say's *Letters to Mr. Malthus* was published and the fourth edition of his *Treatise* was translated into English. This reaction is discussed by Blaug (1958: 43). Oddly, Ricardo failed to respond when he might have done, in the revised third edition of his *Principles* published in 1821.

with a final rejoinder by Ricardo on 21 July 1821. During this correspondence on the law of markets, each wrote two letters.

Malthus opened the discussion on 7 July with the contention that if owners of capital decide to change the direction of their expenditure from unproductive uses to productive, there will be a fall in the demand for the increased output of industry, causing stagnation and unemployment. There will be more output but fewer buyers. To avoid this problem, Malthus argues that there needs to be an increase in unproductive consumption. The issue, as stated by Malthus, is this:

> An attempt to accumulate very rapidly which necessarily implies a considerable diminution of unproductive consumption, by greatly impairing the usual motives to production must prematurely check the progress of wealth.... Under all common circumstances, if an increased power of production be not accompanied by an increase of *unproductive* expenditure, it will inevitably lower profits and throw labourers out of employment. But on the other hand if it be accompanied by a proper proportion of *unproductive* expenditure it will certainly raise both profits and wages and greatly advance the wealth of the country. (Ibid.: 10–11)

Ricardo replied on 9 July that if the question were merely a matter of insufficient motives to produce: 'I should not have a word to say against you' (ibid.: 15). 'But,' he continues:

> I have rather understood you to say that vast powers of production are put into action and the result is unfavourable to the interests of mankind, and you have suggested as a remedy either that less should be produced, or more should be unproductively consumed.... You often appear to me to contend not only that production can go on so far without an adequate motive, but that it actually has done so lately, and that we are now suffering the consequences of it in stagnation of trade, in a want of employment for our labourers &c. &c., and the remedy you propose is an increase of consumption. It is against this latter doctrine that I protest and give my decided opposition. (Ibid.: 15–16)

It is Malthus's recommendation of an increase in consumption to cure recession and unemployment which Ricardo especially rejects. In his reply on 16 July, Malthus speaks of his 'despair' in ever getting Ricardo to understand what he is saying, but seems to repeat exactly what Ricardo had said. Malthus agrees that he does 'recommend a certain proportion of unproductive consumption' because such unproductive consumption 'is absolutely and indispensably necessary to call forth the resources of a country' (ibid.: 19). Malthus lays the issue out again, repeating, exactly as Ricardo had understood him, that the problem is that more might be produced than the community would buy:

> The question is, whether this stagnation of capital, and subsequent stagnation in the demand for labour *arising from increased production* without an adequate proportion of unproductive consumption on the part of the landlords and capitalists, could take place without prejudice to the country. (Ibid.: 20, italics added)

Ricardo replies on 21 July and immediately points out that he (Ricardo) seemed to have understood Malthus very well indeed:

> You seem to be surprised that I should understand you to say in your book 'that vast powers of production are put into action, and the result is unfavourable to the interests of mankind'.... Even as you state your proposition in your present letter, I have a right to conclude that you see great evils in great powers of production, from the quantity of commodities which will be the result, and the low price to which they will fall. Saving, you would say, would first lead to great production – then to low prices, which would necessarily be followed by low profits. With very low profits the motives for saving would cease, and therefore the motives for increased production would also cease. Do you not then say that increased production is often attended with evil consequences to mankind, because it destroys the motives to industry, and to the keeping up of the increased production? Now in much of this I cannot agree with you. (Ibid.: 23–4)

Ricardo then sets out at length to explain why he does not accept that demand failure or too much saving can be genuine explanations for recession. He concludes his analysis by noting that if he thought the problem was too much saving then he would accept the Malthusian remedy of increased consumption:

> I should not make a protest against an increase of consumption, as a remedy to the stagnation of trade, if I thought, as you do, that we were now suffering from too great savings. As I have already said I do not see how stagnation of trade can arise from such a cause. (Ibid.: 26)

If there were over-saving, then, Ricardo agrees, unproductive consumption would be the cure. But, as far as over-saving is concerned:

> Such and such evils may exist, but the question is, do they exist now? I think not, none of the symptoms indicate that they do, and in my opinion increased savings would alleviate rather than aggravate the sufferings of which we have lately had to complain. *Stagnation is a derangement of the system, and not too much general production, arising from too great an accumulation of capital.* (Ibid.: 26–7, italics added)

Both Malthus and Ricardo recognised the existence of a contemporary recession. Malthus believed it to be caused by too much saving. Ricardo believed the cause to lie elsewhere: in a 'derangement of the system'. The difference between them is the causes of recession, not whether they occur at all.

Ricardo's arguments seem to have confounded Malthus to such a great extent that he did not reply, as he normally would have been expected to. On 10 September Ricardo, apparently unused to such delays between letters, wrote again to ask whether his earlier letter had been received. This finally elicited an answer from Malthus (13 September), acknowledging that he had received the earlier letter but had not replied 'partly from a good deal of business of various kinds which I found on arrival, and partly from despair of approaching you much nearer on the question we were then discussing' (ibid.: 63).

Ricardo's letter had left Malthus with no ready answer. It is Malthus who at this point drops the matter and simply changes the subject. In the second round of their personal correspondence on the law of markets, Ricardo carried the day. And in the final analysis, when Keynes came to read over their correspondence more than a century later, it was he who turned out to be 'stone-deaf' to what Ricardo had been saying (cf. *CW* VII: 364 and *CW* X: 98).

RICARDO'S *NOTES ON MALTHUS*

Ricardo's *Notes on Malthus's Principles of Political Economy* provides an unusually rich interpretative source on the actual meaning of Say's Law for classical economists. These 'notes' were a commentary on Malthus's *Principles* which remained unpublished during Ricardo's lifetime. This should not, of course, be taken to mean that they carried no influence. For example, McCulloch was sent the notes and acknowledged his full agreement with their content with regard to the law of markets (Ricardo 1951–73: VIII. 338).

In Malthus we find a succession of arguments all pointing towards a single conclusion: that too much saving will lead to demand deficiency, the remedy for which lies in encouraging unproductive consumption. It is important to bear in mind that at this time 'consumption' did not mean the purchase of a good as modern usage has it, but the use of a good. Goods could be consumed productively, which meant that they were part of a production process, or they could be consumed unproductively, which meant that they were used to satisfy a final demand of some kind. But in either case, consumption meant that the good had been destroyed. Malthus and Ricardo are therefore disagreeing about whether it will enrich a community to use up a larger proportion of available resources in ways which destroy value but which do not create any value in return.

The following quotations from Malthus's *Principles* are, for the most part, taken from Chapter VII[9] section IX, which was to have a profound influence on Keynes.[10]

At the start of section IX, Malthus argues that if there is a shift towards productive uses of labour and away from unproductive uses, the flow of goods and services on to the market will increase at a rapid rate, but demand for the output produced will not keep pace. Therefore, he argues, it is essential that there be a group within the community whose role is to consume without also

---

[9] Milgate (1982: 49n) notes that 'of a total of 315 notes 119 are attached to this chapter'.

[10] In his essay on Malthus, Keynes wrote that this section 'had wholly failed to enter the comprehension of Ricardo just as it has failed to influence the ideas of posterity' (*CW* X: 101). And in a footnote Keynes added, 'I refer the reader to the whole of [Chapter VII] section IX as a masterly exposition of the conditions which determined the *optimum* of Saving in the actual economic system in which we live' (ibid.: 101n).

producing. And the point is that they must not produce, because any additional product they might create would only increase the glut of commodities:[11]

> Under a rapid accumulation of capital, or, more properly speaking, a rapid conversion of unproductive into productive labour, the demand, compared with the supply of material products, would prematurely fail, and the motive to further accumulation be checked.... It follows that...it is absolutely necessary that a country with great powers of production should possess a body of unproductive consumers. (Ricardo 1951–73: II. 421)

About this Ricardo comments:

> A body of unproductive labourers are just as necessary and as useful with a view to future production, as a fire which should consume in the manufacturers warehouse the goods which those unproductive labourers would otherwise consume. (Ibid.: 421n)

Winch (1987b: 83) agrees with Ricardo that, to Malthus, consumption literally meant '"used up" or consumed as in a fire'. Malthus nevertheless argued that a body of consumers who do not produce is absolutely essential as they can create demand without adding to the problem of glutted markets. This too is noted by Winch, who accepts that what Malthus sought was employment which did not add to existing stocks of goods (ibid.).[12] Moreover, Malthus appears to clothe in virtue those who undertake this role of unproductive consumption. An unknown proportion of the community is required to be unproductive consumers to ensure that the economy continues to grow:

> The great laws of nature have provided for the leisure of a certain portion of society; and if this beneficent offer be not accepted by an adequate number of individuals...the rest of society...will be decidedly injured.
> What the proportion is between the productive and unproductive classes of a society, which affords the greatest encouragement to the continued increase of wealth...the resources of political economy are unequal to determine. (Ricardo 1951–73: II. 421–2)

The owners of capital could do the consuming, according to Malthus, but just will not:

> With regard to the capitalists...they have certainly the power of consuming their profits...and if they were to consume it...there might be little occasion for unproductive consumers. But such consumption is not consistent with the actual habits of the generality of capitalists. (Ibid.: 423)

---

[11] Malthus's quotations have been edited so that the argument can be more easily followed.

[12] Meek (1967b: 64) correctly describes Malthus as arguing that 'continued progress required the existence of a vast horde of idlers'.

If the economy becomes too productive there may simply not be enough willingness to consume everything produced. The choice which will then confront the capitalist class will be either to consume more or to produce less. The choice many will take will be to produce less, with the result being that there will be a fall in national wealth. Here is Malthus's logic:

> If the powers of production among capitalists are considerable, the consumption of the landlords, in addition to that of the capitalists themselves and of their workmen, may still be insufficient to keep up and increase the exchangeable value of the whole produce.... And if this be so, the capitalists cannot continue the same habits of saving. They must either consume more, or produce less.... The probability is that a considerable body of them will be induced to prefer the latter alternative, and produce less. But if...a permanent diminution of production takes place...the whole of the national wealth...will be decidedly diminished. (Ibid.: 424)

Malthus applies his approach to the extinction of the national debt, which, he argues, would be catastrophic:

> It is, I know, generally thought that all would be well, if we could but be relieved from the heavy burden of our debt. And yet I feel perfectly convinced that, if a spunge [sic] could be applied to it to-morrow...[the] nation, instead of being enriched, would be impoverished. It is the greatest mistake to suppose that the landlords and capitalists would...be prepared for so great an additional consumption as such a change would require.... The new distribution of produce would diminish the demand for the results of productive labour...and a much greater number of persons would be starving for want of employment, than before the extinction of the debt. (Ibid.: 434–5)

To which Ricardo commented: 'I should think Mr. Malthus must be the only man in England who would expect such effects from such a cause' (ibid.: 435n).[13]

Section IX of Chapter VII ends with a summation in which Malthus again calls for the encouragement of unproductive consumption:

> It is found by experience that, though there may be the power [to consume], there is not the will; and it is to supply this will that a body of unproductive consumers is necessary. Their specific use in encouraging wealth is...to give the greatest exchangeable value to the results of the national industry. (Ibid.: 435–6)

To which Ricardo, in exasperation, replies:

> How can they by their consumption give value to the results of the national industry? It might as justly be contended that an earthquake which overthrows my house and buries my property, gives value to the national industry. (Ibid.: 436)

---

[13] Ricardo was wrong about Malthus's uniqueness. Spence, for example, had also taken a similar position (see Winch 1966: 31).

It was no wonder that Ricardo treated Malthus's views with such disdain. The idea that the economy of England, during the early years of the nineteenth century, had become so productive that markets were glutted due to over-production was preposterous to him. The problem, according to Ricardo, was not too much saving but too little. There was not enough available capital. The abysmal living conditions of the vast majority of the English population was to Ricardo proof beyond argument that what was needed was more output. A theory which, in effect, recommended the wasteful use of resources as a way to create wealth was condemned by Ricardo out of hand.[14]

Ricardo, moreover, had no need of Malthus's theory of recession. The law of markets explicitly ruled out demand deficiency, but that is all it ruled out. Ricardo, in fact, had explanations for the unemployment he saw around him which he discussed in his *Notes on Malthus's Principles*. Ricardo contrasts his own view of why some goods remain unsold with Malthus's:

> If the commodities produced be suited to the wants of the purchasers, they cannot exist in such abundance as not to find a market.
>
> Mistakes may be made, and commodities not suited to the demand may be produced – of these there may be a glut; they may not sell at their usual price; but then this is owing to the mistake, and not to the want of demand for productions. *For every thing produced there must be a proprietor*. Either it is the master, the landlord, or the labourer. Whoever is possessed of a commodity is necessarily a demander, either he wishes to consume the commodity himself, and then no purchaser is wanted; or he wishes to sell it, and purchase some other thing *with the money*, which shall either be consumed by him, or be made instrumental to future productions. The commodity he possesses will obtain him this or it will not. If it will, the object is accomplished, and his commodity has found a market. If it will not what does it prove? that he has not adapted his means well to his end, he has miscalculated.... What I wish to impress on the readers [sic] mind is that *it is at all times the bad adaptation of the commodities produced to the wants of mankind which is the specific evil, and not the abundance of commodities*. (Ricardo 1951–73: II. 304–6, italics added)

Note how Ricardo conceives of the issue. Goods have been produced and at every stage they are owned by someone, whether by master, landlord or labourer. The decision then is whether the goods owned are the specific goods one wishes to keep for oneself. If yes, then there is nothing further to do. But if not, then one

---

[14] Keynes, however, found Malthus's writings completely convincing. In his famous paean to Malthus, Keynes wrote: 'If only Malthus, instead of Ricardo, had been the parent stem from which nineteenth-century economics proceeded, what a much wiser and richer place the world would be to-day' (*CW* X: 100–101). Blaug (1985: 175–6) rightly described Keynes's support for Malthus as 'astounding', the very same word used by Schumpeter (1933: 653). It is not that Keynes misunderstood Malthus's conclusions but that he agreed with them which is so astonishing. While Keynes stated that he preferred that labour be used productively, he also made it clear that if that were not possible, then labour should be used unproductively. In either case, national wealth would be increased (see *CW* VII: 220).

must sell for money what one has and spend these receipts on what is wanted. If one has produced properly, then it will be relatively easy to convert the commodities one owns into money. If, however, the goods produced do not coincide with market demand, then the conversion of goods into money will not be possible at prices which cover costs. But the existence of unsold goods should not be interpreted to mean that production has outrun the demands of the community, only that the wrong goods have been produced.

Ricardo's chapter 'On Sudden Changes in the Channels of Trade' (ibid.: I. 263–72) specifically attributes the causes of recession to miscalculations in production decisions arising from shifts in demand patterns for particular goods.[15] Gluts of manufactured goods will lead to 'considerable distress, and no doubt some loss will be experienced by those who are engaged in the manufacture of such commodities; and it will be felt not only at the time of the change, but through the whole interval during which they are removing their capitals, and the labour which they can command, from one employment to another' (ibid.: 263). Just how slow the adjustment process may be is indicated where Ricardo notes that 'it is often impossible to divert the machinery which may have been erected for one manufacture, to the purposes of another' (ibid.: 266). Sowell (1972: 29) describes this chapter as 'the first systematic attempt to reconcile the facts of depression and unemployment with Say's Law'.

The difference between Ricardo and Malthus was over the nature of recessions, not whether they occurred. In the view of Ricardo, the causes of recession were structural, while, in the eyes of Malthus, they were due to deficient demand. Hollander (1979: 516) notes that Ricardo 'was preoccupied by general unemployment' and that 'his explanation ran in terms of temporary misallocation of resources'. Winch (1987b: 80–81) also recognised this difference between Ricardo and Malthus:

> Whereas Ricardo treated post-war depression and unemployment as a problem of maladjustments due to a mismatch in the demand and supply of individual commodities, Malthus regarded it as evidence of a general deficiency of demand in relation to supply, leading to all markets being overstocked and profits being depressed across the board.

Whatever one might think of Ricardo's views, it is clear that he understood Malthus, both as a theoretician and as a policy maker. He understood Malthus to be concerned with there being too little aggregate demand and he even went so far as to accept that, if that were really the case, then there would be grounds for government spending to ensure full employment.

Moreover, it should be noted that Ricardo's position does not require one to read into the law of markets a necessary belief in wages funds or any other special element of classical economics, such as the distinction between productive and

---

[15] McCulloch wrote to Ricardo to lament that this chapter meant Ricardo had thrown in the towel over the law of markets (Ricardo 1951–73: VIII. 381–2). Ricardo, in reply, denied that he had given anything away to Malthus (ibid.: 387).

unproductive labour. Malthus had stated that demand would not keep pace with supply, so that some group had to consume without producing if wealth creation was to be at a maximum. Ricardo, in turn, replied that demand would never fall short of production if the correct assortment of goods and services were provided to the market. In his view, wasteful spending would reduce wealth creation rather than enhance it. That was the issue. Keynes took Malthus's side and constructed a theory which attempted to show that demand could not be expected to keep pace with supply. The consequence is that, since the publication of the *General Theory*, demand failure is considered by many, if not, indeed, most, economists as a genuine possibility. Thus, through the influence of Keynes, the most widely condemned economic fallacy of the nineteenth century became the mainstream in the twentieth.

4. John Stuart Mill

John Stuart Mill's *Principles of Political Economy* was the standard text on economic theory for a generation after its publication in 1848.[1] While Mill ([1871] 1921: xxvii) characterised himself as doing no more than systematising the views of others, he was, as Stigler (1965: 7) wrote, 'one of the most original economists in the history of the science'. Stigler (ibid.: 10) further argued that Mill's discussion of Say's Law was 'penetrating as well as original'. Sowell (1972: 142), on the other hand, claims that Mill had not appreciated the advances which had been made in discussions on the law of markets, and in his *Principles* 'turned the clock back to a position which remained largely unchallenged until Keynes' *General Theory*'. Whichever might have been the direction the clock was turned, it is certainly true that the position taken by Mill became the standard classical understanding of the law of markets. The theory outlined by Mill would be accepted for almost a century by virtually every English economist.

SOME UNSETTLED QUESTIONS

In his essay 'On the Influence of Consumption on Production', which formed the second essay in *Some Unsettled Questions of Political Economy* ([1874] 1974a: 47–74), Mill set out to demonstrate that recessions and unemployment are not due to failures of effective demand. This classic statement of the meaning of the law of markets was written in 1829–30 but not published until 1844. Sowell (1972: 143) described it as 'perhaps the clearest and most advanced presentation [of Say's Law] in classical economics'. Sir John Hicks referred to it as 'one of the finest products of classical economics' (quoted in Hollander 1985: 484), while Niehans (1990: 114) said that Mill's statement 'is still unsurpassed'. High praise indeed. The question remains, however, whether they actually understood what Mill was trying to say.

Since the publication of the *General Theory* has obscured the meaning of the law of markets, it has become increasingly difficult to comprehend what Mill was

---

[1] See especially Hutchison (1978: 61–2n) for a discussion of Mill's dominance in the latter half of the nineteenth century; also Sowell (1972: 142) and Schwartz (1972:16–17).

saying.[2] If one starts from a Keynesian position, where Say's Law means that recessions cannot occur, then the effort Mill makes in the first half of the essay to deny the possibility of a general glut seems pointless in the face of the second half, where a quite profound explanation for recessions is detailed. The normally very perceptive Hutchison ([1953] 1962: 348–56) finds Mill's discussion incomprehensible, even going so far as to describe it as 'highly problematic and ambivalent, even schizophrenic' (ibid.: 18).

The problem arises from the modern interpretation, which is based on Keynes's argument that acceptance of Say's Law implies full employment. The assumption is made that all income will be spent on receipt, with the further implication that there were no variations in the demand for money. Mill's essay thus provides a conundrum, since it is an apparent defence of the law of markets yet acknowledges the existence of recession and of variations in the demand for money. As Schwartz (1972: 38) has rightly said, 'this work has puzzled many historians'. In his view Mill is 'asserting that Say's law is not always valid in the short run...due to monetary reasons' (ibid.), although, as he hastens to note, this does not turn Mill into a modern macroeconomist. Sowell (1972: 147) interprets the article to mean that Mill had 'limited the principle of the necessary equality of supply and demand to a barter economy'. And the point of origin of this approach to Mill's essay is Becker's and Baumol's (1952: 374) classic article[3] where they wrote:

> J.S. Mill, in the *Principles*, speaks similarly of the 'undersupply of money' during a commercial crisis, this again in connection with a discussion of Say's Law.... But the clearest statement on this point is that in J.S. Mill's second essay in his *Unsettled Questions*.... It is all there and explicitly – Walras' Law, Say's Identity which Mill points out holds only for a barter economy, the 'utility of money' which consists in permitting purchases to be made when convenient, the possibility of (temporary) oversupply of commodities when money is in excess demand, and Say's Equality which makes this only a temporary possibility....
>
> As was the case in other connections, some of the classics may simply not have considered it worth the effort to point out that they were speaking about long-run equilibrium tendencies.

That is, as a long-run tendency, an economy will move towards a full-employment equilibrium although there may be episodes of recession and unemployment. It is this approach which makes the general glut debate appear to be concerned with secular stagnation, since, if both sides agree that unemployment and recession are possible, then the debate must have been over whether they are temporary rather than permanent.

---

[2] Sowell ([1974] 1994: 53) quite rightly wrote: 'Keynes' well-known polemical interpretations of classical monetary theory make it difficult to read classical statements with fresh eyes or in the context in which they were originally made'.

[3] Becker and Baumol (1952) will be discussed more thoroughly in Chapter 9.

Yet this was not the issue.[4] Mill was not trying to show that there are tendencies which return an economy towards full employment (although he, of course, believed there were), but was instead attempting to demonstrate that when recessions occur, it would not be due to failure of effective demand. The consequence of Becker's and Baumol's influence is that even writers who recognise the immediate point Mill is attempting to make, embed their discussion in the classical theory of money and centre their discussion on Say's Identity versus Say's Equality.

In Hollander's *The Economics of John Stuart Mill* (1985), Mill's essay is discussed in the chapter devoted to money and banking. The specific issue Hollander addresses in relation to the essay is how Mill analysed variations in the supply of money (ibid.: 484). In answer, Hollander wrote, 'Mill formally allowed for excess demand for money to hold. The historiographic, analytical and policy implications of his allowance will be our concern in what follows' (ibid.). And indeed, the remainder of the discussion on Say's Law deals with this issue, that is, whether Mill held Say's Identity or Say's Equality. Hollander's conclusion is that Mill ultimately accepted the equality version, although, under the influence of his father, he had accepted Say's Identity to begin with (ibid.: 508). But what is startling is that Hollander, in finishing his overview of Mill's essay, writes that it closes on the 'orthodox theme – there are no constraints to growth emanating from demand deficiency' (ibid.: 506–7). Hollander understands Mill's conclusion, describes it as the 'orthodox theme' and yet appears to see it as a peripheral issue to Mill's discussion of Say's Law.

O'Brien clearly understood the issue underlying the law of markets, and, interestingly, derived his interpretation from a reading of James Mill. Moreover, he specifically denied the relevance of the Say's Identity interpretation:

> What [James] Mill and Say were stressing was the circularity of the economic system. Indeed the discovery of this circularity...involved a major analytical insight. Moreover, *in so far as the proposition related to the impossibility of a failure of aggregate demand*, it was a proposition directed against writers such as Malthus.... However, as interpreted by some modern monetary theorists, this statement is taken to imply firstly that people do not hold cash balances which yield them no utility; secondly, and following from this, that the absolute price level is indeterminate; and thirdly, that money is 'neutral' – i.e. that it does not influence the level of activity. (O'Brien 1975: 160, italics added)

O'Brien understands that Say's Law is intended to show that demand failure is impossible, yet when he comes to discuss Mill's essay, his focus is on the issue of Say's Equality, Say's Identity and the neutrality of money:

---

[4] Malthus himself was keen to point this out. In his *Definitions in Political Economy* he wrote that 'the question of a glut is exclusively whether it may be general as well as particular and not whether it may be permanent as well as temporary. The causes above mentioned act powerfully to prevent the permanence either of glut or scarcity' (Malthus 1986: VIII. 33).

Classical economics did not regard money as neutral. The most striking case here is that of J.S. Mill.... In Mill's *Essays on Some Unsettled Questions of Political Economy*, he distinguished clearly between, on the one hand, the literal interpretation of Say's Law, which could only be true in an economy where money was purely used for accounting purposes (what some commentators have called Say's Identity) and the proposition, applied as an equilibrium proposition only, in a monetary economy – now referred to as Say's Equality. Mill is certainly the clearest writer here. (Ibid.: 161–2)

A further example of the failure to appreciate the focus of Mill's argument may be seen in Bela Balassa's 'John Stuart Mill and the Law of Markets' (1959). Balassa's aim is to resurrect Mill's interpretation, but his starting point is to distinguish between Walras' Law, Say's Identity and Say's Equality (ibid.: 264–5). Balassa argues that the reason Mill accepted Say's Identity on some occasions and Say's Equality on others was due to his having two different concepts of money. On the basis of money as a commodity, Mill's conclusions are along the lines of Say's Identity and over-production is impossible (ibid.: 267). However, where Mill uses the concept of credit money he is adopting Say's Equality, where over-production is possible (ibid.: 268).

But, having made this argument, Balassa must confront the issue of what Mill really meant. As he wrote: 'Why did Mill defend Say's Law against the attacks of Malthus and Sismondi if he recognized the possibility of a general overproduction?' (ibid.: 271–2). His answer is secular stagnation: 'it was the postulation of a permanent glut caused by the deficiency of effective demand that Mill set out to refute' (ibid.: 272). Thus in studying Mill's argument Balassa sees that the issue is deficient demand, but places his emphasis on the permanency of the glut rather than on what might have caused it.

It is no coincidence that Hollander, O'Brien and Balassa each cite Becker and Baumol (1952) during their discussion. Becker's and Baumol's interpretation of Mill's message has become the standard interpretation of not just the essay itself, but also of the classical meaning of the law of markets. Yet the central message of Mill's essay, and indeed of the debate over the law of markets, was not over the issue of money demand but whether demand failure was the cause of recession. That demand failure was the central issue is intimated in the very title of the essay which, in effect, asks what is the influence of the level of demand on the level of economic activity? Mill's answer is that demand has no influence at all, writing, 'what a country wants to make it richer, is never consumption, but production' ([1874] 1974b : 49). That is, to create the conditions for economic growth, what is sought is *never* higher levels of demand but rather higher levels of production. Mill states the practical consequences of this position explicitly:

The legislator, therefore, needs not give himself any concern about consumption.... The legislator has to look solely to two points: that no obstacle shall exist to prevent those who have the means of producing, from employing those means as they find most for their interest; and that those who have not at present the means of producing, to the extent of their desire to consume, shall have every facility afforded to their acquiring the means, that, becoming producers, they may be enabled to consume. (Ibid.: 49–50)

To believe that demand failure was an obstacle to economic growth was, according to Mill, a fundamental error. He labelled as absurd the idea that demand failure might cause recession and, in particular, the idea that government spending might increase the level of economic activity. In commenting on the 'erroneous' views of earlier 'theorists and practical men' (ibid.: 47) who had believed that consumption was necessary to stimulate production,[5] Mill wrote:

> Among the mistakes which were most pernicious in their direct consequences...was the immense importance attached to consumption. The great end of legislation in matters of national wealth, according to the prevalent opinion, was to create consumers. A great and rapid consumption was what the producers, of all classes and denominations, wanted, to enrich themselves and the country. This object...was conceived to be the greatest condition of prosperity.
>
> It is not necessary, in the present state of the science, to contest this doctrine in the most flagrantly absurd of its forms or of its applications. The utility of a large government expenditure, for the purpose of encouraging industry, is no longer maintained. (Ibid.: 47–8)

Mill argued that, whatever may be the intention of those who support increased levels of government spending, the actual consequences are that saving levels are reduced and unproductive expenditure substituted for productive:

> The usual effect of the attempts of government to encourage consumption, is merely to prevent saving; that is, to promote unproductive consumption at the expense of reproductive, and diminish the national wealth by the very means which were intended to increase it. (Ibid.: 48–9)

The classical description of the law of markets was that it denied the possibility of 'general gluts'.[6] Mill used various phrases – 'general glut' (ibid.:

---

[5] Schumpeter, in 1912, was just as incredulous as Mill had been. In discussing Malthus's concept of equilibrium, he wrote that 'this conception led to the proposition, which appears very strange to us today but was very common at the time, that the consumption of unproductive, especially of luxury goods, was necessary' ([1912] 1954: 150).

[6] It is noteworthy that Mill chooses for the most part not to use the term 'general glut'. He more frequently employs the term 'over-production' to refer to the issues surrounding Say's Law. Mill in fact pointed out the possible confusion in using words which implied that too much had been produced when that was not the nature of the problem. He contrasted the possibility of a 'superabundance' of a single commodity, which he regarded as possible, with the superabundance of all commodities together, which he thought of as an absurdity. But in regard to the term itself, he wrote, 'it is, perhaps, a sufficient reason for not using phrases of this description, that they suggest the idea of excessive production' (ibid.: 72). Mill was making the same point where he wrote: 'much apparent difference of opinion has been produced by a mere difference in

53), 'general superabundance' (ibid.: 68), 'general over-production' (ibid.: 73) or simply 'over-production' (ibid.: 74) – but whichever he used, it signified a condition where 'produce in general may, by increasing faster than the demand for it, reduce all producers to distress' (ibid.: 73). By invoking the law of markets, Mill denied that it was possible for total production to outrun total demand, with all markets glutted at one and the same time. Describing Say's Law as the proposition that demand failure is impossible states the law of markets in a way which gets to the essence of what classical economists were trying to say. That is what Mill was trying to clarify in his essay.

When the possibility of over-production was denied, as it was by the overwhelming majority of economists until the publication of the *General Theory*, the point being made was precisely the point made by Mill. But while denying the possibility of over-production, Mill is simultaneously adamant that the law of markets is consistent with the fact of recession. Indeed, he describes the contours of the business cycle, which were already in evidence by 1830:[7]

> General eagerness to buy and general reluctance to buy, succeed one another in a manner more or less marked, at brief intervals. Except during short periods of transition, there is almost always either great briskness of business or great stagnation; either the principal producers of almost all the leading articles of industry have as many orders as they can possibly execute, or the dealers in almost all commodities have their warehouses full of unsold goods.
>
> In this last case, it is commonly said that there is a general superabundance.... Those economists who have contested the possibility of general superabundance, would none of them deny the possibility or even the frequent occurrence of the phenomenon which we have just noticed. (Ibid.: 68)

Mill was compelled to emphasise that denial of over-production did not mean denial of the fact of recession. Indeed, so important was his wish to avoid confusion, that he came back to it in the very last paragraph of the essay where he again stated 'that when properly understood, [the denial of general over-production] in no way contradicts those obvious facts which are universally known and admitted to be not only possible, but of actual and even frequent appearance' (ibid.: 74).

Not only does Mill accept that recessions are possible, he goes on to explain their origins. Recessions arise because of the existence of money, which permits those who have sold to delay using their receipts until a later date. If, for some reason, those with money become reluctant to spend, there is a fall in the level of sales experienced by those with goods to sell (ibid.: 70). The aim is to become more liquid, and the combined endeavour of large numbers of persons to increase their holdings of money leads to a fall in the demand for commodities and services. What some have described as general over-production is in fact a desire

---

the mode of describing the same facts' (ibid.: 69). His aim was to show that expressions such as 'general glut' were 'not applicable to a state of things in which all or most commodities remain unsold' (ibid.: 68).

[7] Blaug (1958: 98) argues that the first cyclical downturn occurred in 1825.

to hold money rather than goods.[8] It is thus quite clear that Mill recognised the possibility and implications of variations in the demand for cash balances. It is noteworthy that Mill even goes so far as to recognise that there can be a desire to hoard money if the situation becomes sufficiently difficult:

> Persons in general, at that particular time, from a general expectation of being called upon to meet sudden demands, liked better to possess money than any other commodity. Money, consequently, was in request, and all other commodities were in comparative disrepute. In extreme cases, money is collected in masses, and hoarded; in the milder cases people merely defer parting with their money, or coming under any new engagements to part with it. But the result is, that all commodities fall in price, or become unsaleable.... It is, however, of the utmost importance to observe that excess of all commodities, in the only sense which it is possible, means only a temporary fall in their value relatively to money. (Ibid.: 72)

Mill emphasises that this situation is only temporary, and is generally followed by very rapid increases in activity. He wrote that 'an overstocked state of the market is always temporary, and is generally followed by a more than common briskness of demand' (ibid.: 71).

One should not, however, conclude from this that the law of markets was devised to deny the possibility of secular stagnation. It is, of course, true that Mill argues that revival follows recession, and therefore secular stagnation is ruled out. But it is ruled out only by implication. This is not the issue addressed, so while one may infer from this argument that Mill saw no reason for concern about secular stagnation, one cannot therefore assume that this was the issue at hand. As its title, 'On the Influence of Consumption on Production', should have made clear, the point of the essay was to rule out demand failure as the cause of recession, not to demonstrate that secular stagnation was of no concern.

To follow Mill's reasoning into the next stage of his argument, it is important to understand what he meant when he referred to 'capital'. Capital, as defined by Mill, consists of all tangible goods which can be used to earn income:[9]

> The capital, whether of an individual or of a nation, consists, we apprehend, of all matters possessing exchangeable value, which the individual or the nation has in his or in its possession for the purpose of reproduction, and not for the purpose of the owner's unproductive enjoyment. (Ibid.: 54)

Thus, when Mill states that fears 'that a country may accumulate capital too fast' are groundless (ibid.: 73), or that 'nothing can be more chimerical than the fear that the accumulation of capital should produce poverty and not wealth' (ibid.), he is stating that there is no need to be concerned with the pace at which capital

---

[8] Cf. Hollander (1985: 506): 'Mill took great pains to insist that recognition of excess demand for money to hold in no way conceded anything to the "general glut" or "over-production" theorists'.

[9] We would today add human capital to the sum total of items from which an income could be earned.

goods are produced. He is further stating that there is therefore no level of production that cannot be absorbed through purchase and sale in an exchange economy. The production of goods creates value. If the goods produced can be sold, then an income can be earned through which other goods can be purchased. The process, as envisaged by Mill, is production followed by sales followed by purchases. It is in this sense that goods buy goods. In this process money is, generally speaking, only a means by which goods are exchanged. Mill explains this process as follows:

> If the producers generally produce *and sell* more and more, they certainly also buy more and more. Each may not want more of what he himself produces, but each wants more of what some other produces; and, by producing what the other wants, *hopes* to obtain what the other produces. (Ibid.: 49, italics added)

The process is not envisaged as barter, but as the conversion of one's production into money. The failure to sell can and does stop the process in its tracks. But if producers do sell, then the receipts earned can be used to make purchases, but, as already noted, may not be used to do so if there is a fall in commercial confidence.

Mill touches briefly on the issue of entrepreneurial miscalculation, the production of the wrong assortment of goods and services, repeating what had been said by James Mill, Ricardo and Torrens:

> Nothing is more true than that it is produce which constitutes the market for produce, and that every increase of production, *if distributed without miscalculation among all kinds of produce in the proportion which private interest would dictate*, creates, or rather constitutes, its own demand. (Ibid.: 73, italics added)

Mill is, in fact, describing a condition which is unlikely to be satisfied for very long in the real world. Miscalculation is likely to occur on a very regular basis, and the correct proportion of supply in relation to demand is unlikely to be maintained beyond a relatively short space of time.

This passage is also noteworthy for a second reason. This may be the origin of Keynes's statement of Say's Law, 'supply creates its own demand'. If one examines a section from the previous passage, it will be seen that the familiar words of Keynes's definition are there, almost verbatim:

> *every increase of production*, if distributed without miscalculation among all kinds of produce in the proportion which private interest would dictate, *creates*, or rather constitutes, *its own demand*. (Ibid., italics added)

That is, 'every increase of production...creates...its own demand'. Whether or not this is the origin of Keynes's form of words, it is the omitted non-italicised words which are critical in understanding the point Mill is trying to make. The importance of producing, in aggregate, exactly the goods and services that those who have earned incomes are prepared to buy in aggregate, takes the issue from the quantum to the specific array of goods and services produced. If there are errors in production, then the conclusion that demand has been created will not hold. There is no inevitability that everything produced will find a market.

MILL'S *PRINCIPLES*

It has been argued that when Mill came to write the *Principles* he had abandoned his earlier views. Hollander (1985: 484–6) provides an interesting discussion of this issue, noting that 'conspicuous in the secondary literature is an opinion that the essay is unique in Mill's voluminous writings on the monetary issues at stake, the argument kept in the shade in the *Principles*' (ibid.: 484). The problem in appreciating the consistency between the essay and the *Principles* is the need to understand the point that Mill was trying to make. In fact, the *Principles* provides the same analysis and the same conclusions are drawn as in the essay, in what is in many ways a more rounded attempt to lay to rest the notion that demand failure can lead to recession and unemployment.

In Book III, Chapter XIV, Mill deals with the law of markets in a chapter entitled 'Of Excess of Supply' ([1871] 1921: 556–63).[10] Again the issue is whether there might be 'a supply of commodities in the aggregate, surpassing the demand; and a consequent depressed condition of all classes of producers' (ibid.: 556–7). Mill feels the entire concept of demand deficiency is so illogical that he fears he may be unable to explain, to their satisfaction, what its advocates have in mind (ibid.: 557). He therefore finds it necessary to provide two possible interpretations of what might have been meant: firstly, whether it is 'possible that there should be a deficiency of demand for all commodities for want of the means of payment' (ibid.) or, as an alternative meaning, whether it is 'the desire to possess that falls short, and that the general produce of industry may be greater than the community desires to consume – the part, at least, of the community which has an equivalent to give' (ibid.: 558).

The first interpretation he rejected because it is goods which buy goods, money being no more than an intermediary. The second argument, which he considered more plausible, he denied by arguing that, while it is theoretically conceivable that the desire to possess may fall short of total production, the very fact that individuals continue to put themselves to the trouble of producing and earning an income shows that they desire more than they already have. He concluded his demonstration by writing:

> Neither of the elements of demand, therefore, can be wanting when there is an additional supply; though it is perfectly possible that the demand may be for one thing, and the supply may unfortunately consist of another. (Ibid.: 559–60)

That is, demand deficiency is impossible (Say's Law) but there may be a mismatch between goods supplied in comparison with the goods demanded (a

---

10 It is from this chapter that the quotation used by Keynes to depict the classical meaning of Say's Law is taken (*CW* VII: 18).

theory of recession). Having dealt with each argument, Mill then asks why so many otherwise learned individuals 'have been led to embrace so irrational a doctrine' (ibid.: 560). His answer is that:

> I conceive them to have been deceived by a mistaken interpretation of certain mercantile facts. They imagined that the possibility of a general over-supply of commodities was proved by experience. They believed that they saw this phenomenon in certain conditions of the markets, the true explanation of which is totally different. (Ibid.)

Mill again explains that the recessions which are misinterpreted as the result of over-production are in fact due to an increase in the demand for money, the solution being the return of business confidence:

> At such times there is really an excess of all commodities above the money demand.... Almost everybody therefore is a seller, and there are scarcely any buyers.... It is a great error to suppose...that a commercial crisis is the effect of a general excess of production. It is simply the consequence of an excess of speculative purchases. It is not a gradual advent of low prices, but a sudden recoil from prices extravagantly high: its immediate cause is a contraction of credit, and the remedy is, not a diminution of supply, but the restoration of confidence. (Ibid.: 561)

Mill then provides a second reason why some economists may have been deceived by the actual workings of the economy into believing that over-production is possible. This is the fall in profits which, Mill states, occurs as a result of the growth in production and population. He writes that this

> is obviously a totally different thing from a want of market for commodities, though often confounded with it in the complaints of the producing and trading classes.... Low profits, however, are a different thing from deficiency of demand; and the production and accumulation which merely reduce profits, cannot be called excess of supply or of production. (Ibid.: 561–2)

Mill concludes by saying:

> I know not of any economical facts, except the two I have specified, which can have given occasion to the opinion that a general over-production of commodities ever presented itself in actual experience. I am convinced that there is no fact in commercial affairs which, in order to its explanation, stands in need of that chimerical supposition. (Ibid.: 562)

Indeed, Mill goes on to describe this as an issue of the most fundamental importance. In doing so, he foreshadows the cleavage between this facet of classical economic theory and the Keynesian theory which displaced it. Most economists, prior to 1936, would have denied that demand failure (i.e. over-production) was a legitimate explanation for recessions and unemployment. In doing so they would have been following Mill, who is crystal clear in setting out just how important this issue is:

> The point is fundamental; any difference of opinion in it involves radically different conceptions of Political Economy, especially in its practical aspect. On the one view, we have only to consider how a sufficient production may be combined with the best possible distribution; but, on the other, there is a third thing to be considered – how a market can be created for produce, or how production can be limited to the capabilities of the market. (Ibid.)

In the continuation of this passage, Mill highlights what he believes to be the consequences for economic theory if one adds demand deficiency to its concerns:

> A theory so essentially self-contradictory cannot intrude itself without carrying confusion into the very heart of the subject, and making it impossible even to conceive with any distinctness many of the more complicated economical workings of society. This error has been, I conceive, fatal to the systems, as systems, of the three distinguished economists to whom I before referred, Malthus, Chalmers, and Sismondi; all of whom have admirably conceived and explained several of the elementary theorems of political economy, but this fatal misconception has spread itself like a veil between them and the more difficult portions of the subject, not suffering one ray of light to penetrate. Still more is this same confused idea constantly crossing and bewildering the speculations of minds inferior to theirs. (Ibid.)

Mill thus went beyond simply stating that demand failure as a theory of the cycle was unnecessary, and argued that to accept such a theory as valid would prevent one from understanding how an economy actually worked.

FOUR PROPOSITIONS ON CAPITAL

But to understand Mill's meaning with regard to Say's Law fully, it is necessary to turn to Book I, Chapter V, Mill's famous chapter on 'Fundamental Propositions Respecting Capital' (ibid.: 63–90).[11] Indeed, the appropriate place to start is the discussion on the meaning of capital in the previous chapter (Book I, Chapter IV) because, as with the essay, it is only through following Mill's definition of capital that the meaning of the law of markets can be understood. Capital, according to Mill, is everything and anything an entrepreneur intends to utilise to earn income. There is nothing intrinsic in an item which makes it capital, but only the intention of its owner. Capital includes not only all tangible goods, but also money and available lines of credit:

---

[11] In his chapter 'On Excess of Supply', Mill had referred to a number of pages of this chapter ([1871] 1921: 557), but in fact the entire chapter is drenched in the law of markets.

The distinction, then, between Capital and Not-capital, does not lie in the kind of commodities, but in the mind of the capitalist – in his will to employ them for one purpose rather than another; and all property, however ill adapted in itself for the use of labourers, is a part of capital so soon as it, or the value to be received from it, is set apart for productive reinvestment. The sum of the values so destined by their respective possessors, composes the capital of the country. (Ibid.: 56)

In Chapter V, Mill provides four propositions with regard to capital which are in his view fundamental for anyone wishing to understand the workings of an economy. The first proposition is that 'industry is limited by capital' (ibid.: 63), of which he wrote:

While, on the one hand, industry is limited by capital, so on the other, every increase of capital gives, or is capable of giving, additional employment to industry; and this without assignable limit. (Ibid.: 66)

In other words, there is no upper limit to production imposed on the demand side. This was the fundamental issue in question during the debates over the validity of the law of markets, and it was to this section of the chapter (pp. 66–8) that Mill referred during his more comprehensive discussion in Book III, Chapter XIV. Mill contrasts this view with the views held by others:

There is not an opinion more general among mankind than this, that the unproductive expenditure of the rich is necessary to the employment of the poor. Before Adam Smith, the doctrine had hardly been questioned; and even since his time, authors of the highest name and great merit[12] have contended, that if consumers were to save and convert into capital more than a limited portion of their income, and were not to devote to unproductive consumption an amount of means bearing a certain ratio to the capital of the country, the extra accumulation would be merely so much waste, since there would be no market for the commodities which the capital so created would produce. (Ibid.: 66–7)

That is, if unproductive consumers decided to invest instead, and therefore used their capital productively rather than merely consuming it, beyond some upper limit the additional output produced would fail to find buyers. Production, on this view, can therefore rise faster than demand, a situation which only an increase in unproductive spending can forestall. It is this proposition which the law of markets was designed to refute.

It is Mill's third theorem on capital which Keynes seized on at the start of his discussion on Say's Law in the *General Theory*. Mill states the theorem a first time and then recasts it later in the chapter, in a single sentence omitting all of the qualifications originally made. It is in this recast mode that it strikes the modern reader as beyond the pale:

---

[12] Here a footnote names 'Mr. Malthus, Dr. Chalmers, M. de Sismondi' ([1871] 1921: 67n).

> To return to our fundamental theorem. Everything which is produced is consumed; both what is saved and what is said to be spent; and the former quite as rapidly as the latter.[13] (Ibid.: 73)

The more complete statement of the theorem comes earlier. In it Mill provides the qualifications which make it perfectly defensible:

> A third fundamental theorem respecting Capital...is, that although saved, and the result of saving, it is nevertheless consumed. The word saving does not imply that what is saved is not consumed, nor even *necessarily* that its consumption is deferred; but only that, *if* consumed immediately, it is not consumed by the person who saves it. *If* merely laid by for future use, it is said to be *hoarded*; and while *hoarded*, is not consumed at all. But *if* employed as capital, it is all consumed, though not by the capitalist. (Ibid.: 70, italics added)

Here Mill argues that the owners of capital have three alternative uses for the capital they possess: they may consume it, or use it as part of the production process, or hoard it and lay their capital by for future use. But, given the continual use of the conditional clause, it is quite clear that there is no necessity that everything produced is immediately consumed.

Mill is attempting to draw the implications of his second theorem, that 'to consume less than is produced, is saving; and that is the process by which capital is increased' (ibid.: 70). He is trying to show that saving does not inevitably imply that some proportion of what has been produced is not put to use:

> To the vulgar, it is not at all apparent that what is saved is consumed. To them, every one who saves appears in the light of a person who hoards: they may think such conduct permissible, or even laudable, when it is to provide for a family, and the like; but they have no conception of it as doing good to other people: saving is to them another word for keeping a thing to oneself; while spending appears to them to be distributing it among others. (Ibid.: 71)

The process of saving and investment can occur, not only through entrepreneurs making decisions to save a larger proportion and then directly investing their increased saving, but also through individuals placing funds with financial institutions. As Mill says of workers:

> If they in their turn save any part, this also is not, *generally speaking, hoarded*, but (through savings banks, benefit clubs, or some other channel) re-employed as capital, and consumed. (Ibid.: 70, italics added)

He concludes that saving ought to be encouraged because it is saving which makes a community wealthier while unproductive consumption only reduces the

---

13 This is the same sentiment expressed by Mill in his essay, where he wrote: 'the person who saves his income is no less a consumer than he who spends it: he consumes it in a different way; it supplies food and clothing to be consumed, tools and materials to be used, by productive labourers' (Mill [1874] 1974b: 48).

capital available for productive uses. Mill's attitude to unproductive consumption reflected the classical view of consumption as a depletion of wealth and production as its creation:

> Saving, in short, enriches, and spending impoverishes, the community along with the individual; which is but saying in other words, that society at large is richer by what it expends in maintaining and aiding productive workers, but poorer by what it consumes in its enjoyment. (Ibid.: 72–3)

Turning to the fourth theorem, Mill asserts that it is the capital which an entrepreneur is willing to devote to the payment of labour which puts workers to work. The gulf between classical and Keynesian theory cannot be wider than at this point.[14] In Mill's famous statement:

> What supports and employs productive labour, is the capital expended in setting it to work, and not the demand of purchasers for the produce of the labour when completed. Demand for commodities is not demand for labour.[15] (Ibid.: 79)

A page later he restates the theorem in this way:

> To purchase produce is not to employ labour...the demand for labour is constituted by the wages which precede the production, and not by the demand which may exist for the commodities resulting from the production. (Ibid.: 80)

This is Mill still dealing with the issues of Say's Law (Thompson 1975: 178; Bladen 1974: 240).[16] He is continuing to demonstrate that it is not demand deficiency which causes unemployment, nor is demand stimulation the cure for

---

[14] Thompson (1975) provides a detailed discussion of the controversy which has surrounded this proposition over the years. He notes that in its own time it was virtually never criticised (179) and that it was defended at different times by Newcomb (181), Marshall (181–2), Pigou (182), Wicksell (182) and Hayek (183–4).

[15] This passage continues: 'The demand for commodities determines in what particular branch of production the labour and capital shall be employed; it determines the *direction* of the labour; but not the more or less of the labour itself, or of the maintenance or payment of the labour. These depend on the amount of capital, or other funds directly devoted to the sustenance and remuneration of labour' ([1871] 1921: 79). While this is obviously related to the wages fund doctrine, there is no implication that there is a fixed fund set aside at the start of the time period which will be paid to labour. It says only that labour will be employed to the extent that those with funds to employ them actually use those funds to do so. Mill is saying that employment depends on the decision of an entrepreneur to offer employment, not on the demand for the products produced by labour. The example (ibid.: 82–4) where there is a change in spending habits from the purchase of velvet to the direct hiring of workers, creating a second fund for employment, indicates that Mill did not think in terms of a constant wages fund.

[16] Mill notes how difficult this proposition is to understand and states that even amongst economists, only 'Mr. Ricardo and M. Say...have kept it constantly and steadily in view' (ibid.: 80).

recession. It is entrepreneurial decisions alone which put workers to work, and the decision involved is the decision to pay workers to produce. It is entrepreneurial willingness to use the capital at their disposal to pay their employees which gives an individual a job, not the purchase of the goods or services sold.[17] Thompson entirely captures Mill's intent: 'Mill defended the theorem largely on the basis of current benefits to labor and flatly denied, on at least two occasions, that spending for consumer goods benefited the laboring class in any way' (ibid.). Thompson may have been referring to passages such as the following where, to underscore his meaning, Mill puts the issue in its converse form:

> The proposition for which I am contending is in reality equivalent to the following, which to some minds will appear a truism, though to others it is a paradox: that a person does good to labourers, not by what he consumes on himself, but solely by what he does not so consume. (Mill [1871] 1921: 84)

Mill demonstrates the validity of this argument by pointing out that the poor rates of his time could raise the standard of living of the poor only by reducing the standard of living of those who were compelled to pay the rates:

> If it be equally for the benefit of the labouring classes whether I consume my means in the form of things purchased for my own use, or set aside a portion in the shape of wages or alms for their direct consumption, on what ground can the policy be justified of taking my money from me to support paupers? since my unproductive expenditure would have equally benefited them, while I should have enjoyed it too. If society can both eat its cake and have it, why should it not be allowed the double indulgence? But common sense tells every one in his own case...that the poor rate which he pays is really subtracted from his own consumption, and that no shifting of payment backwards and forwards will enable two persons to eat the same food. If he had not been required to pay the rate, and had consequently laid out the amount on himself, the poor would have had as much less for their share of the total produce of the country, as he himself would have consumed more. (Ibid.: 84–5)

Mill states that amongst economists virtually all of them at times speak as if buying goods is identical to hiring labour. That is, '[they] occasionally express themselves as if a person who buys commodities, the produce of labour, was an employer of labour, and created a demand for it as really, and in the same sense, as if he bought the labour itself directly, by the payment of wages' (ibid.: 80). Mill finds this form of confusion deadly for a proper understanding of the operation of an economy. He could not have been more clear, nor more scathing:

> It is no wonder that political economy advances slowly, when such a question as this still remains open at its very threshold.... I conceive that a person who buys commodities and consumes them himself, does no good to the labouring classes; and that it is only by what he abstains from consuming, and expends in direct payments to

---

[17] This is along similar lines to the interpretations provided by Schumpeter ([1954] 1986: 644) and Blaug (1985: 184). Thompson (1975: 184–5) believes they are being overly generous to Mill (ibid.: 189).

labourers in exchange for labour, that he benefits the labouring classes, or adds anything to the amount of their employment. (Ibid.: 80–81)

Stimulating demand will do the unemployed no good. Raising consumption may, in fact, lower the ability to employ rather than increase it, if it consumes capital that might otherwise have been diverted into payments to labour. The cure for unemployment does not occur through actions taken on the demand side, but through actions which raise production. And, importantly, this does not rule out a direct role for government in putting people to work. After discussing immigration as a way of activating idle capital, Mill states: 'there is another way in which governments can create additional industry. They can create capital. They may lay on taxes, and employ the amount productively' (ibid.: 86). That is, governments can tax individuals, reduce their unproductive expenditures and spend the money productively by hiring individuals to undertake capital works. This is not an attempt to increase production by increasing demand, but to increase demand by first increasing production. Rather than contradicting the original proposition, it is a conclusion drawn from it.

In the end, Mill's famous four theorems on capital are an extension of, or perhaps the preconditions for understanding, the law of markets. If Say's Law is understood as the proposition that demand failure is not the cause of recessions and unemployment, then it may be seen that the theorems on capital round out what is meant. Towards the end of the chapter on capital, Mill ties the argument on capital together with his classic statement of Say's Law in which, through the medium of money, it is goods which buy goods:

> The demand for commodities is a consideration of importance, rather in the theory of exchange, than in that of production. Looking at things in the aggregate, and permanently, the remuneration of the producer is derived from the productive power of his own capital. *The sale of produce for money, and the subsequent expenditure of the money in buying other commodities*, are a mere exchange of equivalent values for mutual accommodation.... It is production, not exchange, which remunerates labour and capital. (Ibid.: 88, italics added)

Mill is the key to understanding the classical meaning of the law of markets. He sits in a pivotal position at the end of the general glut debates, and his influence was one of the main reasons for its acceptance throughout the remainder of the nineteenth century and well into the twentieth. In both the essay and in his *Principles* he provided a clear exposition of the reasoning behind the law of markets. Mill focused on the impossibility of demand failure as an explanation for recessions, even while fully recognising that recessions regularly occur. Indeed, he even provided explanations for recessions in terms of rising liquidity preference, arguing that a fall in business confidence would lead to an increased demand for money, but the main source of recessions was the miscalculations of producers. Higher levels of unproductive spending were no solution to these problems.

5. Say's Law in English Classical Theory

Keynes argued that acceptance of Say's Law meant that one assumed recessions and involuntary unemployment were impossible. In fact, not only is there no such assumption, the classical theory of the business cycle was founded on the law of markets. This chapter deals with the role of the law of markets in classical economic theory, and in particular its relationship with the theory of the business cycle. This relationship between the law of markets and the theory of recession was well put by Schumpeter in 1912:

> The most important achievement in [the theory of the crisis] was the proof (Say, J. Mill) that a simple theory of over-production was untenable and the clarification of the simple fact, which yet was so often misunderstood, that there can be no supply without a simultaneous demand.... Out of this a positive theory of crisis developed directly: Say's theory of the outlets of trade, *débouchés*, which was widely accepted, especially by Ricardo. This theory maintained that there can be no general over-production and a fundamental disturbance of the economic equilibrium never results from production, therefore, the cause of a crisis can only be found in incorrect conditions of production, in a proportional over-production of one commodity. (Schumpeter [1912] 1954: 150)

One would never know from a reading of the *General Theory* that the place to find Say's Law in classical economic theory was in the theory of the business cycle. As Keynes would have it, acceptance of Say's Law meant that, even when discussing unemployment, economists employed theories in which there was never an obstacle to full employment. Say's Law was the classical economist's 'axiom of parallels' by which involuntary unemployment was rendered impossible. If Keynes were right, the last place to look for Say's Law would have been in the classical theory of the business cycle, and especially in the theory of recession. But that is precisely where it was found.

This chapter will show that discussions of the law of markets in English economic theory was embedded in the theory of the business cycle. This has remained largely unrecognised since the publication of the *General Theory*. This chapter will outline the related propositions attached to the law of markets and will demonstrate that these views were almost universally accepted within mainstream economic theory before 1936.

THE ASSOCIATED CONCEPTS OF THE LAW OF MARKETS

It is one thing to deny the existence of demand deficiency and another to provide a theory of the cycle. Classical economists, because of their acceptance of the law of markets, had to do both. Those who accepted the validity of the law of markets had to explain the fact of recession without reference to demand deficiency or over-production. This was done by explaining recessions as resulting from misdirected production or other factors which drove demand and supply out of alignment.[1] This theory of recession must be seen as an integral part of the matrix of ideas associated with the law of markets since it was this which explained the existence of recession while denying the possibility of deficient demand or over-production. The two concepts, in fact, evolved together and are part of a unified conception of the operation of an economy. The following eight propositions represent the related concepts which make up a complete statement of the law of markets:

1. Demand deficiency is never a correct explanation for recession. Production of more goods and services than will be demanded (i.e. over-production or a general glut) is an impossibility.
2. Goods buy goods through the mediating role of money. The process is one in which one's own goods are converted into money (i.e. sold), and with the money received reconverted back into a different set of goods (C–M–C'). Demand is thus constituted by supply, and purchasing power can never be deficient.
3. An economy can always absorb and employ productively additional quantities of capital.
4. If all goods taken together are produced in the proper proportions to each other, everything produced will find a market at cost-covering prices. This remains true irrespective of how fast production grows or how fast capital is accumulated.
5. Due to entrepreneurial miscalculation, specific goods can be produced in excess (a partial glut). That is, more of a particular good can be produced than can be sold at cost-covering prices.
6. Over-production of particular goods or classes of goods can lead to a general downturn in production. The inability of an initial group of producers to sell and earn incomes can lead to a fall in demand for the products of other producers, and so on through the entire economy. Thus, there can be a

---

[1] Cf. Wesley Mitchell (1927: 8) who wrote, 'to most of the classical economists, the theory of general over-production was a heresy, which they sought to extirpate by demonstrating that the supply of goods of one sort necessarily constitutes demand for goods of other sorts. But maladjusted production they allowed to be possible, and their brief references to crises usually aimed to show how production becomes maladjusted through the sinking of capital in unremunerative investments'.

downturn in production as sales across an economy turn out to be lower than originally anticipated.

7. Recessions, characterised by low levels of production and high levels of unemployment, do occur. Recessions are due, in general, to production moving out of phase with demand in particular sectors. That is, the specific goods produced do not coincide with the goods income earners wish to buy. Recessions are thus due to some form of market 'derangement', not to deficient aggregate demand.

8. If business confidence evaporates resulting in an increased demand for money, or if there is a collapse of credit either as a deliberate act of policy or due to the nature of the credit creation process, reconversion of money receipts back into goods (the second half of the C–M–C' process) takes longer than it normally would and therefore the demand for goods contracts.

These are the propositions which collectively constitute the meaning of Say's Law. The last proposition may appear to be no more than Keynesian liquidity preference theory. Yet, to the extent that this is so, it is Keynes who had adopted classical economic theory. Moreover, this was an aspect of classical theory which was embedded in discussions of the law of markets. Torrens (as noted in Chapter 2) wrote that 'on every occasion of glut or general stagnation, the desire of turning goods into money is rendered more intense than the desire of turning money into goods' ([1821] 1965: 422). John Stuart Mill had said the same where he wrote, in his essay on the law of markets, that what appeared to be demand deficiency occurred because 'persons in general, at that particular time, from a general expectation of being called upon to meet sudden demands, liked better to possess money than any other commodity. Money, consequently, was in request, and all other commodities were in comparative disrepute' ([1874] 1974b: 72). An increase in the demand for money, and a consequent slowing in the demand for goods, were thus not only fully consistent with the law of markets, but were, in fact, part of its very framework.

The eight propositions listed above were the essence of the law of markets. During the latter half of the nineteenth century it would have been well nigh impossible to find a mainstream economist who did not assent to every one of these propositions. Far from the law of markets representing a scattering of ideas which some economists accepted and others denied (Sowell 1972: 12), there was near unanimity in these views across the economics profession. It was this matrix of ideas which underpinned the classical theory of the business cycle.

This cannot be emphasised enough. The law of markets was amongst the most important propositions in classical theory. It was the linchpin of the classical theory of the business cycle. Most fundamentally, it was the basis for the almost universal rejection of demand failure as a cause of recession. It led to a concept of economic relationships in which recession needed to be explained in terms of disharmonies of one kind or another. A theory of demand failure is a theory which explains recession in terms of too little expenditure relative to the flow of product. Goods are not bought in the volumes they are being produced because demanders in aggregate are unwilling to buy everything that is produced.

A classical economist would never have attributed the cause of recessions to demand failure. A recession would have been explained in terms of why the particular goods which happened to have been produced were not the goods which demanders sought to buy at prices which covered the full costs of production. The role of theory was to explain why producers should have made the mistaken judgements they apparently had made in producing unsaleable goods. The kinds of external factors which would have led to such misjudgements included errors of optimism, over-capitalisation of the production process, an insufficiency of available savings to complete an investment programme or a collapse of credit. The fault lay in the structure of economic relationships.

This is fundamentally different from a theory of demand failure. Rather than concentrating on the structure of demand relative to the structure of production, a theory of demand failure concentrates on the level of demand relative to the level of production. The Keynesian-cross analysis captures the essence of demand failure. Recessions occur because the level of spending remains lower than the full-employment level of production. This is not a structural problem in that recession can be explained in terms of how the various parts of the economy mesh. This is, instead, a problem which is literally in terms of the total level of spending.

Because the law of markets placed the focus on production rather than on demand, economic policy concentrated on measures which improved productivity rather than towards measures which would raise demand.

Most discussions of the law of markets in the economic literature finish no later than John Stuart Mill. There is, therefore, little appreciation of the role and importance of the law of markets during the latter half of the nineteenth century and well into the twentieth. Yet, far from its being abandoned, it simply slipped into the background, becoming a part of the fabric of economic thought, accepted by one and all.

Within the English classical school it was understood that demand was constituted by supply and that demand deficiency (or over-production) would, despite superficial appearances, never be the cause of recession. And while during the middle years of the nineteenth century there was a clear understanding that this aspect of theory was related to the law of markets, by the end of the nineteenth century and the start of the twentieth, this appreciation had weakened. There were a number of reasons for this. Firstly, the marginal revolution created a different focus of economic interest, resulting in a reorientation towards microeconomic issues. Secondly, late nineteenth-century economists failed to see the necessary connection between the denial of over-production or demand deficiency and an explanation of recession based on economic disharmonies. The two had developed together because a theory of recession was needed to account for the obvious facts of economic life. By the end of the nineteenth century, while both arguments were accepted, their relationship, with one as the outgrowth of the other, had been generally lost. Thirdly, while the issue denied by the law of markets was demand deficiency, it was generally referred to as over-production. By the time Keynes came to attack Say's Law and focus on the absence of a theory of recession based on effective demand failure, the logical connection between demand failure and over-production seems to have been severed. An interesting example of a distinction being made between over-production and demand deficiency may be found in the following passage from Hawtrey:

> Trade depression cannot be due to over-production; the disparity that arises between supply and demand cannot be due to an excess of supply, but must be due to a deficiency of demand. (Hawtrey [1926] 1954: 345)

Hawtrey explicitly denies the possibility of over-production and, thus far at least, he accepts the classical position on Say's Law. But he also makes an explicit distinction between over-production and demand failure. Although the former is stated to be impossible, the latter is the cause of recession. Recessions are not due to too much having been produced but to too little having been bought.[2]

And indeed, the concepts of demand failure and over-production, although formally identical, conjure up different conceptions of the problem at hand. Over-production locates the fault amongst suppliers. It is the actions of producers which are causing too much to be produced. Demand deficiency, in contrast, locates the problem amongst buyers. Goods remain unsold because of a refusal to purchase, usually due to a preference for saving. Discussions of the *General Theory* did not claim that Keynes had shown 'over-production' to be possible. During the debates which raged around the *General Theory*, the question of over-production was never explicitly discussed.[3]

McCulloch

J.R. McCulloch provides one of the clearest statements of the law of markets amongst the early classical economists.[4] In his discussion of gluts in his *Principles of Political Economy* ([1864] 1965) is found the more mature manifestation of the logic built on the concepts originated by Say and James Mill. Chapter VII deals with the 'causes of gluts'. McCulloch begins the chapter with the statement that 'various bad consequences have been supposed to result from the extension and improvement of machinery' (ibid.: 142).[5] These 'bad consequences' are the destruction of jobs occasioned by increased productivity.

---

[2] Hawtrey's reasoning, although somewhat eccentric, is recognisably part of the classical tradition. Even though he had described the cause of recession as deficiency of demand, he was not abandoning the discipline applied by Say's Law but merely arguing that a fall in credit would lead to a downturn in activity. Hawtrey's approach to 'demand deficiency' will be discussed in the section on Hawtrey at the end of this chapter.

[3] A discussion of the contrast between Keynes and classical views is found in Appendix B.

[4] For other discussions of the law of markets amongst the early classical economists, see Senior (1854: 28–9), Cairnes (1874: 26–34) and Fawcett (1888: 478–83).

[5] Interestingly, McCulloch is writing in reply to Ricardo's discussion 'On Machinery' which was introduced into the third edition of the *Principles*. He is thus defending the law of markets against one of its principal advocates. See their correspondence on this issue (Ricardo 1951–73: VIII. 381–6, 386–91).

McCulloch argues that there is nothing to fear about an economy becoming more productive, and asks rhetorically, what might be the consequences if each worker could produce twice as much as he did: would everything then be bought? Would there be any reason to fear a deficiency of demand? McCulloch wrote:

> It may, however, be asked, would the *demand* be sufficient to take off this increased quantity of commodities? Would their extraordinary multiplication not cause such a glut of the market, as to force their sale at a lower price than would suffice to repay even the diminished cost of their production? (Ibid.: 143)

McCulloch's answer is that, no matter how great the increase in production might be, 'it would not occasion any lasting glut of the market' (ibid.: 144). The reason individuals produce is so that they can consume. Production of one's own goods or services earns the money income which allows an individual to purchase from others. That they have bothered to produce is evidence that they intend to buy. A general glut is, therefore, impossible. Of individual goods, however, a glut is possible due to 'miscalculation' on the part of business people:

> When, however, individuals, instead of directly consuming the produce of their industry, offer it in exchange to others, there may be a glut. Should A, for example, produce articles which are not wanted, instead of those that are, he will not be able to sell them, or to exchange them for those he wished to obtain, so that there will be a glut or excess of his commodities. In such case, A has miscalculated.... Errors of this sort are, however, speedily rectified; for if A find that he cannot attain his object by prosecuting his present employment, he will not fail to abandon it, producing, in time to come, such articles only as he may find a merchant for, as he means to consume. It is clear, therefore, that a *universally* increased facility of production cannot give rise to a permanent over-loading of the market. (Ibid.: 144–5)

But while McCulloch denies the possibility of a universal glut, he does not deny the possibility of recessions. And he is specific that recessions can arise which have nothing to do with monetary disturbances or with government regulation (although, of course, he accepts that both factors can and often do lead to recession). Recessions can arise because the wrong goods and services have been brought to market, and therefore no buyers can be found:

> Setting apart for the moment the influence of sudden changes in the value of money, and of political regulations, if the market be encumbered and a difficulty be experienced in effecting sales, we may be satisfied that the fault is not in producing too much, but in producing articles which do not suit the tastes of buyers, or which we cannot ourselves consume.... We may increase the power of production ten or twenty times, and be as free of all excess as if we diminished it in the same proportion. *A glut never originates in an increase of production; but is, in every case, a consequence of the misapplication of the ability to produce*, that is, of the producers not properly adapting their means to their ends. Let this error be rectified, and the glut will disappear. (Ibid.: 155–6, italics added)

That McCulloch believed he was doing no more than stating the very essence of Say's Law is shown by the footnote placed at the end of this discussion:

> Say was the first who showed, in a full and satisfactory manner, that effective demand depends upon production (see his chapter *de Débouchés*); and that gluts are the result of the misapplication, and not of the increase, of productive power. (Ibid.: 156n)

McCulloch goes on to explain that such 'miscalculations seem generally to originate in some previous change in the usual proportion between supply and demand' (ibid.: 159). He points out that production tends to occur in advance of demand. This can mean that, by the time that the articles produced are brought to market, their demand may have fallen away. But this is not the usual problem, since 'miscalculations and gluts are more frequently produced by an increase than by a decline in the demand for produce' (ibid.: 160). McCulloch describes the effect of 'exaggerated' expectations which arise from an increased demand for some product, which leads to more being produced than can be sold at cost-covering prices:

> The result that every unprejudiced observer would anticipate, almost invariably takes place. A disproportionate quantity of capital being attracted to the lucrative business, a glut of the market, and a ruinous depression of prices, unavoidably follow. (Ibid.: 161)

McCulloch discusses the possibility that money might play a role in causing recession. There are two issues: the amount of money in circulation and changes in the amount of money. With regard to the amount of circulating medium, McCulloch states that it is 'to no purpose to ascribe gluts and revulsions of the market to a permanent deficiency of money' (ibid.: 158). But changes in the volume of money, which lead to changes in its value, can have a devastating effect:

> A contraction and consequent rise in the value of money, being usually accompanied by a sudden collapse of credit...leads sometimes to very extensive revulsions. Such changes cannot, indeed, take place without entailing the most serious losses on all who have on hand considerable stocks of produce; they are also very apt to involve those who have been carrying on their business by the aid of borrowed money in serious difficulties; and if the rise in the value of money be considerable, the influence of the shock given to industry, and the disturbance in commercial channels, may be such as materially to abridge the power of the society to make their accustomed purchases; and may thus occasion a glut of the market. (Ibid.: 158)

McCulloch describes the transmission mechanism from a collapse of credit to business failure to the entire society being unable to buy. Indeed, he extends the analysis to overseas sellers who now find their exports reduced. It is the law of markets: 'effective demand depends on production'; therefore, whatever reduces the level of production must necessarily lower the level of demand.

O'Brien, in his detailed study of McCulloch, examines McCulloch's views within the inappropriate confines of the Becker–Baumol framework. On the one hand, O'Brien argues that McCulloch accepted Say's Identity, since he argued that general gluts are impossible and that demand for particular goods was based on relative prices alone. But O'Brien is also aware that McCulloch had argued that:

> any commodity used as money had to be storeable, he also recognised the importance of hoarding and there can be no doubt of his recognition of the existence of cash balances. The recognition by McCulloch that the velocity of circulation may vary implies also a recognition that the demand for cash balances may vary implying in turn the possibility of an excess demand for money. (O'Brien 1970: 155)

Therefore, O'Brien concludes that McCulloch accepted Say's Equality in regard to disequilibrium situations. Indeed, O'Brien emphasises that 'McCulloch was in fact perfectly explicit that "commercial revulsions" could occur because of sudden changes in the value of money' (ibid.). Indeed, O'Brien goes on to point out that, according to McCulloch, 'sudden changes in the quantity and value of money were only one cause of economic disequilibrium. Confidence was important.... He also seems to have envisaged some kind of trade cycle, and "speculation" and "over-trading" could occur under both a stable and an unstable currency' (ibid.: 155–6).

O'Brien fails to see the full coherence of McCulloch's position because he has looked at McCulloch through the distorting lens of the Say's Identity–Say's Equality framework. O'Brien emphasises that McCulloch was aware of the existence of recessions because one of the legacies of the Keynesian Revolution was the belief that acceptance of Say's Law meant that one always assumed full employment. But when it became obvious that this was untrue, O'Brien merely stated that McCulloch had accepted Say's Equality and framed his discussion in that way, without recognition that the central issue was demand deficiency. It is possible that, had O'Brien written this chapter five years later, when he had come to understand that Say's Law meant 'the impossibility of a failure of effective demand' (O'Brien 1975: 41), he might have taken a different approach.

THE LAW OF MARKETS IN CLASSICAL ENGLISH ECONOMIC THEORY

What follows is an overview of the positions held by a number of leading English economists between 1871 and 1936 on the issues surrounding the law of markets and the origins of recession. From these examples, it will be seen that the law of markets, as outlined above, was a basic frame of reference in their understanding, not just of economic issues in general, but specifically as a fundamental element in the generation of the business cycle.

Jevons

William Stanley Jevons's *The Theory of Political Economy* ([1871] 1970) was a landmark in the history of economic theory. Along with Menger and Walras, Jevons is credited with being a co-discoverer of the theory of marginal utility. It was this book which helped open a new period in economic theorising. Yet in spite of its role in changing the direction of economic theory, and providing a sharper focus on the demand side of the economy, Jevons specifically accepted the law of markets. Black (1983: 20), for example, states that Jevons's 'acceptance of Say's Law was complete'. In *The Theory of Political Economy*, an entire section was devoted to attacking over-production in no uncertain terms:

> Early writers on economics were always in fear of a supposed *glut*, arising from the powers of production surpassing the needs of consumers, so that industry would be stopped, employment fail, and all but the rich would be starved by the superfluity of commodities. The doctrine is evidently absurd and self-contradictory.... Over-production is not possible in all branches of industry at once, but it is possible in some as compared with others. (Jevons [1871] 1970: 212)

In this first major work in English on marginal utility, the conclusions deduced from the law of markets are introduced with perfect logic. There may be diminishing marginal utility for particular goods, but not for goods in general. There may be miscalculation which leads to the marginal utility of various goods being different from each other, and some goods will end up exchanging at prices which do not cover costs. Output must grow 'proportionally'. If it does not, recessions occur along with unemployment. Such recessions are, however, wrongly perceived as 'an apparent glut' but the fault lies in the structure of production, not in a deficiency of demand.

Jevons's support for the law of markets was noted by Hutchison ([1953] 1962: 17–18), who is clearly surprised by this, writing: 'Jevons, almost pathologically ready to attack any doctrine of J.S. Mill, and vigorously assaulting, in particular, Mill's famous four propositions on capital, never questioned or raised the subject of Mill's analysis of "general over-production"' (ibid.: 17). Hutchison recognised the same support in the works of other major names of late nineteenth-century economic theory. Hutchison listed Sidgwick, Wicksteed, Marshall and Edgeworth as others who had accepted Mill's position (ibid.: 18).[6] Hutchison, however, found their acceptance of the law of markets incomprehensible, describing Mill's position as 'combining dogmatism and ambiguity to a quite remarkable degree' (ibid.).

---

[6] For Wicksteed's views, see ([1910] 1950: II. 638–40). For Sidgwick, see (1883: 378–82). Marshall and Edgeworth are discussed below.

Bagehot

In 1873, the then editor of *The Economist*, Walter Bagehot, published his *Lombard Street*, sub-titled, 'A Description of the Money Market'. Chapter VI dealt with the business cycle, and while never mentioning Say or any of the other classical authorities, presented a theory of the cycle fully derived from and consistent with the law of markets.[7] Bagehot began by asking why there are periods when everyone is doing well and other periods when nearly everyone is doing poorly ([1873] 1919: 119). He answered by pointing out that:

> As soon as the division of labour has once established itself in a community, two principles at once begin to be important, of which time is the very essence. These are –
>
> First. That as goods are produced to be exchanged, it is good that they should be exchanged as quickly as possible.
> Secondly. That as every producer is mainly occupied in producing what others want, and not what he wants himself, it is desirable that he should always be able to find, without effort, without delay, and without uncertainty, others who want what he can produce. (Ibid.: 120)

Bagehot's entire book is devoted to discussing the role of the money market, so he can hardly be accused of ignoring the role of money. The very essence of the process envisaged by Bagehot is that one set of goods is exchanged for money as fast as possible so that a second set of goods can be bought with the money receipts. Given these basic principles, Bagehot recognises that there is an intrinsic problem. With the division of labour, one must anticipate what others will be willing to buy, and there is the ever-present danger that producers will miscalculate: 'A produces what he thinks B wants, but it may be a mistake, and B may not want it. A may be able and willing to produce what B wants, but he may not be able to find B – he may not know of his existence' (ibid.). If miscalculation occurs on a large scale, the consequences spill across the economy:

> No single large industry can be depressed without injury to other industries; still less can any great group of industries. Each industry when prosperous buys and consumes the produce probably of most (certainly of very many) other industries, and if industry A fail and is in difficulty, industries B, and C, and D, which used to sell to it, will not be able to sell that which they had produced in reliance on A's demand, and in future they will stand idle till industry A recovers, because in default of A there will be no one to buy the commodities which they create. (Ibid.: 121–2)

---

[7] Bagehot was, however, a student of the history of economics, as may be seen from his collection of essays, *Economic Studies* (1888), in which he discussed the contributions to economics of Smith, Ricardo and Malthus. In his discussion of Malthus, Bagehot wrote: 'To most other parts of Political Economy Mr. Malthus added very little. And on some he supported errors which were even then becoming antiquated. He...believed that the supply of all commodities might exceed the demand, which is as much as to say that there is too much of everything' (ibid.: 148).

'In all this,' Bagehot wrote, 'money is but an instrument' (ibid.: 122). This is part of the conceptual structure behind the law of markets, repeating what Say had originally stated: money is but a form of carriage which facilitates the exchange of goods but does not determine it. This was not to deny that the system of credit creation may not have had a major and critical impact on the level of economic activity. The impact of the system of credit creation could be devastating. Bagehot relates the impact of the system of credit creation back to the two principles cited above. Yet even with the introduction of credit, it is miscalculation on the part of producers which leads to recession:

> The state of credit is thus influential, because of the two principles which have just been explained. In a good state of credit, goods lie on hand a much less time than when credit is bad; sales are quicker; intermediate dealers borrow easily to augment their trade, and so more and more goods are more quickly and more easily transmitted from the producer to the consumer.
>
> These two variable causes are causes of real prosperity. They augment trade and production, and so are plainly beneficial, except where by mistake the wrong things are produced, or where also by mistake misplaced credit is given, and a man who cannot produce anything which is wanted gets the produce of other people's labour upon a false idea that he will produce [what other people want]. (Ibid.: 125–6)

To this form of miscalculation Bagehot adds the greater potential for catastrophe which occurs through large-scale speculation, which is usually induced and encouraged by inflation. Higher prices encourage a false optimism which eventually is overtaken by the actual facts of the situation. Higher prices induce misjudgements, the ultimate outcome of which is an economic crisis and recession (see ibid.: 149–50).

Nor is Bagehot describing a process which is in any way ephemeral or without pain. He wrote that 'it takes two or three years to produce this full calamity, and the recovery from it takes two or three years also' (ibid.: 123–4). This is a process embedded in the law of markets which recognises that economic downturns occur on a regular basis. Miscalculation, plus the effects of the system of credit creation, combine to create the kinds of economic conditions which Keynes insisted classical economists denied. Hutchison ([1953] 1962: 88) argues, moreover, that it was Bagehot's theory of the cycle which Marshall adopted as his own (see also Bridel 1987: 48). In actual fact, Bagehot and Marshall both reflected the classical understanding of the causes of recession.

Marshall

In dealing with Alfred Marshall, the law of markets and Keynes, it is important to keep in mind the sequence in which various publications appeared. In 1879, Marshall discussed the nature of the business cycle, and in so doing quoted a lengthy passage from John Stuart Mill written in 1848. In 1889, J.A. Hobson commented briefly on Marshall's interpretation of Mill, and quoted the same passage from Mill. In 1936 Keynes commented on Hobson's 1889 discussion of

Marshall's 1879 discussion of Mill, and quoted that same passage. And the question at issue was this: did Marshall agree with Mill on Say's Law or did he deviate from what was then the orthodox position?

In 1879, Marshall,[8] in *The Economics of Industry*, quoted a passage from Mill and had then written, 'though men may have the power to purchase, they may not choose to use it' ([1879] 1881: 154). Hobson interpreted this to mean that Marshall had given only qualified acceptance to the law of markets, and suggested that Marshall 'alone amongst economists' had taken a somewhat more sceptical view, since he appeared to suggest that not all income would be spent (Hobson and Mummery 1889: 102n). In Hobson's view, not spending the money one had was forbidden by the law of markets. Hobson's argument was repeated by Keynes in the *General Theory* (*CW* VII: 19n) and the question as to whether Marshall had fully accepted Say's Law has since become controversial. Hansen (1953: 13), Schumpeter ([1954] 1986: 622), Hutchison ([1953] 1962: 88), Eshag (1964: 86–7) and Patinkin (1965: 646–9) argue that Marshall accepted Mill's position. Davis (1979: 659), on the other hand, takes a more agnostic view. He argues that, in the words quoted by Hobson, Marshall could have been interpreting or he could have been taking exception to the mainstream. Bridel (1987: 49) and Bigg (1990: 32), however, agree with Hobson and Keynes in seeing in Marshall some distancing from the orthodox position.

That Marshall accepted Mill's position appears to be highly probable, given the views expressed in an article on Mill's theory of value which he published in 1876.[9] There Marshall wrote:

> We must, of course, always bear in mind *the fundamental truth*, that, to use Mill's words, that 'which constitutes the means of payment for commodities...is simply commodities. Each person's means of paying for the productions of other people consists of those which he himself possesses. All sellers are inevitably, and by the meaning of the word, buyers. Could we suddenly double the productive powers of the country, we should double the supply of commodities in every market: but we should by the same stroke double the purchasing power. Everybody would bring a double demand as well as supply'. (Marshall 1876: 600, italics added)

Marshall quoted, as representing 'fundamental truth', almost the entire passage from Mill which was later to feature in the *General Theory*. He then explained the point in his own words:

> The amount of each commodity which each person would be willing to purchase at a given exchange value would in general be doubled; and the amount which each producer of the commodity would be willing to supply at a given exchange value would be doubled. (Ibid.)

Following the law of markets, Marshall recognised that it is productions which buy productions; a doubling of output leads to a doubling of demand. It is highly

---

[8] Alfred Marshall and Mary Paley Marshall co-authored *The Economics of Industry*.

[9] This was reprinted in Pigou (1925).

unlikely that Marshall would have changed his mind on this fundamental issue between 1876 and 1879. In quoting this passage in 1879, and then by including it in the fifth edition of the *Principles* in 1907, Marshall was endorsing Mill's views, not challenging them. O'Brien (1990: 135) takes the same view, writing that 'Marshall also borrowed from Mill the latter's own particular version of the Law of Markets', while Blaug (1958: 101) states that, in regard to the question of general gluts, 'nothing new was added between 1850 and 1890'.

In *The Economics of Industry*, Marshall describes a boom followed by a collapse ([1879] 1881: 152–3). Credit becomes over-extended and, ultimately, lenders become wary of further lending and boom turns to bust. Marshall then describes the common mis-diagnosis of the ensuing recession in a manner little different from J.S. Mill. Indeed, Schumpeter ([1954] 1986: 747) argues that Marshall's theory of the cycle 'does not amount to more than an elaboration of J.S. Mill's suggestions'. As Marshall wrote:

> After every crisis, in every period of commercial depression, it is said that supply is in excess of demand. Of course there may easily be an excessive supply of some particular commodities; so much cloth and furniture and cutlery may have been made that they cannot be sold at a remunerative price. But something more than this is meant. For after a crisis the warehouses are overstocked with goods in almost every important trade; scarcely any trade can continue undiminished production so as to afford a good rate of profits to capital and a good rate of wages to labour. And it is thought that this state of things is one of general over-production. We shall however find that it really is nothing but a state of commercial disorganisation. (Marshall and Marshall [1879] 1881: 154)

This is a description of events fully consistent with Say's Law.[10] Warehouses full of unsold goods are being wrongly described as 'over-production' (see also Marshall [1920] 1947: 524). The real problem is 'commercial disorganisation'. It is at this stage that Marshall again quotes J.S. Mill, in the passage reproduced in the *General Theory* (*CW* VII: 18), which says that recessions are not due to a deficiency of purchasing power. Marshall then says what Mill himself might have said, which is that individuals may choose not to use the purchasing power they have. Mill had stated that, following a crisis, individuals would choose to hold money rather than buy goods. Marshall ([1879] 1881: 154) wrote, echoing Mill, that 'when confidence has been shaken by failures, capital cannot be got to start new companies or extend old ones'. Marshall then wrote that recessionary conditions flow from industry to industry as the fall in the demand for the goods of one sector leads to a fall in demand elsewhere:[11]

---

[10] Wolfe ([1956] 1982), in discussing 'Marshall and the Trade Cycle', does not refer to the law of markets, nor should this be seen as surprising in light of modern interpretations following Keynes. Wolfe does, however, note that whatever differences there were between Marshall and Keynes, they were not over the possibility of a trade cycle (ibid.: 88).

[11] Bigg (1990: 32) cites a passage from an 1887 article in which Marshall wrote: 'every stoppage of the work in any one trade diminishes the demand for the work of others',

Other trades, finding a poor market for their goods, produce less; they earn less, and therefore they buy less; the diminution of the demand for their wares makes them demand less of other trades. Thus commercial disorganisation spreads, the disorganisation of one trade throws others out of gear, and they react on it and increase its disorganisation. (Ibid.: 154)

This is the transmission mechanism which is part and parcel of the law of markets. Demand and supply are out of phase, with sales not meeting original expectations. Demand, therefore, contracts across the economy because sales have fallen, but the problem is not demand failure as such but market disorganisation. Marshall finally describes the subsequent upturn as confidence returns, production increases and, with the higher level of production, demand increases as well.

The entire process is simply Marshall's depiction of the processes of the law of markets. Marshall quotes Mill, not to contradict him, but as an authority for what he himself is writing. Moreover, this analysis was not just a product of the young Marshall but represents his more mature view as well. The entire discussion, from Mill's quotation through to the description of economic revival, was incorporated into the *Principles* but only from the fifth edition of 1907 (Marshall 1961: II. 713 and noted by Bridel 1979: 660n and Kahn 1984: 13). Moreover, in a footnote to this discussion, Marshall ([1920] 1947: 711–12n) made it clear that, from his perspective, he was following in the tradition of the classical economists who had preceded him.

Once one understands the dynamics of the law of markets it is not difficult to recognise just how orthodox Marshall's position is. Purchasing power is distributed so that everything can be bought, but if there is a failure of confidence, then business people become more hesitant. The desire to hold money rather than to purchase goods begins to dominate until confidence returns and spending begins anew. Bridel (1987: 47), however, argues that Marshall's theory of the cycle is not integrated with his theory of supply, demand and value. He sees the theory as 'a mere descriptive list of particular imperfections which limit in the short run the tendency towards a full-employment competitive equilibrium' (ibid.: 48). Bridel's failure fully to understand the classical theory of the business cycle highlights the degree to which the Keynesian Revolution not only swept aside earlier modes of understanding the nature of recession, but also undermined the ability to reconstruct what pre-Keynesian economists had actually been saying.

What is clear is that Marshall's discussion of the trade cycle makes it difficult to accept Keynes's assertions that classical economists always assumed the existence of full employment (Bridel 1987: 47; O'Brien 1990: 146). The way round this has generally been to differentiate between a short-run theory where Say's Law is abandoned and the longer-run equilibrium towards which the

---

about which he says, 'Marshall thus appears to be fully aware of the interrelatedness of output and demand. However he did not apply this to the long run and hence did not derive the full concept of effective demand' (ibid.). Bigg seems to believe that Marshall's argument represents one step along the road to a theory of effective demand. In fact, it is merely a restatement of Say's Law whereby demand is constituted by supply.

economy is heading. But how long is the short run? Eshag (1964: 40) wrote, in discussing Marshall, that 'the notions of the existence of idle capacity, on a large scale and for any length of time, or of "involuntary unemployment", were generally alien to the classical doctrine'. Compare this with Bigg (1990: 29), whose short term seems to extend for a quite considerable period: 'Full employment remained, for Marshall, the only state of long run equilibrium, however serious and prolonged the short run deviations and attendant problems might be'.

Marshall recognised that recession and involuntary unemployment could occur and endure, taking the same position as Mill. Demand was constituted by supply, and the more that was produced the more would be bought. Over-production was not a realistic concern, but this did not rule out recessions, which were recognised as being caused by disharmonies in the production process with their attendant effects on sales and business confidence.

Edgeworth

Another perspective on the understanding of the law of markets amongst classical economists is provided by the original *Palgrave* entry on 'Over-production', which was written by Francis Ysedro Edgeworth (1845–1926), Drummond Professor of Political Economy at Oxford from 1891 to 1922. He was also co-editor of the *Economic Journal* with Keynes from 1911 to 1926. Edgeworth's best-known association with the law of markets is his review of Hobson and Mummery's *Physiology of Industry* (Edgeworth 1890).[12]

From the very start of his *Palgrave* article, Edgeworth simply denies the existence of over-production in the sense in which it was used by Malthus. And, it should be noted, the author quoted by Edgeworth is John Stuart Mill:

> OVER-PRODUCTION has been supposed to exist both with respect to consumable commodities and capital. But 'the theory of general over-production is an absurdity' (J.S. Mill), in the obvious sense which would justify the recommendation to increase unproductive consumption or to diminish saving. (Edgeworth 1926: 45)

Note that it is the policy conclusion which is the issue. Whatever it is that is happening when recession strikes, it would be an error to attempt to deal with it by encouraging unproductive consumption or a reduction in saving. Edgeworth recognises that there are actual real-world events which might lead one to believe that over-production has occurred, but one would be mistaken to accept the appearance for the underlying reality:

> There are, however, some phenomena which partially resemble the description which is given of over-production. For instance, in a commercial crisis, when there is a deficiency of ready money, there seems to be a plethora of goods; as J.S. Mill pointed out (Essay 2, *Some Unsettled Questions*). A similar appearance, as he

---

[12] Hobson ([1938] 1976: 30–31) believed these critical comments caused him to lose his two extension lecturing positions in London and Oxford.

observed, may be produced by a derangement of currency; and it may be added by an appreciation of money consequent upon a great increase in production. (Ibid.)

There is, moreover, every reason to believe that such occurrences will be accompanied by unemployment. The operation of the law of markets does not in the slightest suggest that recessionary conditions and unemployment might not take place. Indeed, it is conceivable that they may occur on a 'large scale':

> In general, improvement in production, when accompanied with 'sudden changes in the channels of trade' (Ricardo), causes loss to some classes of producers. Workmen may be displaced by machinery...the native workman by the foreigner.... These phenomena, if they occurred on a large scale, might present the appearance of general over-production. (Ibid.)

Edgeworth briefly notes the positions of the two sides in the general glut debates. As he makes clear, in the nineteenth century the overwhelming majority of economists denied that a general glut could occur, while never denying that economic downturns did occur:

> The impossibility of a 'general glut' has been demonstrated by almost all the authorities of last century; with particular clearness by J. MILL, J.B. SAY and J.S. MILL. On the other side are the weighty names of MALTHUS, T. CHALMERS, and SISMONDI; followed by a crowd of inferior writers. (Ibid.)

He goes on to make one final point which, in the light of the subsequent history of Say's Law, contains a good deal of irony. In his concluding statement, Edgeworth observes that one might profitably peruse the writings of Malthus and the others who denied the validity of Say's Law. Examining their arguments, Edgeworth suggests, might be useful because it would ensure that there really is nothing of value in the mistaken views of those who had opposed Say's Law (ibid.).

Beveridge

Beveridge presents an interesting case study, having written separate works on the problem of cyclical fluctuations in 1909 and 1930, and his views are of central interest as he was to be the author of the 1944 'Beveridge Report'.[13] In the 1909 account,[14] he sets out his own theory of recession which is a variant of the misdirected production theory. He describes a situation where there is an increased demand for particular goods which, because of the unplanned nature of production, can lead total supply to overshoot total demand:

---

[13] The *Beveridge Report* provided a third, basically Keynesian, analytical approach to the trade cycle (see Beveridge 1944: 93–7).

[14] Reprinted as the first part of Beveridge (1931).

> The demand is felt and met not by one producer but by many, and not by many each providing a definite share in agreement with the rest, but by many each acting independently and dominated by the desire to do as much business as possible.... Inevitably therefore all the producers together tend to overshoot the demand and to glut the market for a time. (Ibid.: 59)

Far from contradicting the law of markets, this explanation is entirely consistent with it. Producers have miscalculated because they have been unable to gauge correctly how many units of production they can sell. Indeed, Beveridge is very careful to explain that his theory in no way offends the canons of the law of markets:

> Though, however, the theory just propounded does not in itself completely explain simultaneous over-production followed by stagnation in practically all industries, it makes such a result probable. At the same time it in no way offends economic doctrine as to the impossibility of general over-production. (Ibid.: 60–61)

In 1909, Beveridge was content to explain downturns in terms of mutually inconsistent production decisions. In 1930, he took a different approach and explained cyclical activity arising out of 'the inherent instability of credit' (ibid.: 326).[15] What is interesting to note is that the problem is no longer constituted in terms of production decisions as such, but is described as the consequence of an over-extension of credit. The theory as presented by Beveridge is one in which variations in credit cause demand and supply to move out of phase, with demand falling short of the level of production. His explanation traces the movement in credit, following upon a rise in the discount rate:

> There follows a contraction of credit, starting a downward movement of prices which by the inherent instability of credit and prices, brings a further contraction of credit and a further fall. At last a point is reached when bankers feel safe, wish to expand credit again and seek to do so by cheapening it. (Ibid.: 331)

The unstated explanation is that some production must remain unsold because demand is curtailed by the fall in credit. In this, Beveridge is following, in truncated form, one aspect of the standard classical explanation of the cycle.

Robertson

Dennis Robertson holds an interesting position on the questions surrounding the law of markets. In 1914 he had written a critique of Aftalion, who had argued that over-production was possible (Robertson 1914: 84–9), and in the same article had attacked Tugan-Baranowsky for his 'pure misunderstanding' of the 'classical doctrine of markets' (ibid.: 83). In *A Study of Industrial Fluctuation*, Robertson again criticised Aftalion and Tugan-Baranowsky for their 'straw man' versions of

---

[15] Dennis Robertson (1931a: 74) described this as 'one of the best possible books on an economic subject'.

the law of markets (1915: 199n and discussed below). In the same volume he wrote a critique of Hobson and his theory of under-consumption (ibid.: 235–8). In 1929, he wrote an article critical of the views of Catchings and Foster, who had argued that a shortage of money could lead to a deficiency of demand which could then lead to recession. He described their theories as a 'pseudo-scientific apparatus' ([1929] 1931c: 162). It would seem that Robertson accepted the law of markets at least in part, and was a strong enough advocate to have on a number of occasions gone into print on its behalf.[16] For all that, Robertson seems to have had a less than complete grasp of the issues surrounding the law of markets. *Industrial Fluctuation* includes a section headed 'General Depression – The Law of Markets' (1915: 198–205).[17] Robertson argued that, to the extent that the law of markets is intended 'to assert that it is impossible to conceive of an excess of aggregate production over the totality of human wants', then it is 'beyond dispute' (ibid.: 199). He continued:

> It is true of goods in general, though not perhaps of particular goods, that however many of them there are they will not be beyond the physical capacity of the population to absorb.... While it may be to the advantage of particular groups of owners to destroy the stocks of their product rather than dispose of them, it can never be to the advantage of owners in general: if everybody sells freely the various products will provide a market for one another and the aggregate satisfaction of the community derived from the consumption of goods will be greater than it would otherwise have been. (Ibid.: 199–200)

The issue in regard to the law of markets was, however, not whether demand could exceed human wants, which no one had suggested, but whether the economic system would create effective demand for all of the output it was capable of producing. If it were agreed that the purchasing power was available to buy everything produced, then the concern was usually expressed in terms of the consequences of an excessive level of saving. Yet, in dealing with the more detailed aspects of the law of markets, Robertson had a clear understanding of the issues at stake.[18] Having wrongly characterised the law of markets he then correctly sets about demolishing the arguments of Aftalion and Tugan-

---

[16] It is therefore something of a curiosity that Robertson did not focus on the issue of Say's Law in his criticisms of the *General Theory*.

[17] Cannan (1916: 229), in his review of *Industrial Fluctuation*, praised Robertson for making 'clear what are the principal original cause of miscalculation and how the miscalculations work'. In contrast, Wesley Mitchell (1916: 639) was critical of the theoretical aspects of the book, writing: 'since [Robertson] really inquires what would happen in a barter economy run by coöperative laborers he sheds little light on what happens in a real economy run by business men.... We do indeed need analysis of what goes on beneath "the money surface of things"; but the way to get it is to go *through* money to that for which the money stands – not to conjure up a world from which money is excluded'.

[18] Kahn (1984: 15, italics added) noted Robertson's writing showed 'the influence of Say's Law *even* upon the study of the trade cycle'. Kahn obviously found such an idea very peculiar.

Baranowsky in a manner which provides a deeper insight into the classical interpretation:

> I omit the forms in which [the law of markets] is stated in order to be knocked down by M. Aftalion and M. Baranowsky respectively. The former...argues at length that an over-production in one industry does not necessarily imply an actual diminution of output in any other – a proposition never, so far as I know, maintained by any one. The 'under-production' in other industries affirmed to be necessary by the Law of Markets of course merely means a *relative* under-production, due to a misdirection of productive power, and indicated by a rise in the exchange value of their products.
>
> M. Baranowsky...supposes the Law to assert that all consumable goods must always be absorbed in exchange *with other consumable goods*, and advances over its dead body to the triumphant announcement of his 'paradoxical' discovery that owing to the accumulation of fixed capital the aggregate production in a society may exceed its aggregate revenue *in consumable goods* without a rupture of equilibrium between demand in general and supply in general. In this progress he is assisted by his complete misunderstanding of the classical doctrine that 'what is saved affords subsistence to the workman just as much as what is spent'. There seems no reason to believe that the classical school in its most abstract moments was unaware that while the consumable capital 'saved' is consumed by the makers of the instrumental goods for which it is in effect exchanged, these instrumental goods themselves are consumed, i.e., held in use, by the capitalist class; and no reason to suppose that the Law of Markets in any form excludes consumption of this latter kind from its purview. (Robertson 1915: 199n)

Given his previous interest in writers on gluts, it is not entirely surprising that, when Robertson came to give his testimony to the Macmillan Committee in 1930, and faced with the fact of the Great Depression, he looked for an understanding of what was happening in terms of the law of markets.[19] In his memorandum submitted to the Committee, the first section is entitled 'The Gluttability of Wants' ([1930] 1931b: 116). Here Robertson states that not even the most liberal banking system conceivable could overcome 'the tendency to industrial depression' due to 'the failure of private enterprise to absorb spontaneously the increment of saving committed to the charge of the banks' (ibid.: 121). Robinson wrote that 'among the causes of industrial depression I attach leading importance to the temporary gluttability of large groups of particular human wants' (ibid.: 122). While this was true of consumer goods, he found it even more relevant for investment goods.

It is probable that Robertson, in choosing the words 'gluttability of wants', was consciously and publicly distancing himself from the law of markets as he understood it. It is thus arguable that Robertson had rejected Say's Law six years before Keynes. Yet there are reasons to believe he had not. The very way in which Presley describes Robertson's theory of recession makes it clear that Robertson accepted the fundamental position on the trade cycle as it had developed over the previous century:

---

[19] See Presley (1983: 182), where it is argued that Robertson's position was a consequence of his study of Aftalion.

The over-investment theory of a crisis...saw the economy producing more capital goods than would be demanded. There *could* be over-production of such goods. But Robertson went even further than this in agreeing with Aftalion that over-investment could in turn bring a general over-production. (Presley 1983: 186–7; see also 1979: 68)

Elsewhere, Presley described Robertson's position as 'over-investment leads to over-production relative to *particular* demands. This brings depression' (1979: 31, italics added). This is an explanation of the cycle in which a partial glut in the capital goods industry is turned into a downturn of the entire economy. Indeed, Presley (ibid.: 69) wrote that 'the main ingredients of Robertsonian theory are in fact the same as those found in Marshall's work'.

Robertson appeared keen to find a theory on which to hang his desired public policy of increased public spending to combat recession. He wrote that:

> the doctrine of temporary gluttability which I have tried to outline above is in direct conflict not only with the so-called 'Treasury view' that such a policy of promoting public works absorbs resources which would otherwise anyhow be employed by private enterprise, but also with the doctrine, which has been maintained, for instance, by Mr Hawtrey, that the public works are a 'mere piece of ritual', achieving nothing which could not equally well be achieved by the banking system. (Robertson 1931b: 124)

The 'gluttability of wants' was only temporary, according to Robertson, although he thought 'temporary' to be 'in this connection a vague and elastic conception' (ibid.: 125). He was looking for a theoretical understanding of recession which would permit a shorter-run policy to be adopted to alleviate the social disorders associated with unemployment, and he found it in the possibility of glutted markets.[20] But, his choice of words aside, 'temporary' glut is a way of describing Mill's increased desire for money following a drop in business confidence. Indeed, the section in which 'gluttability of wants' is discussed initially deals with the banking system and the effect of falling confidence on the demand for money (1931b: 116–19). Bridel (1987: 81) describes Robertson's attempts to distance himself from Say's Law as 'nothing more than a critique of its short-run validity during each and every phase of the cycle'.

Presley (1983: 186) makes an issue of Robertson's differences with what Presley terms the 'classical strawman model', arguing that Robertson was no slave to the classical version of Say's Law. Presley is, however, prevented from fully understanding the issues at stake because of his Keynesian approach. He wrote that Robertson 'did not accept the validity of Say's Law, he disputed the

---

[20] In his *Banking Policy and the Price Level*, Robertson (1926: 95–6) had written: 'the primary reason for constructional depression is a perfectly sensible downward revaluation, on the part of private individuals and corporations, of the advantage of possessing instruments. If this view is accepted, there is nothing inherently foolish about attempts to organise a *collective* desire (say for municipal lavatories) to take the place of a private desire (say for factories) which has temporarily failed'.

existence of any automatic mechanism generating full employment' (1979: 82; also 216). Presley thus has difficulty in reconciling the recognition of recession in classical writings with their simultaneous upholding of Say's Law (ibid.: 68). Robertson, with his focus on forced savings and excess production of capital goods, understood recession in terms of the structure of production rather than the volume of demand.

Pigou

A.C. Pigou was for Keynes the very embodiment of classical economics (see *CW* VII: 3n and 19–20). In particular, Pigou was accused of ignoring, as did all other classical economists, the consequences of variations in effective demand. Keynes wrote that due to the influence of Ricardo, 'the great puzzle of Effective Demand with which Malthus had wrestled vanished from economic literature. You will not find it mentioned even once in the whole works of Marshall, Edgeworth and Professor Pigou' (ibid.: 32). And, in a letter to Robertson a few months before publication of the *General Theory*, Keynes wrote that 'I have still failed to find anything relevant to the matters I discuss in [Pigou's] *Industrial Fluctuations*. You are more learned in that matter than I am, so, if you can easily direct me to a passage, I will be grateful' (*CW* XIII: 524). To which Robertson replied: 'I think I think [sic] that pretty well the whole of *Industrial Fluctuations*, being a study of the variations in Effective Demand, is relevant to your theme' (ibid.). It is little wonder that Pigou (1936) was so aggrieved in his review of the *General Theory*.[21]

According to Pigou, the problem in recession is that there is not enough aggregate demand, and the practical remedies are related to whether the level of demand can be increased. Pigou writes that there are two distinct issues which must be dealt with in answering this question. The first is whether it is even possible to create demand from scratch or, at the very least, transfer demand from good times to bad. The second question is whether doing so will provide any social benefit. When *Industrial Fluctuations* was first published in 1927, the 1929 'Treasury View' had, of course, not by then been advanced. Pigou instead provided an example of an argument that demand cannot be raised by quoting a passage from the *Report of the Transvaal Indigency Commission* (1929: 316):[22]

---

[21] See Hutchison (1978: 165–6 and ch. 6) for a strong defence of Pigou against Keynes's criticisms; also Corry (1978: 9–12) and Collard (1983: 124–30). Interestingly, Harrod had begun his review of Pigou's *Theory of Unemployment* (1933) by describing it as 'a supreme intellectual achievement, a masterpiece of close and coherent reasoning' (1934a: 19). Given that Keynes used Pigou as the representative follower of Say's Law amongst his contemporaries, it is interesting that Pigou is the most difficult of Keynes's contemporaries with which to demonstrate an association with Say's Law. Hansen (1953: 16–20) provides a comprehensive discussion of Say's Law in Pigou's work from a Keynesian perspective.

[22] Pigou had cited the same report in his *Unemployment* (1914: 171–5; cf. Hutchison 1978: 162). Pigou's position in *Unemployment* was supported by Beveridge in his review (1914: 252).

Wealth is the only source from which wages are paid, and the State must levy taxation (or raise loans) in order to pay wages to its workmen. When, therefore, a Government gives work to the unemployed, it is simply transferring wage-giving power from the individual to itself. It is diminishing employment with one hand while it increases it with the other. It takes work from people employed by private individuals, and gives it to people selected by the State.

It is this argument which Pigou wishes to refute. His aim is to demonstrate that those who contend that a government cannot increase employment during recession are wrong, and he presents an argument to demonstrate that demand creation is possible. From this he turns to demonstrate that the private sector will not have already produced to the maximum extent given current conditions:

> We have thus found that the creation of demand in bad times, and, therefore, also the transfer of demand from good times to bad, in such wise as to lessen the amplitude of industrial fluctuations, is possible. We have now to consider the suggestion that whatever transfer is sociably desirable...will already have been made under the influence of private self-regarding motives. It can easily be shown that this suggestion is incorrect. (Ibid. 320)

Pigou thus argues that recessions can be alleviated by a programme of public sector works. And the issue, from Pigou's perspective, is literally the need to raise 'aggregate demand'.[23]

Yet Pigou seems to understand demand in a Say's Law sense. Demand is embedded in supply; the more that is produced, the more that can be demanded. When he seeks an increase in 'demand', Pigou seeks an increase in the supply of publicly owned goods, rather than an increase in purchases from existing stocks.[24] The chapter on 'Repercussions' (ibid.: 57–71) is cast in real terms, such that

---

[23] An interesting example of the parallel views of Keynes and Pigou is provided by a letter written to *The Times*. On 17 October 1932, a letter was published over the signatures of six prominent economists: D.H. Macgregor, A.C. Pigou, J.M. Keynes, Walter Layton, Arthur Salter and J.C. Stamp (*CW* XXI: 138–9), stating that in the face of high levels of unemployment, increasing the level of savings would only exacerbate the problem. It was therefore necessary that higher levels of spending occur, both by private individuals and by governments. The prescriptions towards higher spending and less saving sound entirely 'Keynesian'. But as Keynesian as the letter to *The Times* may sound, it was written not by Keynes but by Pigou. Pigou's authorship is noted by Moggridge (*CW* XXI: 137–8).

[24] Pigou (1929: 329) discusses public sector demand for ships, schools and roads, which clearly means placing orders for their construction. He is more explicit in detailing what private producers do when he discusses how an employer of labour can shift his 'production' from good times to bad (ibid.: 323). But Pigou also included the straightforward purchase of goods offered for sale by those with incomes from business, and implies that deficit financing may be appropriate for the public sector (ibid.: 330).

goods are bought from each other with the goods each has individually produced.[25]

It is also notable that the basic mechanism of industrial fluctuations is seen by Pigou in terms of 'miscalculation'. With production generally in advance of sales, there are forecasting errors which lead to even more pronounced fluctuations, either upwards or downwards, depending on the psychology of market participants. The chapter headings provide the sense of his approach to fundamentals. Chapter VI: 'The Structure of Modern Industry and Opportunities for Errors of Forecast'; Chapter VII: 'The Mutual Generation of Errors of Optimism and Pessimism'; Chapter VIII: 'Autonomous Monetary Causes of Industrial Fluctuations'. Forecasting errors and monetary causes are the basic initiating causes of recession, though other factors contribute, and increase the amplitude. But what is also evident is that neither demand failure nor over-production are identified as initiating causes or even as contributing factors. While the generation of additional demand is seen as helping to alleviate the consequences of recession, considerations of demand-side failure are not included amongst the causes.

An earlier discussion by Pigou along the same lines may be found in his 'Unemployment and the Great Slump' ([1921] 1923). There he traces how a partial glut, where 'the output of one of the groups in the country...falls off in consequence of bad harvests, war, labour troubles, or some other cause' (ibid.: 35), can lead to a general downturn across all industries. The recession of 1921 occurred because 'the *world* fell out of joint' (ibid.: 38) due to the nature of the boom which had preceded it. That is, the recession was due to structural disharmonies.

Pigou, in his writings, was disciplined by the logic of the law of markets. His theoretical approach to recession and unemployment was within the parameters defined by J.S. Mill, Torrens and Marshall. Pigou discussed practical remedies in terms of increasing demand, but there was always a close recognition that to raise demand there had also to be an increase in production. Virtually none of the calumny heaped on Pigou's head by Keynes seems to have reflected an accurate judgement of Pigou's views.[26]

---

[25] Take, for example, the following description of exchange which is in the format C–M–C': 'If A makes his offer in the form of 2000 pounds, he makes it in substance in the 2000 pounds worth of A goods that B buys with the 2000 pounds. When B has handed over his extra product, received 2000 pounds for it, and spent the 2000 pounds in buying A goods, the money counters return to their old seats, and the real transaction has been completed' (Pigou 1929: 64).

[26] Collard (1996: 923–4) discusses Pigou's theory of the business cycle writing, that 'in the present rather unsettled state of business cycle theory there are still lessons to be learned from the eclectic approach taken by Pigou in *Industrial Fluctuations*'.

Hawtrey (1933)

Ralph Hawtrey's *Trade Depression and the Way Out* was published in 1933 in the depths of the Great Depression and, as its title indicates, it was concerned with the appropriate policies for dealing with depression. This was a revised and extended version of a pamphlet which had been published in 1931. And while it contains all of the views associated with the law of markets, its opening paragraph might lead one to the conclusion that Hawtrey took the same position that Keynes would take three years later in the *General Theory*:

> Trade depression has many symptoms, but perhaps the most characteristic of all is the shortage of demand. Those who produce or buy goods with a view to sale are faced with a difficulty of selling them. Production is restricted and prices are reduced, and still it is found that sales fall short of output. Thus the under-employment of labour, the fall of prices and the accumulation of unsold goods are all related to the shrinkage of demand. (Hawtrey 1933: 1)

In the next paragraph, however, Hawtrey defines demand as he intends to use it, in a way which is related to, if not actually identical with, the concept underlying the law of markets. Demand is constituted by the money receipts earned by selling in the marketplace:

> Where does demand come from? Clearly from people's incomes, and incomes are derived from production. People get their incomes by working, or else by letting their property or capital be used productively. The traders who sell things apply the proceeds of sale to paying the costs of production, and retain the balance as profit. The profit supplies the traders' incomes, and the costs are composed of other people's incomes in the form of wages, salaries, interest, etc. In fact, the whole income of the community is composed of the proceeds of sale of all the goods and services which constitute its output. One trader's outlay on materials or intermediate products goes to pay the incomes of those employed by others to produce these goods. Such incomes as old age pensions and the interest on the national debt, which are not paid in return for any current contribution towards the productive output of the community, are charged by taxation, etc., on the productive incomes. The consuming power of the latter is diminished by the amount of the former. The total consuming power of the community is therefore equal to its output. (Ibid.)

Demand comes from incomes and incomes come from production. By casting demand as constituted by production, Hawtrey commences from a thoroughly classical position.[27] The upper limit to the level of demand is given by the level of production, and the process envisaged is from production to demand. But at the same time, by casting the argument in terms of demand shortage, the approach adopted is, at least superficially, Keynesian. That Hawtrey remains on the side of classical analysis is indicated by the question Hawtrey asks:

---

[27] Keynes, in his correspondence following publication of the *General Theory*, attempted to absolve Hawtrey from being a classical economist (*CW* XIV: 15). Hawtrey, in his reply, insisted that he was precisely that (ibid.: 19).

> If consuming power is equal to output, how can there ever be a failure of demand?...
> *What we have to explain is how the shrinkage in both output and demand starts.*
> (Ibid.: 2, italics added)

That Hawtrey inextricably links demand with production suggests that demand is inseparable in his mind from the production which underpins it. And, as a further indication that he is aware that he is dealing with the issues surrounding the law of markets, he immediately discusses the question of 'over-production'. He notes first that output exceeding demand, *on an industry by industry basis*, is often attributed to over-production. He then mentions, in a single sentence, the classical position on the impossibility of general gluts, which he accepts as valid but, in this context, thinks of as beside the point (ibid.).

In Hawtrey's view, a general glut cannot occur but partial gluts can. It is these partial gluts, where demand falls short of supply in particular industries, which set up a chain reaction, where there are further reductions in demand and, therefore, further reductions in the flow of output. Miscalculation by producers in various industries leads to production exceeding the level of sales, and ultimately results in a general downturn in the economy:

> Suppose that over-production occurs in *some* industries.[28] Those industries find that they cannot sell their output. They restrict production and reduce prices. The fund out of which the incomes of the industries are paid is thereby doubly reduced, on account of smaller quantities and of lower prices. There is less employment and there are lower profits. The result of this reduction of incomes is that the demand for the products *of all other industries* contracts. They in turn, finding their sales declining, suffer a reduction of income, which means a further reduction of demand for products in general. (Ibid.: 2)

This is the process of economic contraction which had been highlighted by classical economists for more than a century. Hawtrey, in typical classical fashion, then proceeds to extend his analysis to the problems created by the system of credit creation. Indeed, it is Hawtrey's fundamental position that the system of credit creation is the determinant of the flow of demand. It is demand, in the form of money payments, which is the basis for sale and expenditure, and therefore 'the banks, by restricting credit, can start the vicious circle of deflation' (ibid.: 8). Moreover, Hawtrey connects the problems caused by the credit creation process to the superficial appearance of over-production:

> Whenever there is delay in reducing prices to the point at which consumption keeps pace with output an accumulation of goods in stock begins.... The accumulation of stocks of goods is apt to be regarded as a symptom of 'over-production'. The stock of a product at any moment represents excess of production over sales. If the excess is due to a shrinkage of sales, the term 'over-production' if unqualified becomes

---

28 It is noteworthy that Hawtrey italicised the word 'some'. He seems to have gone out of his way to demonstrate that he was not taking issue with the question of whether there can be a general glut.

inappropriate, though there may fairly be said to be a *relative* over-production. If the demand for a particular product is falling off, then producers ought to reduce their output to whatever extent is requisite to re-establish equilibrium between prices and costs. If they fail to do so, they have produced too much.

If it is not the demand for a particular product but the demand in terms of monetary units for *all* products that falls off, **then though a part of output remains unsold there cannot be said to be over-production at all**. The normal balance, by which production generates incomes just sufficient to buy the products, has been interfered with. Money that ought to be passing through incomes to form demand is intercepted and either extinguished by repayments of bank advances or held idle in balances. The shortage of demand is thus caused by a hitch in the credit system. (Ibid.: 39, bold added)

This is an analysis of recession carved out of the law of markets. The existence of general over-production is denied. Partial gluts, due to business errors, have led to excess supply of certain products. Production in those industries must now be curtailed, which will commence a downward spiral of contraction. And while production is recognised as the basis of demand, the system of credit creation reduces the flow of money payments, exacerbating the original problem. Hawtrey casts the argument in terms of demand, yet the problem, as he describes it, is decidedly not demand deficiency in the Keynesian sense, but the consequences of the structure of supply failing to match the structure of demand.

Indeed, Hawtrey works to dispel the notion that depression is due to gluts in either consumption or capital goods. And he specifically uses the word 'glut' to describe the kind of situation whose existence he emphatically denies. In dealing with the question as to whether there had been 'a glut of consumable goods' (ibid.: 81) in the United States at the onset of the Great Depression, he writes: 'it is quite certain that no such glut existed or impended in the United States at the end of 1929' (ibid.: 83). And in dealing with the possibility of a 'glut of capital' he not only denies it as a possibility, but he does so by employing the saving-is-spending argument Keynes was at pains to discredit:

As improvements [in production] reduce the real cost of consumable goods, and people spend a smaller proportion of their incomes upon them, the surplus incomes not required for consumable goods will be saved. But this does not mean that the money saved will be held idle. In general, money saved is *spent*; it is invested, and is passed on through the investment market to be spent on capital goods. (Ibid.: 85)

Hawtrey agrees that, if there were a glut of capital:

we could no longer say that money saved is spent, and it follows that savings would cause a deficiency of purchasing power. The demand for goods would fall short of the total of incomes, and therefore of the value of goods produced, and a portion of the goods produced would remain unsold. (Ibid.: 87)

But while agreeing that in theory a glut of capital could lead to output exceeding the level of demand, in practical terms Hawtrey totally dismisses this as a genuine possibility, and in no uncertain terms:

> When glut occurs, and changes of economic organisation become necessary, there will be visible symptoms pointing to the requisite action, *provided* that the economic system is functioning normally at the time. But it would be a grave blunder to mistake the symptoms of depression for the symptoms of glut. Before we can tell whether the symptoms of glut are appearing, we must first escape from the depression.
>
> And in reality it does not seem likely that a state of universal glut is at all near.... Modern methods of production may tend to cause a real glut of factory productions, of staple foods and materials and in general of everything in which there is scope for highly capitalised production. But that is far from exhausting the entire economic field. Social progress constantly offers new openings for more skilled and more individual economic activity. (Ibid.: 92)

Hawtrey's *Trade Depression and the Way Out* is a thoroughly classical analysis of the down phase of the business cycle,[29] drenched in the analytics associated with the law of markets.[30] Demand is defined in terms of supply, and while the aim of policy is seen to be an increase in demand, in the sense of a flow of money payments, demand must nevertheless be ratified by a flow of production.[31] Hawtrey has provided a theory of recession not only consistent with the law of markets but, in fact, based on it.

Hawtrey's reliance on Say's Law was, in fact, recognised by Keynes. A year after the publication of the *General Theory*, in a letter to Hugh Townshend, Keynes referred to Say's Law in Hawtrey's *Capital and Employment* (1937), writing 'on page 102 to 104, he is practically assuming Say's Law, and an appropriate fall in the rate of interest whenever there are idle savings' (*CW* XXIX: 259).

Hawtrey's arguments found on these pages of *Capital and Employment* are little different from his views in *Trade Depression and the Way Out*. He again states that although a glut of capital exists as a 'theoretical possibility' (1937: 103), it has 'never yet occurred and so has nothing to do with the trade cycle' (ibid.: 104). Which leads him to conclude:

---

[29] Cannan (1932) in his review of the first edition, and Harrod (1934b) in his review of the second, found nothing to criticise with regard to the economic theory. They clearly saw nothing unusual in the structure of Hawtrey's arguments. Indeed, Harrod states that in terms of theory, although there is not much, the aim is 'to wage constant warfare with the hosts of follies and fallacies that beset monetary theory. On the whole he is admirably successful' (ibid.: 280).

[30] Hawtrey was himself unaware of the origins of his ideas, as shown in his description of Say's Law as 'applicable primarily to a non-monetary system' (*CW* XIV: 32). Both Klein (1968: 45–6) and Deutscher (1990: 241–2) argue that Hawtrey accepted Say's Law.

[31] See Hawtrey's discussion of the 'Quantity of Money and the Price Level' (1933: 7–8) in which the relationship between money, output and prices is discussed.

Apart from the special case of a temporary glut of capital caused by extreme depression, we can assume that the investment market will succeed in finding an outlet in capital outlay for all the resources it receives and there need not be an absorption or release of cash by the market on any important scale. (Ibid.)

Keynes is quite right to see in this a rejection of his own position and the acceptance by Hawtrey of the classical position on Say's Law. Hawtrey's view is that the capital market brings available savings and investment together. Acceptance of this position means rejection of the central argument of the *General Theory*.

CONCLUDING COMMENT

The above discussion has focused on the core acceptance of Say's Law by mainstream English economists from the early nineteenth century through to the publication of the *General Theory*. Within the normal range of differences, there is a broad thread which connects them, which has as its core the proposition that demand deficiency (i.e. general glut) is not an acceptable explanation of recession and unemployment. The basis for this judgement was that demand was constituted by supply, so that the appearance of demand failure was, in reality, a problem associated with production. And it was further understood that production failure generally originated in miscalculations on the part of producers or through problems associated with the process of credit creation. It was the structure of demand relative to supply, rather than the weakness of demand in general, which was the cause of recession. Recession was discussed in terms of what might cause production miscalculation, in which the role of the credit creation machinery played a prominent part.

Keynes's attack on classical economics was utterly misguided. His argument, that acceptance of Say's Law meant that an economist assumed full employment from the outset, was simply wrong. What makes this especially ironical was that, not only was Say's Law not an obstacle to understanding that recessions and unemployment could and did occur, but it was that self same Say's Law which formed an integral part of the generally accepted explanation of why recessions and unemployment actually took place in the real world.

6. Say's Law in the Classical Theory of the Business Cycle

This chapter provides an extended analysis of four works which specifically demonstrate the inadequacies of Keynes's understanding of Say's Law and the role it played within classical economic analysis. Each of the works, in its own way, underscores the importance of the law of markets, not only in making sense of the economy generally, but as a means of understanding the nature of recession and unemployment. These analyses show that, not only was Keynes wrong in his assessment of Say's Law, but that in presenting the arguments in the *General Theory* as an attack on Say's Law, he altered fundamentally the way in which economists understood the nature of the business cycle. Not only did he present a theory of his own, but he also placed an almost insurmountable obstacle in the way of understanding how economists had previously understood the causes of recession.

The four works under review in this chapter are Henry Clay's *Economics: An Introduction for the General Reader* (1916), Frederick Lavington's *The Trade Cycle* (1922), Wilhelm Röpke's *Crises and Cycles* (1936) and Gottfried Haberler's *Prosperity and Depression* (1937).

HENRY CLAY: *ECONOMICS: AN INTRODUCTION FOR THE GENERAL READER* (1916)

An important understanding of the way in which Say's Law was used by those who employed it in the early years of the twentieth century is provided in the text *Economics: An Introduction for the General Reader* written by Henry Clay in 1916, and reprinted a number of times throughout the 1920s and 1930s.[1] (A second revised edition was published in 1942.) This was a very commonly used

---

[1] Henry Clay (1883–1954) was Professor of Economics at Manchester University from 1922 to 1930 and is mostly remembered today for his work on industrial relations. He joined the Bank of England in 1930 and became its economic adviser in 1933, which he remained until 1944.

text[2] and presented a non-controversial explanation of the facts of economic life as they were understood during the first third of the twentieth century.[3] The value of the text today is that it provides a more than usually thorough discussion of an exchange economy, and presents its detail in the very way caricatured in the *General Theory*. The explanation of the processes of the economy provided by Clay is thoroughly drenched in the law of markets, and indeed states, almost word for word, Keynes's accusation that, to the classical economist, saving was the same as investing. Yet, as is quite clear from the text, not only did this view of economic life not lead to a belief that unemployment could not occur, but it was actually used to explain why unemployment comes about.

Clay approaches his study of wealth creation along the same lines as Torrens and John Stuart Mill. The definition of capital employed is that of Mill in the *Principles*. Clay points out, following Mill, that 'capital is not certain forms of wealth, but any form of wealth put to a certain use, namely that of assisting the production of further wealth' (Clay [1916] 1924: 234). Clay explicitly states that what is saved is spent. Keynes had chosen the Marshalls as his example of this form of reasoning because, he wrote, 'the doctrine is never stated to-day in this crude form' (*CW* VII: 19). Here, however, it *is* stated by Clay:

> That part of income that is devoted to aiding future production is said to be saved. That does not mean it is not spent or consumed; it means that it is spent or consumed to aid further production. If the income has been received in cash, the saved portion is put in a bank and the bank lends it to business men who use it to aid their work of production; or it is invested; that is, the owner puts it into a business which uses it to buy buildings, plant, materials, etc. We may put the case concretely by saying 'savings' constitute a demand for buildings, machines, materials, and stock-in-trade, while the rest of income is a demand for food, clothing, shelter, and other goods and services for immediate consumption; both are spent, but the object of spending is different in the two cases. (Clay [1916] 1924: 235)

This is the classical approach to saving and investment highlighted by Keynes. It is arguable that the passage contains a tacit assumption of full employment, but it is just as possible that it assumes no more than an equilibrium of a kind where all that is produced is put to use. But whatever else there is in it, it is not a statement about Say's Law. This comes next.

From his discussion of spending and saving, Clay goes on to discuss 'the National Dividend or Income'. It is in this discussion that Say's Law is introduced. Clay's argument is that there is no upper limit on national income, limiting employment to a fixed number of workers. There is always room for an increase in production because there is no need to fear that it will not be bought.

---

[2] Brown (1988: 22) records that it was used as a text at Oxford in the 1930s. It is also mentioned in *The Great Gatsby* where Gatsby is found looking 'with vacant eyes through a copy of Clay's *Economics*' (Fitzgerald [1926] 1990: 82).

[3] The review in the *Economic Journal* stated: 'Mr Clay has written a first rate book, and one covering, at any rate in outline, the whole field of economic inquiry' (Furniss 1916: 350–51).

And the explanation for this is drenched in the Say's Law concept that demand is constituted by supply:

> There is always a demand for this additional product, because the addition to society's income enables society to pay the additional workers or machines or organizers.... What we call 'Supply' and 'Demand' are the same things looked at from the different standpoints of consumer and producer; and consumers and producers are the same persons. The real National Income is the goods and services produced to satisfy the nation's wants; it is these that land, labour, and capital produce, and it is with these that land, labour, and capital are paid: any increase in the product is an increase in the payments....
>
> It is only because our exchanges are made through money that we have any difficulty in perceiving that an increase in supply is (not 'causes') an increase in demand.... Thus an increase in the supply of cloth is an increase in the demand for other things; and *vice versa*, an increase in the supply of anything else may constitute an increase in the demand for cloth. What is divided amongst the members of society is the goods and services produced to satisfy its wants; and the same goods and services are both the Supply and Demand. (Ibid.: 241–2)

An increase in supply *is* an increase in demand. The account of how productions buy productions is, in all important respects, identical with the explanation given by J.B. Say or James Mill.

Yet if one continues with the argument presented by Clay, there is no question that the application of Say's Law does not lead to a denial of the possibility of involuntary unemployment. People can be made unemployed against their own desires, when they would be content to work not only at the going real wage, but even at a lower real wage.

Clay specifically discusses the origins of unemployment. The following chapter is entitled 'Unemployment and Over-Production'.[4] In this chapter, not only is involuntary unemployment shown to be consistent with Say's Law, but Say's Law is employed to provide an understanding of the processes by which unemployment occurs. Clay opens the chapter by noting that the 'sketch' of economic processes he has provided is 'defective in one important respect'. What the sketch did not do, he writes, was:

> indicate how there comes to be any unemployment; how it comes about, in other words, that a system which regularly absorbs the new generation coming into industry every year is unable to absorb, however busy it may be, the whole of the workers who are willing and anxious to find work. Nor does it explain the regular recurrence of the related phenomenon, which we call, according to the point of view, over-production or under-consumption.... All that will be attempted in this chapter is to show that they are not inconsistent with the account of the working of the economic system, given in the last chapter. (Ibid.: 244)

---

[4] Mills (1916: 879), in his review in the *American Economic Review*, described Clay's treatment of unemployment as 'fresh, clear and seemingly well suited to the general reader'.

To understand why the entire apparatus of economic relationships may break down into high rates of unemployment requires an understanding that the 'whole system is based on specialization' (ibid.: 245). It is co-operation amongst individuals who specialise in different tasks that allows the economy to operate at all. But sometimes it breaks down. The issue is the structure of production. Referring to the aggregation of firms which make up an economy, Clay writes that 'their operations must have a certain proportion to one another, each stage of the industry must be adjusted to the wants and capacities of the other stages, or their co-operation will be defective' (ibid.: 246).

Changing demand patterns, and the timing of the supplier response, can cause the production of various goods and services to move out of phase with each other:

> The different industries are one another's customers and colleagues; an expansion of one, if it is not to be checked, calls for a corresponding expansion of others. But the *different industries require different lengths of time for the delivery of their products.* It is difficult therefore to ensure among them the harmonious co-operation which the modern industrial system requires. (Ibid.: 247)

Lack of mobility of the factors of production is specified as a major difficulty in the way of achieving harmony amongst producers. Factors of production are not perfectly malleable.[5] It takes time to transform the skills of the workforce, or the capital structure of business, to match the changes in the economic environment, whether on the demand side or on the supply side. The imperfect adjustment of means to ends means 'there will be unemployment and other dislocation' (ibid.: 248).

But this is by no means the only, or even the major, cause of unemployment. Clay turns to examine the consequences of imperfections on the part of business in anticipating the level of demand for the goods and services it produces:

> The second principle of the present organization that bears on the problems we are studying is the principle that production as a whole is carried on in anticipation of demand. Specialization has been carried so far, and has resulted in an organization so complex, that the production of most commodities begins many months before they are required. (Ibid.)

Normally demand is stable and can be reasonably predicted, but not always:

> Mistakes are bound to be made. Things are made, which, when made, are not wanted, or are not wanted so much as other things that have not been made.... When we consider the variety of goods ready for sale in retail shops and the complexity of the

---

[5] In a 1928 article criticising Pigou's *Industrial Fluctuations*, Clay (1928: 10) argued that 'maldistribution of labour [was] the principal influence causing the present unemployment'. It was, therefore, 'not possible to say either that the general or average level of wages is "too high" or that it is lower than it ought to be'. Clay was not prepared to lay the blame for unemployment on wage rates alone (ibid.: 13–14).

organization needed to produce each of them, and realize at the same time that that organization has been brought into being and applied to the production of the goods without any expressed demand for them, it becomes matter for surprise, not that the productive organization is occasionally misdirected, but that it hits its mark so often as it does. (Ibid.)

Clay then defines over-production as a glut of a particular product:

Let us be quite clear what we mean by over-production. It does not mean that more of the article has been produced than can be consumed or used; it does not even mean that more has been produced than can be sold. Any quantity of a thing that has a use can be sold, if the price be put low enough. What over-production of an article means is that more of the article has been produced than can be sold at a price big enough to repay its makers the cost of production, plus sufficient profit to induce them to go on producing at the same rate; all that has been produced can be sold, but only at a loss. (Ibid.)

Businesses regularly fail to anticipate correctly what the public actually wants. Over-production of individual products leads to sellers not realising their costs. Contrary to Keynes's assertion, in a world in which Say's Law operates, the total cost of production does not necessarily have to be matched by the resulting sales revenue. This is because production occurs in advance of demand:

Over-production and under-production occur because supply has to be adjusted to demand ahead of demand, on an estimate of it, not in response to an ascertained and definite demand. (Ibid.: 251)

From this Clay goes on to discuss cyclical trade fluctuations. He notes, to begin with, that failure to anticipate demand correctly can explain the ups and downs of a single industry. But a fuller explanation is needed for the problems of the economy as a whole. He describes these alterations in the level of activity, and in the level of involuntary unemployment, in the following terms:

The circulation of wealth is subject to general fluctuations, the most marked symptoms of which are alternating periods of overtime and unemployment. At one time producers in *all* trades cannot work fast enough to satisfy the demands of the market, employers in all trades cannot get the operatives they want; at another time producers in *all* trades cannot find a market for the goods they are producing, and employers in all trades dismiss or put on short time their operatives. (Ibid.: 252)

Clay admits that he cannot give a full answer to why this is so, but offers some suggestions. The first is the transmission mechanism identified by Torrens: each industry is the customer of other industries, and once an industry begins to contract, the demands placed upon other industries similarly contract:

The separate trades are one another's customers, so that depression in one affects the others. Producers are also consumers; if therefore the producers in one trade are getting lower wages and lower profits, they can spend less on the products of other trades. (Ibid.)

But this is not, in Clay's view, a sufficient explanation of the speed with which contraction overtakes the business world. There is also a psychological dimension. Given that production largely takes place in anticipation of demand, a fall in confidence will translate itself into an actual fall in the level of activity:

> A market is a crowd, and has the psychological characteristic of the crowd, that the general opinion imposes itself on the individual members with extraordinary force and rapidity.... [Consequently] an opinion that demand is falling off will impose itself on the business community. (Ibid.: 253)

Once the ball starts rolling, there is a chain of reductions in demand from one firm to another as sales fail to match expectations. This downturn will be accentuated by refusals on the part of sellers to lower their prices. Note the role of Say's Law in the following passage, where the failure to turn one's stocks of goods into money is seen as the cause of the fall in demand elsewhere:

> They hold out for the high prices which are now a thing of the past; *being unable to sell, they are unable to buy,* and the circulation of wealth is checked until they give way. (Ibid.: 254, italics added)

Clay is, however, dissatisfied with this explanation. Following on from the above discussion of the transmission of recession from one firm to the next, he therefore goes on to say:

> This suggested explanation has been given more or less in the terms of the market; to relate it to the sketch of industry given in the last chapter, it is necessary to eliminate the references to purchase, sale, and price, and to think of the transactions as exchanges of goods and services between groups of specialized producers – an aspect of them which the use of money as a medium of exchange conceals. (Ibid.: 254)

At this point he drops money from the discussion and formulates his argument as follows:

> We should say that producers can always find consumers who will give them something in exchange for their products, but producer and consumer cannot always agree on the terms of the exchange. The regular process of exchange is checked because the exchangers cannot come to terms; and exchange being checked, the production of wealth for exchange is checked. (Ibid.: 254–5)

At the end of the chapter, one additional factor is raised. Clay refers to the credit system as a factor which accentuates booms and depressions. Here he describes the role of the banking system in deepening recessions:

In times of waning confidence banks, by restricting advances, deprive business men of an aid that is essential if they are to carry on business on their usual scale, and they depress prices. A sudden restriction of credit may even drive some firms into bankruptcy, and so shake confidence that not merely financial depression, but general industrial depression ensues. Probably no class therefore can do so much to exaggerate trade fluctuations as the bankers; a cautious and conservative policy in the giving of credit is essential to the stability not only of the banks and their allies, but of the whole industrial community. (Ibid.: 256)

It is clear that when Clay wrote his text in 1916, understanding, accepting and applying Say's Law did not imply that involuntary unemployment was impossible. Indeed, an understanding of Say's Law provided a satisfying, and reasonably complete, explanation of the business cycle, including the origins of depression with mass unemployment in all industries.

FREDERICK LAVINGTON: *THE TRADE CYCLE* (1922)

Frederick Lavington's *The Trade Cycle* provides an unusually clear and to the point example of the use of the law of markets to explain fluctuations in output and employment.[6] But it does more than that. It also connects the classical theory of the cycle, embedded as it was in the law of markets, with the modern theories of Robert Clower. The following casual remark by Clower has the most critical significance for an understanding of his critique of the modern interpretation of macroeconomic theory:

> I was fascinated recently by Frederick Lavington's book on the trade cycle, a short little book. It repays reading now. It was published in the early 1920s. It's a far more intelligent account of the general theory than the *General Theory* is. It covers much of the same ground as the *General Theory* and covers it with a focus that is dead right, expressed in a way that the most casual business person or common reader could instantly grasp. The language is straightforward, the background is there, the theory that is needed to understand what he's doing is set forth. (Clower 1989: 26)

Clower thus appears to believe that Lavington stated what Keynes meant to say. Perhaps; but what Lavington did was provide a theory of the cycle built on the typically classical constituent elements of the law of markets. We shall return to this issue when discussing Clower in Chapter 11.

Clower's views notwithstanding, Lavington's *The Trade Cycle*, which has as its sub-title, 'An Account of the Causes Producing Rhythmical Changes in the

---

[6] Frederick Lavington (1881–1927) was lecturer in economics at Emmanuel College, Cambridge, from 1918 until his death in 1927. Moggridge (1992: 213) lists him as a personal friend of Keynes and notes that he had been one of Keynes's pupils before 1914 (ibid.: 434). Skidelsky (1992: 699) describes him as the 'most orthodox of the Cambridge economists of the 1920s'.

Activity of Business' ([1922] 1938: 3), is a thoroughly classical account of the theory of the cycle.[7] The theoretical aspect of the book begins with a discussion of the fundamental identity of buyer and seller which is the very essence of the law of markets. Chapter III is entitled 'Essential Conditions of Organisation' and is devoted to some basic propositions which underlie his theory of the trade cycle. Here Lavington writes of 'another condition of fundamental importance to the genesis of the business cycle' (ibid.: 22), this being the implications that follow from goods buying goods. The passages in bold type below emphasise the essence of the law of markets, where demand is clearly seen to be constituted by supply:

> When each producing group under the command of an entrepreneur specialises in the production of a narrow range of commodities, each must sell its products for those of other groups; in other words, **the ability of each to market its own products depends on the output by other groups of the goods with which their products are bought; its own activity is dependent on the activity of all others.**
>
> This mutual dependence among business firms is more intimate and far-reaching than is apparent without some reflection. It is almost literally true that each producing group constituting an industry forms a market for the products, not only of associated industries, but of every other industry in the country. For in general the capitalists, entrepreneurs, and work-people who form that group are a fair sample of the whole community in its aspect as a consumer, **and therefore purchase, with the proceeds of their own activities, a fraction of the output of all other industries....**
>
> In order to come a little closer to the facts on which this general statement rests, consider the position of any representative entrepreneur in a time of marked depression such as the present. The producing group under his command is working at low pressure because it has no reasonable expectation that if it produces more it will be able to sell the additional output. If it is asked why this additional output cannot be sold, the answer is that consumers will not buy it. **And if the further question is asked (as it should be asked) why consumers will not buy, the answer is because they are not able to –** *because they themselves are not producing.*
>
> **In a problem of the kind we are considering, therefore, the party known as the 'consumer' hardly possesses any independent existence. His proper name is 'other producers'.** In so far as concerns his *will* to buy he is a real person, but in so far as concerns his *power* to buy he is only an aspect in which other producers are seen. **His power to act as a consumer is derived from his own activity as producer, whether as capitalist, entrepreneur, or workman.** That being so, the original question may be answered very simply. **In a time of general depression the individual firm is working at low pressure because other firms are working at low pressure. Each is inactive because the general power to consume has fallen; and the general power to consume has fallen because of and in proportion to the general decline in the activity of production.** The inactivity of all is the cause of the inactivity of each. No entrepreneur can safely expand his output until other entrepreneurs can safely expand their output; or more exactly and more significantly, no entrepreneur can safely expand his output until he has a reasonable expectation that others will be more active at the time when his additional output is ready for the market. (Ibid.: 22–4, bold added)

---

[7] In the preface Lavington cites Marshall, Pigou, Robertson, Wesley Mitchell and Aftalion as sources for his ideas ([1922] 1938: 7).

We see here a chain of argument which is held together with links forged from the basic premise of the law of markets, namely that goods are bought with goods and that demand is constituted by supply. Why are people not buying? – because they are not selling. Where does the power to consume originate? – from one's own activity as a producer. We thus have the law of markets embedded as a necessary component in the explanation of the business cycle, as the unifying element which connects one person's bad trade with another's. Hutt (1963: 350n) also cites this passage, stating that in it Lavington 'tacitly recognises the importance of the Say Law'.

Lavington's explanation is a fundamentally real explanation, which is deepened by an understanding of how the banking and credit creation systems can amplify cyclical activity. The basis for cyclical activity is errors of judgement by entrepreneurs, reinforced by further errors of pessimism and optimism.[8] As Bigg (1990: 51) puts it, 'entrepreneurs' decisions are based on conjecture and thus are subject to error'.[9] It is during boom periods, according to Lavington, that 'maladjustments' occur (Lavington [1922] 1938: 66), which ultimately bring the upswing to an end and lead to recession. Lavington first specifies the influences which arise from the monetary system:

---

[8] Haberler, in *Prosperity and Depression*, placed Lavington's argument within his discussion of 'psychological theories' (1937: 134, 138).

[9] Lavington had a long-standing interest in the issue of decision making under conditions of uncertainty. For example, in 1912 he argued that, 'the future can be foreseen only imperfectly, and the adjustment of methods of living is at best a succession of approximations; incessant change followed by incessant readaptation, and the cost of imperfect foresight is a continuous maladjustment of resources – which is irregularly distributed over individuals in the form of gain and loss' (1912: 398). Nor should this be thought of as mere calculable risk. Lavington is discussing a condition in which the future is unknowable, where there is an incalculable degree of uncertainty. He wrote that 'the changing environment is a condition resulting in a continuous maladjustment of resources, and hence in a continuous social waste, the amount of which is determined on the one hand by the extent of Ignorance and on the other by the immobility of invested resources.... Uncertainty is then the result of a particular form of Ignorance.... It is a condition of exposure to events of which the prospective net effects compensate for the state of imperfect knowledge as to their importance and date of occurrence' (ibid.: 399–400). And in a later article he wrote: 'the immense complexity of the processes by which the future grows out of the present inevitably makes impossible any full understanding of the conditions determining the economic results of productive operations and renders these results partially incalculable.... The presence of this incalculability impairs the close and continuous adjustment of means to ends' (1925: 187). And further on, he states: 'it seems clear that in the actual business world the set of prospective returns offered by any venture cannot very usefully be conceived as having an actuarial value determined by objective calculations and expressed as a single quantity' (ibid.: 197). This should be compared with Keynes's discussion in 'The General Theory of Employment', where the unknowable future is discussed in terms similar to Lavington's (*CW* XIV: 112–15).

In a country with a modern monetary system in normal operation a cyclical condition of extreme business activity engenders financial causes which inevitably bring about its termination. But as, in the opinion of economists, the influence of the monetary system is to be regarded not as the primary, but as a reinforcing cause of business cycles, this explanation may not be an adequate one. (Ibid.: 68)

The inadequacy leads Lavington to ask a 'narrower' question: 'Does the phase of marked business activity engender any real, as distinct from monetary, cause which prevents its own continuance indefinitely?' (ibid.: 68). Lavington's answer is a clear yes, and he sees the first clue in the greater volatility of the 'constructional trades'. It may well be that investment is being carried on at too great a rate relative to the flow of saving, which ultimately slows, if not actually stops, the rate of investment (ibid.: 69).[10] Lavington, however, argues that the cause of cyclical activity lies elsewhere. He notes that in pre-World War I days, something like one-sixth of aggregate income was saved and that 'this immense annual volume of new savings was smoothly and continuously absorbed' (ibid.: 70). Since the war, savings have been growing more slowly, with a resulting rise in rates of interest. He makes this point because he wishes to establish two conclusions. The first conclusion is this:

that although there is a recondite sense in which there can be an 'excess of savings', there cannot be such an excess in the sense that new supplies of capital are not marketable; history and common sense alike show that indefinite quantities of new capital can be absorbed and can be made to yield a return, though possibly of smaller amount than before. For this and other reasons, no explanation of the termination of boom is looked for on that line of inquiry. (Ibid.: 71)

This takes the argument back to the original general glut debate, where the issue was whether an economy could absorb all of the capital available to it. Lavington unquestionably sides with Say, Ricardo and Mill. Lavington is clear that all new savings can be soaked up, even as he is providing an explanation of the downturn of the business cycle. This leads to his second conclusion, which is:

unless there is at least a proportionate growth in the volume of new uses for capital, *any additional supply, whether in the world as a whole, in the home market of this country, or in a particular industry, must press its way into uses in which it yields a lower return than before.* (Ibid.: 71)

Lavington compares the expected return with the actual to demonstrate the implications of the lower return to additional flows of capital. In the midst of a boom, if such new flows of capital move into industries which are expanding at a rapid rate, then one may take as a working hypothesis that 'the *actual realised yield* on the new supplies in the particular industries in question, must be lower than before, and very much lower than the extravagant anticipations of those who called the capital equipment into being' (ibid.: 72). The result would be that, as

---

[10] Lavington ([1922] 1938: 69) cites Dennis Robertson as holding this view.

the new capital equipment came on stream, there would be a wide recognition of 'frustrated expectations' (ibid.). It is in fact the very coming on stream of this new plant and machinery which 'corresponds with the end of the boom' (ibid.). This has a number of effects. Firstly, it leads to a fall in demand for new capital equipment. Secondly, business confidence is reduced, adding to the uncertainty with which business people look at economic prospects. Thirdly, and most importantly from a Say's Law perspective, there is a recognition that there have been past errors in production which will cause losses to those who have called those particular forms of production into existence:

> The condition is not one in which there is realised a general uniform fall in prospective profits. It is almost certainly marked by the exposure of business errors due to a disproportionate volume of investment in particular industries. In so far as undue optimism has given rise to such errors the situation is aggravated, and confidence further shaken, by the prospective financial difficulties of particular individual firms. (Ibid.: 73)

This 'disproportionate' production causes a further set of influences to come into play. The fall off in production leads to a fall in demand as the depression grows in intensity. The fall in investment leads to an anticipated fall in demand for consumption goods and there is therefore a slackening in the production of goods which are normally purchased by consumers (ibid.: 81). But it is the fact that different parts of the economy are out of phase which leads to depressions reaching their lower depths. It is here that the implication of supply constituting demand is shown to be so critical:

> This tendency to a fall in the current output of producers generally is reinforced by the declining faith in the future of markets due to the earlier recognition of maladjustments of productive capacity. It is likely to be reinforced further by the fact that, as the business atmosphere changes, forecasts are becoming tinged by a growing error of pessimism, which still further limits the willingness of entrepreneurs to assume the risks of producing in anticipation of demand. In this way, the declining output of each entrepreneur, by reducing the consuming power of the group he controls, narrows the markets for the products of others; the inability of the markets to absorb the output of goods further lessens confidence; and lessened confidence, acting through a decline in business orders, shows itself in a further decline in current output. (Ibid.)

Note that it is the declining *output* which reduces the *consuming power*. Lavington returns to this point when he comes to summarise his discussion of the course of the trade cycle. He discusses the circumstances surrounding the entrepreneur which he places at the centre of the economic system:

> Among the most important of these circumstances is the condition of mutual interdependence among individual producers. The output of each producing group, constituting as it does the earnings of that group, constitutes also the consuming power of the group for the output of all others. Hence the total output of all the

producing groups within the area of exchange constitutes the total power to buy. (Ibid.: 88)

This is the law of markets embedded in a theory of the business cycle in which it is a necessary component. If the purchase and sale aspect of the law of markets is removed, the downturn in production in one part of the economy cannot be transmitted to other parts of the economy. But once it is understood that the power to demand arises from the ability to produce and sell, then the dynamics of the business cycle are seen in a different light. Recessions develop from 'partial gluts'. Partial gluts occur due to monetary factors, past errors in business decision making and a fall off in business confidence. But once this partial downturn commences, the initial fall in production constitutes a further fall in demand in other parts of the economy and the cycle is deepened.

It cannot be said that, for Lavington, acceptance of Say's Law meant that there was no obstacle to full employment or that involuntary unemployment is impossible. As the discussion in his final chapter shows, for him unemployment is an 'evil' with 'disastrous' consequences (see particularly 102–3). The law of markets, recession and involuntary unemployment are all simultaneously compatible in Lavington's model of the trade cycle.[11]

Curiously, Bigg (1990: 51) makes only one mention of Say's Law in his entire work on the collapse of Marshallian macroeconomics, and it is to argue that, because Lavington had stressed that business decisions were based on conjectures of the future, he was therefore moving towards a denial of Say's Law. Bigg understands Lavington in this way because, following Keynes, he interprets Say's Law as guaranteeing full employment. He therefore argues that, because there was 'no necessary reason why the entrepreneurs' expectations and rational judgements should lead to full employment, at least in the short run' (ibid.: 51–2), Lavington was moving away from acceptance of Say's Law. But, in so arguing, Bigg misunderstands the ancestry of Lavington's position, and wrongly sees it as a denial of Say's Law rather than as a reflection of it.

Lavington must be seen as being in a direct line of descent from Marshall (see especially Bridel 1987: 204n7). Indeed, in his preface to *The Trade Cycle* Lavington writes that 'most of the leading ideas have been drawn from the writings of Dr. Marshall, Professor Pigou and Mr. D. H. Robertson' (op. cit.: 7). In saying this, Lavington was emphasising his classical roots, and however much Clower may wish to describe Lavington's theory of the cycle as a prototype *General Theory*, the facts are that Lavington belongs inside the orthodox tradition and within the compass of the law of markets.

---

[11] Moreover, Milgate (1982: 73) rightly states of Lavington's theory of the cycle that in the context of the period in which it was written 'none of [it was] either extraordinary or unorthodox'.

WILHELM RÖPKE: *CRISES AND CYCLES* (1936)

Wilhelm Röpke's *Crises and Cycles* was the last major work on the business cycle in English whose arguments were totally uninfluenced by the Keynes of the *General Theory*.[12] The arguments advanced are thus not intended to refute the arguments which would be raised by Keynes. It is therefore deeply interesting that Röpke presented his arguments in a way which emphasised the role of the law of markets in making the nature of the business cycle comprehensible. Chapter IV is entitled 'The Causes of Crises and Cycles' (Röpke 1936: 61). Its particular interest is that it quite self-consciously builds a theory of recession on the law of markets.[13] Röpke begins with a statement which flatly contradicts, to its very core, the Keynesian view of the world:[14]

> The history of doctrines which have attempted to clear up the mystery of recurrent disturbances of economic equilibrium is now more than one century old, Jean Baptiste Say and David Ricardo being perhaps the first to grasp the real problems involved. (Ibid.: 61)

Röpke rejects, in advance, Keynes's assertion that classical economists had denied the possibility of involuntary unemployment, and had used models which assumed full employment, even when discussing the problems of recession and depression. Röpke, very much the classical economist, could however write:

> The paradoxical nature of the crisis is characterised by the fact that production is curtailed in every direction, and there is no work anywhere, while so far as the economic position of millions of people is concerned, we could really be doing nothing better than getting every ounce of product out of men and machines. (Ibid.: 77)

---

[12] Wilhelm Röpke (1899–1966) was Professor of Economics at the University of Marburg until the arrival of the Nazis in government in 1933. He then became professor at the University of Istanbul until 1937 when he went to the Graduate Institute in Geneva where he remained till his death. Blaug and Sturges (1983: 323) describe him as an 'extremely prolific and wide-ranging writer whose chief aim was the rehabilitation of the market economy.... Through his close friendship with Ludwig Erhard he was a major architect of the "German miracle"'.

[13] It is similarly interesting that the division in economic theory between classical and Keynesian economists was reflected in two reviews of the book. Howard Ellis (1936: 762) wrote of *Crises and Cycles* that 'it is certainly one of the best "all-round" general treatises upon the subject in contemporary literature'. Meade (1936: 695), while acknowledging the orthodoxy of Röpke's arguments, stakes out the then emerging Keynesian position: 'Professor Röpke's view has, of course, the support of many weighty authorities; but a bare assertion is not sufficient to convince those, who are of the opposite opinion'.

[14] Röpke might well have been talking about Keynes (although he wasn't) when he wrote that 'it is all too common that an economist...wants to make himself immortal by presenting a brand-new theory of cycles and making room for it by abusing all the others and emphasizing the differences rather than the similarities' (1936: 62).

Moreover, Röpke adds, although to all appearances the problem is one of over-production, the actual explanation for recession has in fact nothing at all do with it. Over-production, according to Röpke, 'is the most popular crisis theory at all times of crisis' (ibid.: 77–8). Röpke specifically denies that the problem is due to a general glutting of markets:

> It is an indisputable fact that a general slump, which does not permit of the scale of production reached in the boom being maintained, sets in during the crisis, and it is equally indisputable that this general slump is the result of the total demand suddenly falling behind the total supply. But let us make sure what this means and what it does not mean.[15] Under no circumstances can it mean that the *cause* of the general slump is to be sought in the fact that production has outstripped consumption and that too many of all goods at once are being produced. Closer consideration shows that there is no logic in such a view. (Ibid.: 78)

But if supply exceeding demand is not due to over-production, then where does the explanation for recession lie? It is here that Röpke brings forward a structural explanation. It is not the *level* of demand which creates recession, he argues, but the *structure* of demand relative to production:

> An economic crisis (that of to-day like those of the past) can therefore not be interpreted as a general over-production of all goods at once, a surpassing of the possibilities of consumption by the possibilities of production, but only as a lack of proportion between the different lines of production, in short, as a functional disturbance with the highly complicated modern exchange economy. The disparity between the goods at our disposal and our unsatisfied wants is more obvious than ever, but the wheels of the machine which delivers the goods do not fit together properly at times of crisis. (Ibid.: 79)

Röpke discusses 'the over-production myth' (ibid.: 79, 80). His reasoning to explain why over-production cannot occur is framed along the lines set out by the law of markets, by which demand is constituted by supply, that is, by the receipts from sales of one's own goods and services. He is quite categorical that there is no limit to production on the demand side, and that where recession and unemployment occur, they are not due to a failure of demand, but rather to an incorrect composition of goods for sale:

> The incomes with which the goods produced are bought come ultimately from the production itself, and the total sum of the incomes is also determined by the total sum of the production. If we follow these relationships to their logical conclusion, we find that production is not determined by consumption, but consumption by production. That is to say, there is no limit to profitable production as a whole (i.e., apart from the question of the correct composition of the total production), since the saturation point of human wants is immeasurably far off, but there is, unfortunately, a limit to

---

[15] At this point Röpke inserts a footnote which lists a series of references, the first one being Say's 1803 *Treatise*. He describes the works listed as being 'anti-idiotica' (1936: 78n).

consumption, which is determined by the utmost we can produce with our limited forces and means. (Ibid.: 80)

Röpke states that 'all these considerations are old-established propositions of political economy' (ibid.: 81). And, lest anyone doubt what these propositions he is referring to are, he specifically quotes, and at length, Ricardo's famous defence of the law of markets.[16] Röpke goes on to dismiss the possibility of a general glut, and in doing so, rules out both the lack of will to consume or the lack of power. He specifically makes the point that supply will constitute demand if, but only if, the goods produced coincide with the goods which others wish to buy:

> It should be beyond all doubt that a general over-production relative to the desire and the capacity to consume is inconceivable. When we consider that purchasing power is created afresh with production, it follows furthermore that it is equally impossible to produce too many of all kinds of goods at once in relation to purchasing power. It is inconceivable that all producers can have produced an excess and that they cannot mutually exchange the surpluses provided that they have adjusted their production correctly to the corresponding demand. (Ibid.: 82)

This leads to the conclusion that recessions are not due to producing too much, but are due to producing the wrong things. He emphasises that, in dismissing over-production as an explanation of recession, he is neither denying the possibility of recession nor indicating that recession is of no concern. His aim only is to demonstrate that this particular explanation of recession is 'impossible':

> The essence of all these considerations is this: A depression is a time of a general glutting of the market, which can be described as the exceeding of total demand by total supply and expresses itself in a general price fall. But the glutting of the market is caused not by a general over-production (of all conceivable goods) but by a disproportionality disruptive of the equilibrium of the economic system in the composition of total production, in other words a partial over-production, which by reason of the mutual interdependence of all producers finally leads to a glutting of markets, that is, to a lagging of total demand behind total supply extending to all branches of the economy.
>
> This elementary consideration must form the starting point of any adequate theory of cycles and crises. It is the task of this theory to show how a disproportionality destructive of equilibrium comes about. The rejection of the over-production theory does in no way imply that the crisis is unobjectionable. It simply dismisses an impossible explanation. (Ibid.: 82)

Röpke explains the root causes of the imbalances found in disequilibrium. It had, from the start, been a facet of the law of markets that over-production in some

---

[16] Röpke (1936: 80) specifically quotes Ricardo's defence of the law of markets in Chapter XXI of the *Principles* which begins: 'Productions are always bought by productions, or by services; money is only the medium by which the exchange is effected'.

areas of the economy was offset by too little production in others. He points out that this imbalance has to be understood as notional:

> Neither should it be imagined that the partial over-production (disproportionality), which leads eventually to the general glutting of the market, still manifests itself in the crisis in such a way that those who produce too much find their counterpart in those who produce too little. This disproportionality develops in the upward swing of the cycle, but in the depression it is in vain to look round for branches of production where too little is being produced. The foregoing analysis will have made it clear why this is so: the disruption of the equilibrium in the economic system has disturbed the process of exchange all along the line, a disturbance in which the whole production is involved. The requisite additional production has become a mere latent possibility which only comes to light with the restoration of equilibrium.[17]   (Ibid.: 83)

Röpke goes on to discuss what he describes as the 'secondary contraction' in which the only adequate means of characterisation 'is to point to the *contraction of the total demand*' (1936: 122).[18] It is demand failure, but set in the very processes of classical economic theory, in which the secondary contraction occurs with a series of lags characterised by disharmonies between the different parts of the economy. As Röpke wrote, 'in the first case, it is the disproportion between supply and demand, and, in the second case, it is the disproportion between costs and prices' (ibid.: 122). Röpke argues that the 'whole trouble may be ascribed to the disastrous *destruction of that harmony between the process of the formation of incomes and the process of the utilisation of incomes*' (ibid.).

Röpke notes, in a manner no different from J.S. Mill, that there are huge sums of money being held in idle accounts by businesses 'which are holding themselves as liquid as possible instead of using their funds for replacing old machinery let alone for making additional investments' (ibid.: 123).[19] And finally, and most remarkably, he writes:

> Money is being saved in a form, and under circumstances, which largely prevent it from being invested, so that the *rate of saving is continuously greater than the rate of investment*. As long as this is the case, savings not only add nothing to the wealth of the community but are positively harmful for economic welfare. Saving in this case is not only 'abortive'...but downright destructive – always in the relative sense that the money saved finds no outlet in new investments. Or in other words: *money is*

---

[17] This may be compared with Clower ([1967] 1984b: 53), where he wrote, 'the dual-decision hypothesis effectively implies that Walras' law, although valid as usual with reference to *notional* market excess demands is in general irrelevant to any but full employment situations. *Contrary to the findings of traditional theory, excess demand may fail to appear anywhere in the economy under conditions of less than full employment*'.

[18] Haberler (1937: 54–7) discusses the idea of secondary deflation, also noting that the concept had been 'frequently' employed (ibid.: 223n).

[19] Röpke (1933: 435) adopted this same approach in his discussion of German business cycle policy.

withheld from expenditure on consumption goods, without any compensation for this
non-consumption taking place in the form of investments in capital goods. The
general contraction of demand is, then, tantamount to an excess of savings over
investment. By force of logic, these two things must be identical.[20] (Ibid.: 123–4)

Indeed, Röpke specifically notes that in the depths of recession, very low rates of
interest may still not induce business to invest. In the following passage, he is for
all intents and purposes, describing the mechanism of the Keynesian liquidity
trap:

> Even a rate of interest which approaches zero may be insufficient...to induce
> entrepreneurs to enter upon new investment. If in such a situation the elasticity of
> demand for credit becomes almost absolutely rigid, attempts at credit expansion will
> not lead to the desired expansion of the total demand for commodities, but merely to
> an increase of general liquidity. (Ibid.: 125)

One might draw the conclusion that Röpke must reject Say's Law. If he
recognises that there is more production than demand, and he states that the
problem consists of more saving than the willingness to invest those savings, then
he must agree with Keynes in arguing that the problem actually consists of an
under-employment equilibrium because the level of national saving exceeds the
aggregate willingness to invest. In this case, the economy would contract until the
level of saving was in equilibrium with the level of demand, and there the
economy would rest.

This is an over-saving argument[21] and Röpke will have none of it. In the
following passage, he rejects the over-saving argument in precisely the form it
was later raised by Keynes in the *General Theory*:

> Some...even go to the length of asserting that there is a permanent tendency for
> investment to be outrun by savings and therefore a tendency towards a chronic
> depression which is only interrupted by short-lived fits of concentrated investment.
> According to these gloomy pessimists – mostly sanguine inflationists in disguise, if
> not actually prophets of the end of capitalism – our economic system is headed for a
> sort of economic 'entropy' where all economic energy will be paralysed by a
> suffocating excess of savings....
>
> Enough has been said on these points to make a refutation of such wild surmises
> hardly necessary. It all boils down to the question as to whether it is conceivable that
> savings can ever become so abundant that we do not know what to do with them even
> at a rate of interest approaching zero. To this question, of course, only one answer is
> possible. Over-saving as such is an inconceivable thing, belonging to the same
> species as other economic scares like over-production. (Röpke ibid.: 131)

---

[20] In a footnote, Röpke (1936: 124n) adds that 'Mr. Keynes has succeeded in making this
process particularly clear' in his *Treatise on Money*. In light of Röpke's subsequent
deeply critical views of the *General Theory*, it is interesting to find that he refers to the
Treatise as 'this great work' (ibid.: 133).
[21] See Haberler (1941: 233–5).

This discussion should be seen in the context of Röpke's analysis of over-saving (ibid.: 90–92). There, in dealing with the causes of cycles, Röpke discusses the typical premises of those who have argued on behalf of various theories of over-saving. He notes that theorists who support the notion of over-saving 'do not deny that saving is necessary for adding to the productive wealth of society, but since saving means essentially non-consumption, thus creating a deficiency of consumers' demand, it is believed that it tends to defeat its own final purpose' (ibid.: 92). He then went on to add:

> The gravest defect of most of these theories, however, seems to be the confusion of a static with a dynamic point of view. In other words they fail clearly to distinguish between the effects of saving *per se* and the effects of an increase in the *rate* of saving. As regards the effects of saving *per se*, i.e., a uniform or even gradually increasing rate of saving, it must be vigorously denied that it can disrupt economic equilibrium. In this 'static' sense there certainly exists no problem of over-saving with reference to a maximum which cannot be exceeded without destroying economic equilibrium. On the other hand, it cannot be denied, however, that a sudden and marked increase of the rate of saving presents a real problem. (Ibid.)

Röpke takes a position at all times consistent with the law of markets, and yet one which fully appreciates the depths of recession, and the immense problems of returning to economic growth and full employment. But his understanding of the nature of recession leads him in different directions from Keynes. Because Röpke sees recession in the context of the business cycle, he locates the cause of recession in the preceding phase.

So what can be done? In the first instance, Röpke recommends a non-interventionist approach (ibid.). But, he adds, 'the present depression shows...there are cases where positive measures as well may be apt.... In particular the giving of relief to the masses of unemployed is a task which must be carried out somehow even if no direct remedy for the depression is discoverable' (ibid.: 147). And indeed, Röpke is quite categorical that a properly constructed public sector programme of deficit spending has a role to play. In what he describes as a 'compensatory budget policy' (see discussion, ibid.: 155–8), he states that governments should spend greater amounts during recessions and reduce their expenditure during the upswing of the cycle. He sees such a policy as a 'useful principle among others, without making it the dominant principle of trade-cycle policy' (ibid.: 158). He remains sceptical of the value of such a principle because of the likelihood of planning error due to political pressures (ibid.: 157), and because it will be difficult to get governments to lower expenditure during the eventual upswing (ibid.: 158).

Because Röpke thinks of the process of recession in terms of disharmonies, he conceives of recession in terms of businesses being lost and in need of direction. He recognises two tendencies amongst economic theorists: those who remain in favour of a restrictive policy, and those who favour a more expansionist approach. He places himself in the expansionist camp and outlines the kinds of approach, with emphasis on credit expansion, that need to be adopted to get an economy moving once again. But he confronts the possibility that credit expansion will not of itself lead to a renewal of investment. In those circumstances, there is a major role for fiscal policy (ibid.: 199).

This may be described as a 'Keynesian' policy but it comes from a different context and with far more sombre overtones. It is not presented as a panacea, but as a policy which must be adopted given the extreme nature of the Great Depression. And it is presented with due regard to the risks being run. Röpke first notes that 'it takes strong nerves cold-bloodedly to stand the sight of such a budget deficit in all its naked horror' (ibid.: 200). But the more important danger is that eventually people will become used to such deficits and make 'the spirit of financial recklessness respectable' (ibid.: 201).

Finally, it is noteworthy that Röpke explicitly rejects a policy of lowering wages. He makes it clear that lowering real wages during the secondary recession will do nothing to lower unemployment, and his case is similar to that of Keynes:

> [The question to be answered is] whether in the last phase of the depression the lowering of the general level of wages is a measure suitable to preparing the way towards economic revival. This question must be answered in the negative so long as the 'slack' created by the cut in wages does not give an incentive to the revival of activity in other parts of the economic system. So long as this is not the case, all cuts lead only to an aggravation of the depression since they cause a falling off in demand without putting any new demand in its place in other spheres. In other words, pursued within the framework of a restrictionist policy and without simultaneous measures of expansion, wage-cutting is liable to aggravate the depression. (Ibid.: 184)

It is clear that Röpke accepts that there are circumstances where lower wages can assist economic recovery. Those conditions simply do not appear at the bottom of the depression. But what is also clear is that the remedy put forward does not encompass an adjustment to wages because the problem is deeper and lies elsewhere. We are dealing with involuntary unemployment, and the only solution is a revival of investment, not a further fall in real wages. And all of this is fully consistent with the law of markets.

The value in Röpke's treatment is that he has presented a theory of the business cycle which stretches back through time, consciously related to the theories of Say and Ricardo, and in its specifics congruent with the theory of the cycle put forward by Torrens. There can be no question that Röpke's theory of the cycle is based on an acceptance that depressions can be deep, prolonged and lead to extremely high levels of unemployment. It is also the work of a scholar who understood the historic antecedents to his own theories, which makes this work a rich source of understanding of the role that the law of markets played in classical economic theory.

As Röpke's discussion demonstrates, Keynes totally misrepresented the nature of Say's Law and the implications it had for an understanding of recession and unemployment. Röpke, even in the midst of the Great Depression, continued to describe over-production as a myth and characterised the notion of over-saving as fallacious. Yet he was able to provide a profound theoretical explanation for the

Depression, and came to the conclusion that there might be value in public works financed by budget deficits. It was not the level of demand which was at fault. It was instead the low level of business confidence which undermined the willingness of entrepreneurs to produce. The problem was thus not to be found on the demand side of the economy, but on the supply side. And all of this was specifically related back to the insights provided more than a century before by J.B. Say and David Ricardo.

Crises and Cycles is also a remarkable historic document in that it was the last major work on the business cycle published in English entirely uninfluenced by the *General Theory*. That it pointed to the law of markets as the guide to understanding the nature of the business cycle makes it a fitting end to the theory of the cycle which was first developed at the start of the nineteenth century. All that was about to change. The publication of the *General Theory* marked the end of the theory of the cycle as it had developed since the time of J.B Say. It was to be replaced by the very theory that the law of markets had been designed to reject.

GOTTFRIED HABERLER: *PROSPERITY AND DEPRESSION* (1937)

In 1930, Gottfried Haberler, then only thirty years old, was commissioned by the League of Nations 'to co-ordinate the analytical work then being done on the problem of the recurrence of periods of economic depression' (Haberler 1937: iii).[22] The result was *Prosperity and Depression*, one of the most astonishing documents in the history of economics. It is a survey of all of the theories of recession as they were discussed by economists in the 1930s.[23] In it is found the theory of recession which can be traced back to J.S. Mill and Say, essentially a theory based on the structure of production being out of phase with the structure of demand. What is additionally remarkable about this text is that its two later editions, published in 1939 and 1941, show the phenomenally rapid advance of Keynesian theory. In a little over half a decade, the accumulated understanding of the business cycle, which had developed since the start of the nineteenth century, was swept aside to be replaced by the one theory virtually all economists had, until then, rejected as fallacious. And what may be the most remarkable aspect of all is the way in which the ideas of the *General Theory* permeated even the first edition in a manner which remained imperceptible even to Haberler himself.

---

[22] Gottfried Haberler (1900–1995) was born and educated in Austria and his approach to economic issues was within the 'Austrian' school. Most of Haberler's work centred around the theory of international trade but he also made contributions in index number theory and in the theory of inflation. He was Professor Emeritus at Harvard.

[23] Hansen (1938, 124n) described *Prosperity and Depression* as 'the most authoritative statement of this extremely complex subject which has yet appeared'. Hawtrey (1938: 93) wrote that 'the first part is a brilliant achievement, a lucid and concise survey of theories of multifarious variety and some of them of great complexity'.

The first edition of *Prosperity and Depression* was published in 1937. In it, the *General Theory* is seen as the latest in a line of theories of the cycle, and not recognised by Haberler as being particularly important. In this first edition, the theories of the cycle, as presented, are direct descendants of the theories based on the law of markets, although never explicitly stated as such. It is important to recognise, as Haberler notes in his introduction, that Part I was 'substantially' completed by December 1935, and Part II in May 1936 (Haberler 1937: 2).[24] The straddling of the publication date of the *General Theory* meant that most of *Prosperity and Depression* was written prior to the publication of the *General Theory*, but that there was also time to add further material to take up points raised by Keynes. Keynes's influence on the first edition was thus minimal in terms of the number of pages devoted to discussing the *General Theory*, but, as will be seen, was quite important all the same.

By 1939, the whirlwind acceptance of the arguments of the *General Theory* required Haberler to add a chapter of nearly one hundred pages, devoted almost entirely to it. By 1941, a further revised edition needed to be published, in which an entire Part III was added to the first two, also dealing with the analysis of the *General Theory*.[25]

What we thus have is a work which documents the transformation from the system as it had developed until 1936 into the system of ideas which then replaced it. Haberler, as a scholar of pre-Keynesian business cycle theory, was able to survey with great accuracy the theories as they existed prior to the publication of the *General Theory*. But what may be the most extraordinary aspect of the book was that, while superficially resisting the pull of Keynesian economic theory, Haberler in fact adopted it wholly.[26]

The following discussion will be entirely based on the first edition of 1937. Part I contains a 'Systematic Analysis of the Theories of the Business Cycle', in which Haberler outlines the traditional classical theories which had been developed since the start of the nineteenth century. These were, firstly, the purely monetary theories, whose explanations for cyclical movements were based on variations in the availability of credit and, secondly, theories in which explanations of the cycle were based on structural imbalances and entrepreneurial

---

[24] Brandis (1985: 649) plausibly suggests that Haberler specified the timing of the completion of the manuscript 'with an eye to the impact of the *General Theory*'.

[25] See Marget ([1942] 1966b: xi–xii) for a contemporary account of the pace at which Keynesian theory came to dominate the economics profession. This is also discussed by Blaug (1991b: 175).

[26] Keynes recognised this himself in a letter to Austin Robinson following the publication of the second edition of *Prosperity and Depression* in 1939:

Indeed the truth is that [Haberler] has come the whole way round and swallows the book bait, hook and line. But his digestion tells him that it is all very familiar diet. His method of showing this is to demonstrate that not everything said hitherto is false, at any rate garnished with the proper qualifications, and that such previous remarks and explanations as are, properly qualified, can be shown to be compatible with my theory, – with all of which I cordially agree. (*CW* XIV: 274)

misjudgement. It is to these that Haberler gave the greatest credence. Each of the other explanations – under-consumption, psychological theories and harvest theories – in his view provided insights and partial explanations, but could not fully account for cyclical variations in economic activity. Only Haberler's discussion of the structural causes of depression will be outlined in what follows.

The longest chapter in Part I deals with theories of 'over-investment', and covers just under half of all pages devoted to discussing the various theories. In the introduction to this chapter, Haberler discusses the 'general characteristics' of theories of over-production. The central cause of recession is that, during the upturn in activity, the various parts of the economy move out of phase with each other. It is thus the structure of demand which causes recession, rather than the level. Structure of production is the key concept. Put simply, production must be so constituted that the incomes earned by those engaged in production will be used in such a way as to buy precisely those goods and services which have been produced. Those incomes may be spent directly on consumption goods, or they may be lent to others to purchase investment goods. But the total flow of money expenditure must be used to buy just those goods and services which have been produced. This is explained by Haberler as follows:

> Equilibrium in the structure of production will be preserved, if the allocation of the factors of production to various employments correspond to the expected distribution of the money flow – *i.e.*, the monetary demand for the products of the different branches of industry. This distribution is, broadly speaking, determined by (1) the decisions of the population as to spending and saving, (2) the decisions of consumers as to the distribution of expenditure between various lines of consumption goods, and (3) the decisions of producers at every stage as to the distribution of their cost expenditure between different forms of input. (Haberler 1937: 28)

Recessions are caused by a 'real maladjustment in the structure of production' (ibid.), and are of two kinds: vertical and horizontal. In a continuation of the above passage, Haberler explains the difference between the two forms:

> If the structure of production does not correspond to the first set of decisions, we have a *vertical* maladjustment – vertical because the industries which are not harmoniously developed are related to each other in a 'vertical' order, as cost and product.... If the structure of production does not correspond to the second or third set of decisions, we have a *horizontal* disproportion – a disproportion between industries of the same 'rank' as measured by distance from consumption. (Ibid.)

This is J.S. Mill brought up to date and in a more sophisticated form. Mill had written that 'every increase of production, *if distributed without miscalculation among all kinds of produce in the proportion which private interest would dictate*...constitutes its own demand' ([1874] 1974b: 73, italics added). Recessions occur when miscalculation occurs, that is, when the structure of demand is different from the structure of supply. The goods which have been produced do not coincide with the goods which consumers and investors wish to buy, and some goods remain unsold. This is, in its essentials, the basis for the theory of over-investment as outlined by Haberler. The structure of demand in the economy as a whole is different from the supply. Consumers wish to spend too much and save too little, or they wish to spend on a different array of goods than the array which has been produced, or producers have sunk their funds into capital works which do not return what they cost to produce. But, one way or another, the proportions in which goods have been produced do not coincide with the goods that those who have incomes or borrowed funds wish to buy.

And, in true classical form, Haberler notes that these theories do not depend on monetary instability, but can be exacerbated by monetary instability:

> According to these theories, the business cycle is not a purely monetary phenomenon. But that does not preclude the possibility of money's playing a decisive role in bringing about the cycle and causing periodically a real maladjustment. (Haberler 1937: 29)

Haberler discusses three variants of the 'over-investment' theory. These are, firstly, monetary over-investment theories (ibid.: 31–68), in which the vertical maladjustments are due to instability related to the system of credit; secondly, non-monetary over-investment theories (ibid.: 68–80), which are based on the ebb and flow of new investment opportunities; and thirdly, theories which depend on 'the acceleration principle and the magnification of derived demand' (ibid.: 80–98). All forms of the over-investment theory explain why demand and supply may move out of phase with each other, but the third, based on the acceleration principle, may need further amplification to demonstrate its consistency with the law of markets.

The acceleration principle is the proposition that changes in demand for consumption goods lead to much larger proportional changes in the demand for capital goods. Therefore, a fall or even a slowing in demand for consumer items may lead to a more than proportional fall in the demand for capital goods and, therefore, to a more rapid downturn in economic activity than the fall in consumer demand might otherwise have occasioned. Thus, if the law of markets means that recessions are not due to demand failure, it might at first sight appear that the acceleration principle is contradictory to that principle.

This is, on closer analysis, not so. The issue of demand failure is the equivalent of over-production, that is, too much being produced relative to demand. The acceleration principle, in contrast, is related to the structure of demand rather than to its level. The acceleration principle posits a functional relationship between the demand for capital goods and the demand for consumer goods such that, if the demand for consumer goods should slow, there is a more rapid slowing in demand for capital goods. While it is true that, in this circumstance, the effect on the economy is a fall in demand for some forms of capital equipment, it is a failure not due to too much having been produced, but rather to the fact that the wrong assortment of goods has been produced. This is but one further example of an economic downturn occurring due to structural maladjustment.

After dealing with vertical maladjustments, Haberler, in Chapter 4, turns to 'Changes in Cost, Horizontal Maladjustments and Over-indebtedness as Causes of Crises and Depression' (ibid.: 99–110). Here he discusses horizontal maladjustment, which he also refers to as 'error theories' (ibid.: 104). The terms of description are those of the earliest classical writers on the cycle, and are derived directly from the law of markets. Because the economy is interdependent, and perfect knowledge about prices and demand is unobtainable, during the upswing of the cycle some expenditures turn out to have been misconceived. Therefore, supply and demand fail to mesh, and there is a resulting contraction in activity:[27]

> These theories [Haberler wrote] stress the great complexity of our economic system, the lack of knowledge, the difficulties in foreseeing correctly the future demand for various products. One producer does not know what the other is doing. A given demand cannot be satisfied by producer A; producers B, C, D etc., are accordingly called upon to satisfy it, and this creates an exaggerated impression of its volume and urgency. This leads to competitive duplication of plant and equipment, involving errors in the estimation of future wants. (Ibid.)

While the distinction between horizontal and vertical maladjustment is worth making, this is a distinction not made by the earlier classical economists. Both forms of maladjustment are, however, consistent with the theories these earlier economists had advanced, since both forms of maladjustment envisage the structure of demand being different from the supply. And indeed, Haberler himself notes the somewhat arbitrary distinction he has made:

> The border-line between horizontal and vertical maladjustment is sometimes difficult to draw. But since the two are not mutually exclusive, since they can, and probably frequently do, coexist and reinforce one another, the fact that classification is sometimes difficult in concrete cases does not weigh too heavily in the balance. (Ibid.: 105)

The maladaptation of supply to demand was the theory of recession which grew out of the classical rejection of demand failure as an accepted theory. The fact that some goods remained unsold had to be accounted for, and in the theory of the business cycle, miscalculation became the explanation of the down phase of the cycle. Haberler's discussion provided a more detailed, more nuanced assessment of these theories as they were held during the 1930s in comparison with a century before. Their origins, however, can be seen in the classical theories which were explicitly associated with the law of markets during the early part of the nineteenth century.

In the second half of the book, Haberler provided his own synthesis of the theories he had discussed. In it he provided an outline of the theory of the cycle which has roots in the earliest discussions on the nature and causes of recession. It is a theory built on business miscalculation which can be, but is not necessarily, exacerbated by credit contraction. The origins of the crisis and subsequent

---

[27] Keynes also discussed the contribution to recession of 'misdirected investment' (*CW* VII: 321).

downturn are located in the processes of the upturn. Various forces are set in motion while the economy is expanding which ultimately create stresses on the economic system. The longer an expansion has gone on, the more vulnerable the economy becomes to the forces of adversity. In classical fashion, the downturn can commence in one or two areas, and then spread through the economy. As Haberler wrote:

> This discussion leaves us with the conclusion that a breakdown in an individual industry may very well cause at least a temporary fall in total demand below the level at which it would otherwise stand.... [If] the expansion has already lost its *élan*, the economic system will be vulnerable and may easily be plunged into a process of general contraction. (Ibid.: 252–3)

The question Haberler addresses is whether the process of contraction is endogenous to the economic system. He discusses two possible sources of the downturn, the first being the 'purely monetary explanation'. This explanation Haberler described as 'not very convincing' (ibid.: 261). Of the alternative explanation, he wrote:

> The other and...much more promising hypothesis is that, as a result of the maladjustments in the structure of production which are inevitable in any expansion, some particular industry or group of industries is forced to curtail output and employment, and thereby start a general contraction. (Ibid.: 260–61)

Haberler explains the nature of the problem in terms of the structure of demand. This expresses the classical theory of recession and disequilibrium:

> The flow of goods does not correspond in all its ramifications to the flow of money and its divisions, and therefore in some lines of production demand does not cover cost. (Ibid.: 262)

'Distortions in the structure of production' appear. The goods produced do not correspond to the goods demanded. It can be the wrong consumer goods or investment goods, but the goods which the community wishes to buy are different from the goods which are being produced, and a proportion of production cannot be sold at cost-covering prices. Haberler describes, in some detail, the ensuing contraction process (ibid.: 224–6). The following passage provides the essence of his description:

> When demand flags at various points, merchants will give lower orders to producers, production will be curtailed and workers will be dismissed. This reduces income. When incomes fall, the demand for all kinds of goods is further reduced and depression spreads to other parts of the system. (Ibid.: 224)

Haberler states that his 'general description of the contraction process may probably be taken as a correct description of the *common opinion* on the matter' (ibid.: 226, italics added). That is, the classical theory of recession, from initiating causes through to the spreading deflation and including the transmission mechanism, occurs through the law of markets. Demand being constituted by supply, as production contracts incomes contract. With the fall in incomes, demand for other goods and services contracts. Superficially, it may appear that there has been an overall fall in demand, but the underlying reality is that the various parts of the economy have gone out of phase. The economic system is no longer synchronised, and at least some parts must contract. A period of deflation occurs which may continue for a considerable period of time. Ultimately, the trough will be reached and a revival will occur. Haberler's discussion thus contradicts Keynes's statements that classical economists assumed full employment, and this assumption was due to their tacit acceptance of Say's Law. The reality is that classical economists assumed that recessions were almost certainly inevitable. As Haberler wrote:

> Is it possible to say generally that such maladjustments are bound to occur during any expansion?... We can only say that there is a *prima facie* probability that they are. We can figure out the consequences approximately – always again in terms of possibilities and probabilities: but only extensive empirical studies can show whether *the contention of so many well-known writers* is correct, and it is actually a fact that processes of expansion regularly develop this type of maladjustment and in turn are brought to an end by them. (Ibid.: 274, italics added)

An acceptance of Say's Law did not lead classical economists to believe there was no obstacle to full employment. The grand irony remains that it was their understanding of Say's Law which was the basis for their understanding of the nature of recessions and indeed of the business cycle as a whole.

Haberler and Keynesian Economics

But while Haberler was able to survey accurately the theories of his contemporaries, he was less capable of understanding the historical origins of the theories he was outlining and was completely unaware just how different the theory advanced in the *General Theory* was. Part I of *Prosperity and Depression* was largely completed in December 1935, but there are a number of references to the *General Theory*, mostly in footnotes, to indicate that amendments were possible after that date. Most of the references to the *General Theory* are unexceptionable, but there is one sequence in the argument of Part I which stands out as having been influenced by Keynes. At the start of his chapter on under-consumption, Haberler had made the following observation about the *General Theory*: 'Mr. Keynes has laid great stress on the deflationary character of acts of saving' (ibid.: 111n). And in the midst of his discussion of under-consumption he takes up the argument in a way which had never been traditionally addressed by mainstream economists. Haberler carefully distinguishes this argument from two others which are characterised as 'the heart of the under-consumption or over-saving theory' (ibid.: 117). This one he recognises as different:

Saving may lead to depression because savings do not find an outlet in investment. There may be an excess of savings over new investment which will be intensified by every additional act of saving, at any rate where saving extends beyond a certain limit. In other words, saving produces a deflation, a decrease in *aggregate demand* for goods. (Ibid.: 116, italics added)

Note Haberler's use of the term 'aggregate demand' in the midst of a passage which is, to all intents and purposes, a summary of the central argument of the *General Theory*. Note, too, that this passage is different from the argument made by Röpke. Röpke had accepted that once in the midst of recession, saving could make matters worse. Here Haberler is arguing that 'saving may lead to depression', a very different thing. It is also notable that Haberler did not see this particular theory fitting comfortably into the theory of under-consumption. He placed this argument within the compass of monetary and over-investment theories (ibid.). Although Haberler had refused to accept that the productive system would collapse because there was too little consumer demand, he was far less dismissive about this form of the over-saving argument. He accepted that, from a theoretical point of view, there is nothing that ensures all savings will smoothly enter the spending stream. If investment falls short of savings then it is possible that there may be a destruction of purchasing power which will lead to a fall in investment. Thus, unlike Röpke, for whom the confusion caused by an already existing recession may lead to savings running to ground, with Haberler the crucial next step is taken. Here the recession is itself caused by savings in excess of investment. This is a rejection of the law of markets. Unbeknownst to Haberler, he had entirely adopted the argument of the *General Theory*.

This is shown to an even greater extent in Part II. The first draft was completed in May 1936, three months after the publication of the *General Theory*. In Chapter 9, in the midst of a discussion on the expansion process, we find Haberler echoing Keynes on the deflationary effects of saving. The following passage presents the multiplier process, where saving is a leakage from the spending stream:

If we look at saving only in its aspect of a reduction of expenditure – for example, if we suppose that money saved is simply destroyed or hoarded – it is obvious that, even in the absence of money-scarcity, credit restrictions and a rise in the rate of interest, a habit on the part of the public of saving a certain proportion of its income will tend to damp down, and finally extinguish, this increase in money income. (Ibid.: 214)

'Obviously,' Haberler wrote, ' continual additions by way of investment will have to be made to the income stream in order to counteract the deflationary pressure of saving' (ibid.: 214–15). He asks whether an act of saving will lead to a parallel act of investment. His answer shows he has accepted, in full, Keynes's refutation of Say's Law. He believes himself to be disagreeing with Keynes, but the fact is that in accepting any part of the demand deficiency argument he has swallowed the hook. Haberler wrote:

The question then arises whether an act of saving in itself tends to produce an act of investment. Answers to this question are usually of an extreme nature. Some economists, of whom Mr J.M. Keynes is not the least eminent, reply that saving has no immediate effect on investment and that its ultimate effect, owing to the deflation which it induces, is to diminish the incentive to invest. Others[28] assume that in normal conditions saving will give rise to an equivalent amount of investment.

The truth probably lies somewhere between these two extremes. (Ibid.: 215)

If the truth does not lie at the 'extreme' in which these 'others' are found, then even in the 'normal' conditions of an expanding economy, an act of saving cannot be counted upon to end up as investment. The law of markets is then wrong. Demand deficiency can be a serious problem which will limit the economy's growth. Nor is Haberler half-hearted in putting forward this view. He wrote: 'always and in all circumstances...saving must tend to reduce the total demand for goods in terms of money' (ibid.: 216). Nor does he believe that it is a circumstance which is limited to first round effects.

An increase of saving, we have found, normally exercises a deflationary effect at the moment of its appearance.... If we pursue the consequence of this saving in subsequent periods, we find the deflationary effect is, as it were, cumulated. A relative fall in demand now leads to a relative fall in investment later, this to a further fall in demand and so on.

If the increase in saving is repeated in subsequent periods, it may not merely slow down the expansion but even prevent it from reaching the height it would otherwise attain, and finally turn it into a decline.... The expansion will cease when saving catches up with investment, and the higher the proportion of income saved the lower will be the income level at which the expansion will cease.

The general conclusion of the foregoing argument is that saving which is in progress during an expansion process tends to slow down the expansion. *Ceteris paribus*, the more people save the slower the expansion, and the less they save the more rapid the expansion. (Ibid.: 216–17)

Haberler had no idea he was saying something totally contrary to the spirit and letter of the classical theorists he had been assessing. When he came face to face with the very argument the law of markets was designed to refute, he not only accepted it as valid, but insisted that this was all part of the ancient lore of economic theory.

---

[28] Pigou, and Pigou alone, is specifically named in a footnote.

7. Keynes's Discovery of Say's Law

Prior to updating his essay on Malthus for *Essays in Persuasion*, Keynes had limited interest in Malthus's economic theories. As this chapter will demonstrate, it was reading Malthus's letters to Ricardo during the depths of the Great Depression in late 1932 that crystallised in Keynes's mind the importance of effective demand. It was out of this first acquaintance with the law of markets that the *General Theory* would grow.

To most economists the use of aggregate demand is so completely natural that it is difficult to imagine economic theory without it. Yet prior to the publication of the *General Theory* not only was the concept of aggregate demand seldom employed by economists,[1] but its use as an important operational variable was specifically denied. It was to deny the need for aggregate demand, or effective demand as it was then generally called, that the law of markets was invoked. Keynes was completely correct when he wrote that the vast majority of his contemporaries believed they could 'safely neglect the aggregate demand function' (*CW* VII: 32).

In the *Treatise on Money* Keynes had made no use of aggregate demand. In contrast, the *General Theory* is primarily about its importance. There has been a considerable literature on the intellectual steps taken by Keynes between the *Treatise* and the *General Theory*. And while there is general agreement that Keynes began to focus on effective or aggregate demand at the end of 1932 or the beginning of 1933, explanations of why this change in direction took place at that time have been generally vague. This chapter addresses the change in the direction of Keynes's thought, a change which has had the most profound implications for economic theory down to our very day. It will be shown that Keynes developed a theory of fluctuations in aggregate demand to explain fluctuations in output and employment because of the influence on him of the writings of Thomas Robert Malthus which Keynes had been reading during October and November 1932 while updating his essay on Malthus for inclusion in *Essays in Biography* (1933).

---

[1] Patinkin (1976: 83) provides a vivid account of how peculiar it was to have the concept of aggregate demand introduced into economic theory.

THE TRADITIONAL ARGUMENT

It has been traditionally argued that Keynes arrived at his conception of 'effective demand' independently, and only afterwards realised that others had had similar ideas before him. Among those to whom Keynes was said to have given such credit was Thomas Robert Malthus.[2] In contrast to this traditional position, it will be argued in what follows that it was reading the Malthus side of the Malthus–Ricardo correspondence which led Keynes to the idea of effective demand. It was because Keynes was reading this correspondence in late 1932, at the height of the Great Depression, that the *General Theory* was written as it was, focusing on effective demand as the central issue in the theory of depressions and unemployment. It follows that, had Keynes not read Malthus, it is virtually certain he would never have written a book attacking Say's Law, or attributing recessions and depressions to failure of effective demand.

The orthodox view was put by Moggridge in his shorter biography of Keynes:

> Another indication of Keynes's growing confidence in his new ideas was that he began to find predecessors for them. In preparing his *Essays in Biography* for the press during the autumn and winter of 1932–3, he revived a 1922 essay on T.R. Malthus, the early Cambridge economist, which he had originally prepared for the London Political Economy Club and had read at intervals to various societies in Cambridge during the 1920s. Taking advantage of the contemporaneous work by Piero Sraffa, who was editing the works of David Ricardo for the Royal Economic Society, he revised the essay, but then, at the last possible moment, he added additional passages which seemed to give Malthus the germs of Keynes's own recently worked out views, particularly as regards effective demand. (Moggridge 1980: 109)

This has been the traditional view. Keynes, it is said, attributed to Malthus ideas similar to those he had independently worked out himself. A survey of the literature reveals that little attention has been paid to a possible Malthusian influence on Keynes. Moggridge (1973), in his chronological discussion of the development of Keynes's views between the *Treatise* and the *General Theory*, gives only passing reference to the updating of the Malthus essay. It is mentioned as having occurred, but is not presented as having had any influence one way or the other on Keynes's thinking (ibid.: 81).

In his extended biography of Keynes, Moggridge (1992) refines his ideas further. In this later work, Keynes's key analytical discovery in the *General Theory* is specified as the 'output equilibrating model' (ibid.: 562). Moggridge writes that 'we can date Keynes's adoption of his output equilibrating model to late 1932 or early 1933 *at the latest*' (ibid.). It is only to provide evidence for this dating that Moggridge cites Keynes's essay on Malthus.

Patinkin (1993), in his chronology of the steps between the *Treatise* and the *General Theory*, mentions neither Malthus nor Keynes's biographical essay on

---

[2] Rashid ([1977] 1986: 224) sums up the literature on Keynes's 'generous praise' for Malthus, writing that Keynes's 'good will outran the bounds of accurate scholarship'.

Malthus. Patinkin does, however, provide a discussion (ibid.: 656) of when he, Dimand (1988), and Moggridge (1992) believe that Keynes began to formulate a theory of effective demand. Patinkin believes the dating to be in early 1933.[3] Patinkin notes that both Dimand and Moggridge accept that Keynes became interested in effective demand after the last of his Michaelmas lectures on 28 November 1932.[4] Patinkin does not, however, relate the timing of Keynes's sudden interest in effective demand to Keynes's immediately prior work on the economics of Malthus.

In his *Keynesian Revolution in the Making* Clarke (1988) comes close to recognising the critical role which Malthus played in forming Keynes's thinking. Yet, in the end, Clarke accepts the orthodox view in seeing the sequence of events as Keynes first formulating his theory and then discovering a predecessor in Malthus (ibid.: 266). For Clarke, it is 'overwhelmingly likely' that it was in the summer of 1932 that Keynes first conceived the theory of effective demand (ibid.: 263). Clarke sees Malthus as having provided an inspiration of sorts, but not in terms of the actual development of Keynesian thought. According to Clarke, Keynes's reading of the Ricardo–Malthus correspondence was to 'give him a name for his new concept – effective demand' (ibid.: 267), but it was not the inspiration for the concept itself.

In his *Origins of the Keynesian Revolution* Dimand (1988) makes only two passing references to Malthus. There is no suggestion that a reading of Malthus had any influence on the direction taken by Keynes in the *General Theory*. The same may be said of Bridel, who devotes an entire chapter to 'The *General Theory* and the Principle of Effective Demand' (1987: 157–87).

Some, however, have recognised the possibility of a causal relationship between Malthus and Keynes. O'Leary (1942), in his discussion of the influence of Malthus on Keynes, spends the bulk of his paper pointing out the similarities between 'Malthus's general theory and that of Keynes' (ibid.: 901). O'Leary notes that 'the theory of effective demand is the heart of Keynes's general theory' (ibid.: 908), which is similar to the role effective demand played in Malthus's theories (ibid.: 909). This leads him to raise an additional issue:

> In view of the degree to which Malthus anticipated Keynes's general theory, it seems pertinent to examine into the question of whether Malthus had any influence upon Keynes's thinking. (Ibid.: 917)

O'Leary recognises that Keynes had been updating his 'Essay on Malthus' for the *Essays in Biography*. He notes, in this context, that Keynes had recognised that the term 'effective demand' had been used by Malthus as early as 1800 (ibid.). He points out that 'Keynes's *Essay* is replete with praise for Malthus's work' (ibid.: 918), and notes that 'Keynes's references to Malthus in his *General Theory* are disappointingly casual' (ibid.) and that, in fact, Keynes is dismissive of 'the

---

[3] The same dating is found in Patinkin (1976: 72–3).
[4] Patinkin notes that Clarke (1988) chooses a slightly earlier dating.

importance of Malthus's contribution' (ibid.). In the end, O'Leary merely concludes:

> There can be little doubt that Keynes was influenced by Malthus' ideas, but it is impossible to say to what extent. It does appear, however, that there is more of Malthus in Keynes's *General Theory* than Keynes himself has realized. (Ibid.: 919)

Klein (1968) is also in no doubt that Keynes was influenced by his reading of Malthus, saying, in regard to Malthus, that 'in one instance, we can be reasonably sure that Keynes derived a profound inspiration' (ibid.: 125) from one of his classical forebears. But while Klein recognises the influence, he is ambiguous about the extent to which Malthus influenced Keynes. He notes the existence of this influence, and the similarities between Keynes and Malthus, in that both deal with effective demand and Say's Law. Klein cannot, however, be interpreted as claiming that Keynes discovered the idea of effective demand by reading Malthus, as he writes only that 'Keynes was aware of this historical similarity and must have profited much from a perusal of the early literature' (ibid.: 125).[5]

Brandis (1985) also sees Keynes as receiving an inspiration from Malthus. He argues that it was the reading of Malthus which gave Keynes a new tack but not a new theory. Brandis actually makes of Keynes a quite cynical publicist, writing:

> Keynes, at some time after April 1932, may have concluded that he had to find a new angle of attack on the ruling economics establishment if his voice were to be more than merely one of a number that were listened to more or less respectfully on the subject of unemployment – either on the level of theory or, especially, of policy. (Ibid.: 654).

In Brandis's view, Keynes learned from the example set by Joan Robinson in attacking Marshall in *The Economics of Imperfect Competition* and was then in need of someone that he too could challenge. He came across Say and Say's Law while reading Malthus and used this as his straw man because it would then allow him to pit himself against the entire classical tradition (ibid.: 654–5). All this was, however, merely a means to differentiate his views from those of others. But because Brandis thinks of Say's Law in the way it was portrayed in the *General Theory*, that is, as ruling out unemployment (ibid.: 652–3), he cannot see any relationship between Keynes's reading of Malthus and the theory which emerged. Instead he writes:

---

[5] Hollander (1997) argues that Klein had recognised that Keynes received his initial inspiration from Malthus, citing this same passage as evidence. However, to have written that Keynes had been 'aware of this historical similarity', as Klein does, actually indicates that Klein believed that Keynes had reached the same conclusion independently. Klein would not have described the close relationship between the ideas of Keynes and Malthus as an 'historical similarity' if he had believed that Keynes had taken his original idea directly from Malthus.

There *was* a Keynesian Revolution, as we are all aware. It freed us, or seemed to free us, from the basic pessimism of business cycle theory. I do not say 'freed us from Say's Law', for I do not believe that is what was shackling us in the 1930s. (Ibid.: 655)

Brandis thus recognises that Keynes drew the idea to attack Say's Law from reading Malthus. But Brandis misunderstands what in fact Say's Law means and therefore can see no more in the relationship than a way by which Keynes could gain attention for theories he had more or less already presented in the *Treatise* (ibid.: 651, 654) and which were anyway by then old hat (ibid.: 652).

Skidelsky (1992) takes an interesting position and actually acknowledges the possibility that Keynes may have been 'influenced by the Malthus of Effective Demand, rather than, as has hitherto been supposed, discovering him after he had developed the principle independently himself' (ibid.: 417). Skidelsky, however, suggests that this influence may date back to 1924, because, in a speech given in that year, Keynes quoted a passage on demand failure from a letter written by Malthus to Ricardo. Yet the context of the speech indicates that the passage quoted would have merely illustrated that Ricardo and Malthus had 'frequently differed on points of economic theory and method' (KP: PS/2). Indeed, far from seeing Malthus as underrated and Ricardo as disastrous for economic theory, in that same speech Keynes praised Ricardo by describing him as 'the most powerful abstract intelligence which has found Economics worthy of it' (ibid.). In the final analysis, Skidelsky has raised the Malthusian influence only as a possibility. That he devotes only a single paragraph to this possibility suggests that he views the influence as marginal. Indeed, when Skidelsky came to discuss Keynes's final Michaelmas lecture in 1932, he adopted the traditional view by stating that Keynes 'felt for the first time the need to place himself in a tradition or perhaps to invent a tradition in which he could place himself. Malthus, whom he had always admired, fitted the bill' (ibid.: 464).

Overall, there has been little suggestion in the literature that Malthus had an important influence on Keynes. It will be the aim of this chapter to demonstrate, not only the existence of this influence, but also how critically important that influence was.

THE OVERLAP BETWEEN MALTHUS AND KEYNES

That there are strong similarities between the *General Theory* and Malthus's economic views is not in doubt. Keynes himself establishes this connection in Chapter 23, where he includes Malthus in his 'brave army of heretics' (*CW* VII: 371). But while Malthus might have been included, he is referred to only in a perfunctory manner, just one of a number. It is true that Keynes states he is devoting less space to Malthus because he has dealt with him in the *Essays in Biography* (ibid.: 362). Nevertheless, this very brief reference would provide no indication that Malthus played a particularly important role in the development of Keynes's thinking.

There is, in fact, an extraordinary degree of overlap if both Keynes and Malthus actually reached the same conclusions independently. Note the following areas of similarity. Firstly, both Malthus and Keynes argue that it is the reliance by others on Say's Law that creates fundamental misunderstandings about the nature of the economy. For Malthus, it was the belief in the law of markets by Say, Ricardo and James Mill. For Keynes, it was just about all of his contemporaries who, more or less unwittingly, were still following in the footsteps of Ricardo in accepting Say's Law. Secondly, there is the issue of effective demand. Where Say's Law breaks down is in situations where output is greater than the willingness to purchase that output. In both Malthus and Keynes, it is precisely the unwillingness to purchase all that the fully employed economy can produce which causes the economic system to falter. Thirdly, both Malthus and Keynes attribute the problem of demand failure to decisions to save. In Malthus, the cause of the problem is related to decisions to increase savings. Decisions to save lead to interruptions in the demand for consumer goods, which then lead to progressive reductions in demand throughout the economy, which, in turn, cause less to be produced in succeeding periods. In Keynes, it is the failure of investment to soak up all of the savings which have been generated. The deficiency of investment relative to saving causes the economy to contract.

REFUTING SAY'S LAW

That Keynes even mentions Say's Law, never mind that he set out to disprove it, provides strong evidence that reading Malthus had a major influence on the development of Keynes's thought. When Malthus was writing, he was in the midst of the general glut debates of the early nineteenth century. Indeed, his correspondence with Ricardo was one facet of that debate. Virtually all economists of importance were involved in the question of whether demand failure was a cause of recession. During the 1930s, however, Say's Law was not a mainstream issue. Little attention has been devoted to answering the question as to why Keynes suddenly turned to a discussion of Say's Law when he had never previously shown any interest in this issue. If, however, one assumes that Keynes read Malthus and then, because of this reading, devoted the *General Theory* to effective demand, then the answer is indeed obvious.

What Keynes was doing, unknown to his contemporaries, was resurrecting the general glut debate of the early nineteenth century. Keynes was wading in on the side of Malthus in an almost totally forgotten controversy. He was arguing that Malthus had been right all along in arguing that demand failure might occur. Keynes's aim was to refute the view that failure of effective demand could not cause recession. By 1936, this had been a settled conclusion amongst economists for more than a century. It was only as a consequence of the *General Theory* that this settled conclusion was overturned.

Because Keynes was taking his starting point from Malthus, he set out to prove, as Malthus had attempted to do, that more could be produced than the community was willing to buy. This is the issue of demand failure, and it is the point Ricardo understood Malthus to be making. As already discussed in Chapter 3, Ricardo had categorically denied the possibility of demand failure in his correspondence with Malthus, and it was the Malthus side of this correspondence which Keynes read in late 1932, as the quotations in his essay on Malthus show. Keynes himself was in no doubt that he was taking a Malthusian interpretation of effective demand. In a letter to Ralph Hawtrey, dated 8 November 1935, Keynes specifically stated that he was taking his lead from Malthus:

> *Effective demand.* In modern economics this term has gone out of use and that is part of my defence for reviving it in my own sense, but my own sense seems to me to bear an exceedingly close family resemblance to what Malthus meant by it. (*CW* XIII: 602)

In adopting the Malthusian meaning of effective demand, Keynes began from the premise that more could be produced than the community wanted to buy. That is, the community had the power to buy but lacked the will.

WRITING THE ESSAY ON MALTHUS

There is no controversy over when Keynes was preparing his essay on Malthus. The essay was written during October and November 1932. There is also general agreement over when the idea of effective demand occurred to Keynes, most authorities placing it towards the end of 1932 or at the beginning of 1933. We are therefore dealing either with one of the most unlikely coincidences in the history of the sciences or with a cause and effect relationship. One may argue that Keynes discovered the idea of effective demand and then almost immediately happened to be updating his essay on Malthus. Or one may, instead, argue that it was because Keynes was updating his essay that he was struck by the idea of effective demand, which he then adopted as his own.

We know that it was in the latter half of 1932 and early 1933 that Keynes was working on his *Essays in Biography*. The preface to the *Essays* was written in February 1933, making this the last possible date. But there is other evidence which can help to pinpoint more accurately when he was working on Malthus. There are, firstly, letters to his wife. On 30 October 1932, Keynes wrote to her as follows:

> My dearest sweet duck,
>   I have become completely absorbed in re-writing my life of Malthus, and sit by the hour by my desk copying bits out and composing sentences and wanting to do nothing else with stacks of books round me. What a relief not to be writing arguments! What an easy and agreeable life fanciful writers must have! (KP: JMK to LL)

On 20 November 1932, Keynes writes of his Malthus essay again. Lydia is at this time visiting Russia, which is why Keynes refers to the quiet life he is leading: 'I have got back to my Malthus Essay and have been writing it, very quiet by myself, all day with much enjoyment' (ibid.).

There is also surviving correspondence between Keynes and James Bonar, who had, in 1885, written a book entitled *Malthus and His Work* which had been reprinted in 1924 with additional material. The first letter from Keynes to Bonar is dated 3 November 1932 (KP: B/1). Keynes states that he is interested in adding something about Malthus, although what this something is he does not reveal. But there are two points of great significance. One is a query asking whether Bonar has the transcripts of letters from Malthus which he had quoted in his revised book, showing Keynes's interest in Malthus's correspondence. The other point of significance is that Keynes states that he and Sraffa are to visit Malthus's old home in the following week.

If Keynes is interested in Malthus's letters, there is no better source for some of them than his companion of the following week. One may easily deduce that by this stage, early in November 1932, Keynes had in his hands the letters which Malthus had written to Ricardo, and almost as surely had by then read them closely. It is asking too much to believe that Keynes would write to Bonar seeking transcripts of Malthus's letters but not also have gone through the letters closest to hand. One may therefore assume that by 3 November 1932 Keynes had read the Malthus correspondence with Ricardo which was to feature in his essay on Malthus.

Correspondence between Keynes and Sraffa also exists. Sraffa was the editor of Ricardo's collected works and it is precisely because of this that Keynes wrote to him. The letter sent by Keynes is not in the archive at King's College, Cambridge. But from the letter in reply, dated 20 December 1932 (KP: B/1), it is clear that Keynes had sent Sraffa an early draft of the essay on Malthus. It is also clear that Keynes had been reading the Malthus side of the correspondence with Ricardo which was to be excerpted in the essay, and the purpose of the letter was to seek permission to quote from Malthus's letters.[6]

One additional feature is very important. Sraffa readily gives his permission to Keynes to quote from the letters, but adds, 'Only don't treat too ill my David!'. That is, Sraffa asks Keynes to treat Ricardo kindly. Either from the letter which Keynes had sent, or from previous discussions in Cambridge, Sraffa is aware that Keynes has an unfavourable view of Ricardo, or at least of Ricardian economics.[7]

From the correspondence, Keynes is seen to have been working on his essay on Malthus from at least the end of October 1932, and is interested in Malthus's correspondence from at least the start of November 1932. It is more than likely that Keynes had looked at this material some time before these dates, but almost certainly by this time Keynes is familiar with the material in the Ricardo–Malthus

---

[6] Keynes would have been very privileged in enjoying access to these letters in 1932. Malthus's letters to Ricardo were not published until the 1950s.

[7] How recent that attitude was in Keynes is a moot point. Lydia used Ricardo as the standard of economic excellence in a letter to Keynes on 24 April 1932, where she wrote that a friend of hers had 'found a subject for Handel Ballet, good part for me, it is from a book of a famous maitre de ballet, whom we revere like your Ricardo' (KP: LL to JMK).

correspondence. It is reasonable to assume that the Malthus correspondence he had looked at by this time included the material which was to be incorporated in the final published version of the essay. If so, by late 1932 Keynes had been looking at the Malthus side of the Ricardo correspondence dealing with the questions of over-saving, Say's Law and effective demand.

Clarke (1988: 266) is quite specific that all the important additions to the essay on Malthus had been completed by the end of November 1932. According to Clarke, the draft essay had been virtually completed by the time Keynes gave his final 1932 Michaelmas lecture, on 28 November. Yet, in most respects, the actual timing of the additions to the essay is of secondary importance. In dating Malthus's influence on Keynes, it is not when Keynes was writing the essay but when Keynes was reading Malthus that is critical. And as the letters to his wife, Bonar and Sraffa make clear, Keynes had been reading Malthus's correspondence from at least the end of October 1932.

EFFECTIVE DEMAND

Prior to the publication of the *General Theory*, demand-side considerations were of minor importance in business cycle analysis. It is the major theoretical innovation of the *General Theory* that the theory of recession and unemployment became the focus of the demand side of the economy. It is the reorientation of economic theory to the demand side which represents the critical contribution of the Keynesian Revolution. Keynes himself made clear the monumental importance of effective demand in a letter to Harrod in August 1936:

> You don't mention *effective demand* or, more precisely, the demand schedule for output as a whole, except in so far as it is implicit in the multiplier. To me, regarded historically, the most extraordinary thing is the complete disappearance of the theory of the demand and supply for output as a whole, i.e. the theory of employment, *after* it had been for a quarter of a century the most discussed thing in economics. One of the most important transitions for me, after my *Treatise on Money* had been published, was suddenly realizing this. (*CW* XIV: 85)

Many others have recognised effective demand as Keynes's essential contribution. Peter Clarke, in his *The Keynesian Revolution in the Making: 1924– 1936* (1988), when he moves from his discussion of the *Treatise* in Chapter 10, entitles Chapter 11 'The Making of the Theory of Effective Demand'. Patinkin, in his *Anticipations of the 'General Theory'?* (1982), after a long discussion of what constitutes the central message of the *General Theory*, and after looking at a number of possibilities, finally concludes as follows:

> This leaves the theory of effective demand as the distinctive analytical contribution of the *General Theory*. That this is its central message is also clear from the *General Theory* itself. (Ibid.: 9)

In his chronology of the *General Theory*'s development, Patinkin (1993: 647) continues to argue the central importance of aggregate demand along with the equilibrating role of changes in output.

Samuelson, in 1947, wrote:

> I myself believe the broad significance of the *General Theory* to be in the fact that it provides a relatively realistic, complete system for analyzing the level of effective demand and its fluctuations. (Samuelson [1947] 1960: 150–51)

According to Bridel (1987: 158), Keynes believed effective demand to be his 'fundamental theoretical novelty'. And while the structure of the *General Theory* was new, aside from effective demand, the kinds of arguments Keynes advanced were not. Even the argument that full employment was embedded in classical theory had been stated previously. For example, in an article in the *Evening Standard* on 19 March 1929, in an analysis of the Liberal Party pamphlet, *We Can Conquer Unemployment*, Keynes wrote, 'the orthodox theory *assumes* that everyone is employed' (*CW* XIX: 807; see also *CW* XIX: 811). Nor was Keynes's position on the effect of the different motives to save and invest new in the *General Theory*, as may be seen from Stamp's review of the *Treatise*:

> The essence of Mr Keynes' theory is that the decision to save instead of spending money on consumption-goods is made by a different set of minds and on different principles (in the way it divides purchasing power) from the decision to spend on production-goods (i.e. to invest)...and there is nothing immediately to compel investment to be equal to savings. The whole of the theory is bound up with the results of these disequilibria. The performance of the act of saving is in itself no guarantee that the stock of capital goods will be correspondingly increased. (Stamp 1931: 244)

What was new was effective demand. It is this which sets the *General Theory* apart from all of Keynes's previous work, and which sets the *General Theory* apart from almost the whole of orthodox economic theory which came before. The constraints imposed by Say's Law had until then prevented mainstream economists from presenting a theory of recession based on demand failure, and while fluctuations in demand in aggregate may appear like second nature to an economist educated since the publication of the *General Theory*, it was a concept almost entirely foreign to economic theory prior to 1936. Keynes's initial mention of the phrase 'effective demand' can therefore be used to identify, within reasonably narrow limits, the moment when Keynes made his discovery of effective demand. To understand how significant this use of the term 'effective demand' was even for Keynes, it needs to be appreciated that he had never discussed effective demand in any of his theoretical works prior to November

1932. From the end of 1932 onwards, the use of the phrase 'effective demand' explodes through his writing.[8]

THE MICHAELMAS LECTURES OF 1932

Most scholars agree that Keynes showed no evidence of having turned towards the *General Theory* during the lectures given in May 1932. There is general agreement that, at the time of the May lectures, Keynes was still enveloped in the form of thinking attached to the *Treatise*. The earliest sightings of a change in direction are found in the late summer or early autumn of 1932, with most preferring a later dating (see Dimand 1988: 155; Kahn 1984: 113; Moggridge 1992: 562; Patinkin 1993: 656). It is here argued that an accurate dating of the moment of conception can be found in November 1932. Prior to November 1932, Keynes was still locked into the conceptual apparatus of the *Treatise*. From November onwards, Keynes was developing the concepts which were to culminate in the publication of the *General Theory*.

The first of the Michaelmas lectures was delivered on 10 October 1932 and the last on 28 November 1932. Keynes opened the first lecture by announcing he was in the process of writing a new book, and gave these lectures the same title he was intending to give his book: *The Monetary Theory of Production*. Three sets of notes taken by students of these 1932 lectures survive. These are by Robert Bryce, (Sir) Alec Cairncross and (Professor) Lorie Tarshis.[9]

There is little in the first seven lectures to remind one of anything more than a rudimentary version of the *General Theory*. This changes completely with Lecture VIII, delivered on 28 November 1932. Suddenly, we are into the opening chapters of the *General Theory*. One no longer has to read between lines, or look for ideas which provide a faint echo of the book to come. Unmistakably, we are in the midst of the real thing. And it is here that Keynes, for the first time, uses the term 'effective demand'.

The surviving lecture notes provide clear guidance as to where Keynes was heading as of 28 November 1932. There are a number of significant points raised in the lecture which provide evidence that, firstly, Keynes had decisively turned the corner towards the *General Theory* and, secondly, it had been the reading of Malthus which influenced the direction of his thought. Note all of the following from this eighth Michaelmas lecture of 1932. The name of the notetaker and the page reference in Rymes's (1988) transcriptions of the notes are provided:

- Keynes discusses book collecting and the habit of 'browsing among old books to get ideas' [Bryce: 48]. He contrasts his own attitudes with the

---

[8] The index to the *General Theory* provides eighteen separate references to effective demand, three of them more than ten pages in length. In contrast, there are only four single-page references to aggregate demand.

[9] I am grateful to Professor T. Rymes of Carleton University, Ottawa, for making available his transcriptions of the original lecture notes.

attitude he believes prevalent at Cambridge, where past thoughts on economic matters are neglected. Keynes implies that he does not neglect past thoughts.

- Keynes deals with certain ideas which had been held in the past which were denied by his contemporaries. The first of these older ideas he takes from Adam Smith who, Keynes states, understood that 'savings did not always find [their] way into investment' [Tarshis: 27].

- The second old idea discussed is Mercantilist thought which, according to Keynes, had a sound basis. He criticises free trade arguments which assume 'that all factors are fully employed'. Keynes notes that, in the past, the 'optimum output is the exception rather than the rule' [Tarshis: 27].

- The third of the sound but discarded past ideas is that 'spending is good for trade' [Cairncross: 22; Tarshis: 28; Bryce: 50]. Keynes criticises economists for believing that saving is economically beneficial. Indeed, 'only economists believe that saving would be good' [Bryce: 50]. Where saving does not get taken up in investment, 'the spendthrift is helping the community' [Bryce: 50].

- In the fourth of the discarded ideas, Keynes refers to 'effective demand' [Cairncross: 22; Tarshis: 28]. Tarshis's notes have Keynes stating that 'the explanation of prices was to be found in effective demand' [Tarshis: 28].

- Keynes explicitly associates the principle of effective demand with Malthus. Cairncross's notes read: 'cf. also Malthus on effective demand' [Cairncross: 22].

- Keynes sides with Malthus against Ricardo: 'Malthus held this Ricardo destroyed it' [sic; Bryce: 51].

Keynes has become a rudimentary 'Keynesian' no later than 28 November 1932. The lecture marks a watershed. It is possible to argue an earlier date. But given the contents of Lecture VIII of the Michaelmas term, 1932, Keynes is on the road to writing the *General Theory* from that moment onwards.

THE ESSAY ON MALTHUS

The essay on Malthus provides further strong evidence that Keynes, in November 1932 is, for the first time in his life, attempting to understand the problems associated with recession and unemployment in terms of effective demand. There is no controversy over the dating of the essay as having been prepared for publication during the period between October 1932 and February 1933. There is also no controversy over which material Keynes added at this stage. In point of fact, all of the economic material in the essay was introduced at this time. Moggridge (*CW* X: 71n) provides an outline showing which sections were added in late 1932 or early 1933. Until the additions were made at the end of 1932, there had been no economic material in the essay.

The contents of the new inclusions are themselves strong evidence that it was effective demand that Keynes was plucking from Malthus. Keynes's essay on Malthus attributes an over-saving argument to Malthus, and the essay was being written at exactly the moment when Keynes began to discuss recessions in terms of deficient effective demand. The fact that Keynes had previously had his own saving–investment apparatus, and believed in public sector stimulus, would have made the Malthusian addition of effective demand attractive to him. In the final analysis, it is not whether Keynes interpreted Malthus correctly that especially matters, but simply whether Keynes was led in the direction of effective demand by what he read in Malthus. And this would be the case even if that reading had been a misreading of Malthus's intent, which it was not.

If one looks at the essay (*CW* X: 71–103), concentrating only on those parts written prior to its being sent to the printer, parts which were probably being written before the end of November 1932 (for a discussion of the dating, see Clarke 1988: 266), we find Keynes dealing with effective demand (*CW* X: 88), an issue never previously discussed by him. Keynes cites letters from Malthus to Ricardo 'to show Malthus's complete comprehension of the effects of excessive saving on output *via* its effect on profit' (ibid.: 99). Keynes chooses the following excerpt from a letter from Malthus to Ricardo to illustrate his point:

> I confess indeed that I know no other cause for the fall of profits which I believe you will allow generally takes place from accumulation than that the...*effective* demand is diminished. (Malthus, quoted in ibid.: 99)

In the final section, added at the galley stage, probably early in 1933, further light is cast on Keynes's interpretation of Malthus in relation to saving and effective demand. In this section of the essay, Keynes states that the quoted letters were only restating the arguments found in Chapter VII, section IX of Malthus's *Principles*. Keynes then writes in a footnote:

> I refer the reader to the whole of section IX as a masterly exposition of the conditions which determine the *optimum* of Saving in the actual economic system in which we live. (*CW* X: 101n)

The section of Malthus's *Principles* referred to by Keynes is devoted to demonstrating that, because of the excessive level of saving, 'a country with great power of production should possess a body of unproductive consumers' (Malthus, quoted in Ricardo 1951–73: II. 421). Malthus then states, by way of a conclusion:

But it appears to me perfectly clear in theory, and universally confirmed by experience, that the employment of a capital, *too rapidly increased by parsimonious habits*, may find a limit, and does, in fact, often find a limit, long before there is any real difficulty in procuring the means of subsistence; and that both capital and population may be at the same time, and for a period of great length, redundant, compared with the *effective demand* for produce.[10] (Ibid.: 427, italics added)

That Malthus had a different theory of deficient 'effective demand' from that which Keynes would ultimately develop is beside the point.[11] What Keynes takes from Malthus is the desire to demonstrate the importance of effective demand, and therefore to refute Say's Law. This is the critical issue. It is Keynes's determination to refute Say's Law which becomes the central theme of the *General Theory*. Keynes understands Malthus to be developing a theory of deficient effective demand due to excess saving. It is exactly this that Keynes from then on endeavours to develop for himself. If one follows the train of argument Keynes ascribes to Malthus, Keynes understands Malthus's argument as proceeding from excessive saving, to a fall in effective demand, to a fall in profits, to a fall in output. There is a good deal of refinement between this 1932 essay and the *General Theory* itself, but this summary captures the central theme of what was to be developed in the *General Theory*.

It is interesting to note that Keynes's reference to Malthus's *Principles* is to the first edition and not the second. The long quotation in the *General Theory* (*CW* VIII: 363–4) is found only in the first edition of the *Principles* but was omitted in the second! In the first edition, Malthus, in a footnote, attacks Say and the law of markets (Ricardo 1951–73: II. 318n). In the second edition, this first footnote is replaced, and Malthus instead discusses the importance of money in determining the flows of economic activity. One may then wonder whether Keynes's own thought might have evolved differently had he read the second edition instead of the first, which is a much softer argument and which does not push the unproductive consumer argument to the same extent. Compare the opening of Chapter VII section IX in the first edition with the same opening in the second. In the first edition, Malthus wrote:

The third main cause which tends to keep up and increase the value of produce by favouring its distribution is the employment of unproductive labour, or the maintenance of an adequate proportion of unproductive consumers. (Malthus, in ibid.: 421)

---

[10] It is interesting that, in the very next paragraph, Malthus uses the phrase 'propensity to spend'.

[11] This has been argued by many; for example, Schumpeter ([1954] 1986: 481); Blaug (1958: 238–40); Corry (1962: 126) and Black (1967: 63). A contrary view has been put by Hollander (1962). Hollander (1997) again argues that Keynes's debt to Malthus is lessened if Keynes ultimately arrived at a different theory of effective demand from Malthus. Yet the only debt that matters is that Keynes drew from Malthus the idea of demonstrating that effective demand might be deficient. That Keynes was able to convince others that he had succeeded is what constitutes the Keynesian Revolution.

This was substantially revised in the second edition:

> The third main cause which tends to keep up and increase the value of produce by favouring its distribution is the employment of individuals in personal services, or the maintenance of an adequate proportion of consumers not directly productive of material objects. (Malthus 1986: 6. 398)

Ricardo argued that promoting consumption by unproductive labourers was nonsensical. In the second edition, Malthus argues that demand is enhanced by an increasing number of providers of personal services and an 'adequate proportion' who do not themselves directly produce goods. The phrasing applied to the second group suggests that they must in some way be indirectly productive of commodities, such as the sweeper in a factory. But both groups are adding value by their activities, neither is unproductive and it is unlikely that Ricardo would have objected to this statement. Ricardo's question was: 'In what way can a man's consuming my produce, without making me *any* return whatever, enable me to make a fortune?' (Ricardo 1951–73: II. 422n, italics added). The provision of services or indirect involvement in the production process does provide a return. An exchange involving goods against productive services would not have attracted Ricardo's indignation. Malthus, in his second edition, was more than clarifying what he had first written. He had changed his position and had come most of the way towards Ricardo.

THE *GENERAL THEORY* INTERPRETED

The *General Theory* has a straightforward and natural interpretation if seen in the light of its Malthusian ancestry, particularly in the light of Malthus's attempts to refute Say's Law. The point Malthus was attempting to establish was that demand deficiency of itself could be the cause of recession and unemployment. Keynes therefore attempted to demonstrate that there is no certainty, even in the best of times, that a community will buy everything it can produce. This is the requisite demonstration needed to refute Say's Law. Since Say's Law denied the possibility of demand-side failure, Keynes needed to provide a framework in which depression could occur through endogenous factors on the demand side.

To prove that insufficiency of effective demand is a chronic problem, and that the richer the community the more chronic the problem becomes, Keynes developed three conceptions. These were enumerated in order of discovery in his letter to Harrod referred to above. They were, firstly, 'the psychological law that, when income increases, the gap between income and consumption will increase'; secondly, 'the notion of interest as being the measure of liquidity preference'; and, thirdly, 'the proper definition of the marginal efficiency of capital' (*CW* XIV: 85).[12] Each of these is part of an explanation of why the demand for output

---

[12] This letter to Harrod is quoted in Moggridge (1980: 104) and Clarke (1988: 260) as presenting the ordering in which Keynes developed his ideas. The full text of the letter is

may be less than the total level of production. It is through manipulating these concepts that Keynes attempted to refute Say's Law.[13]

The fact that the marginal propensity to consume is less than unity meant that, as income increased, the total level of consumer expenditure did not rise to the same extent. There was, therefore, a widening gap between total incomes received and total consumption. It was Keynes's contention that, even in the normal course of events, particularly in wealthier communities, this gap would not be closed by a sufficient level of investment. Therefore, the actual level of production would (or at least could) chronically remain below the full-employment level of production.

Liquidity preference and the marginal efficiency of capital provided explanations of why investment would remain below the full-employment level. Keynes's aim was to explain why savings would not be soaked up in investment. He defined liquidity preference as the amount of 'resources' an individual 'will wish to retain in the form of money in different sets of circumstances' (*CW* VII: 166). Interest rates, in this Keynesian theory, are determined by liquidity preference and not by the demand for, and supply of, savings. Interest is paid to induce individuals to part with their liquidity. Given the stock of money, liquidity preference alone determines interest rates. Given the high degree of liquidity preference, interest rates are kept higher than the rate which would need to prevail if all savings were to be used. Recession therefore necessitates the Malthusian solution: increases in effective demand. In the Keynesian approach, the state must become the purchaser of last resort. Otherwise demand will fall short of production, and the economy will be condemned to a chronic state of less than full employment.

CONCLUSION

There should be little doubt that it was only because Keynes read Malthus's letters to Ricardo in late 1932 that he eventually focused on effective demand in the *General Theory*. Because of his reading of Malthus, Keynes attacked Say's Law and wrote the *General Theory* to establish variations in effective demand as the major cause of fluctuations in economic activity. This was the crucial issue underlying the law of markets.

The story of how the *General Theory* came to be written cannot therefore be understood in isolation from Malthus's role, nor is it possible to understand the *General Theory* itself without seeing it in relation to Keynes's interpretation of Malthus. Indeed, it follows from the arguments in this chapter that the continuing

---

found in *CW* (XIV: 84–86). This is similar to the *General Theory* itself, where Keynes wrote: 'The analysis of the propensity to consume, the definition of the marginal efficiency of capital and the theory of the rate of interest are the three main gaps in our existing knowledge which it will be necessary to fill' (*CW* VII: 31).

[13] For a brief but well-stated account of how Keynes constructs his argument from these three elements, see Williams ([1941] 1954: 278–9).

focus on aggregate demand by macro and business cycle theorists is due largely to Keynes's interpretation of Malthus, which he derived from his reading of the Malthus side of the Malthus–Ricardo correspondence during the months of October and November 1932.

8. Influences Deepening Keynes's Understanding of Say's Law

Until the end of 1932, Keynes had shown no interest in the issues surrounding Say's Law and had at no stage written on the subject. Thus, when he encountered Say's Law in reading Malthus's correspondence, he was entering an area which would have been largely unknown to him. It would therefore have been necessary for him to undertake further investigation to understand more completely the nature of the issues he had accidentally come upon.

As is well known, part of the research effort underlying the *General Theory* was undertaken by others.[1] But in regard to Say's Law, it is likely that Keynes conducted most of his researches himself. Firstly, he was deeply interested in what he had discovered. His excitement is shown in the manner in which he commended the whole of Chapter VII, section IX of Malthus's *Principles* to readers of his essay on Malthus (*CW* X: 101n). It is unlikely he would have done so had he not read these passages himself. Secondly, there is no record that any of the early discussions within his coterie at Cambridge revolved around Say's Law, a strong indication that the research that Keynes conducted on Say's Law during 1932 and 1933 was undertaken largely on his own without consultation with his contemporaries.[2] Thirdly, whatever assistance he might have received from others, the importance Keynes clearly attached to the issue of Say's Law and effective demand would have ensured that he would have closely studied the material he had uncovered.

Once Keynes had taken his inspiration from Malthus, he made a further effort to understand more completely the issues surrounding Say's Law. It is likely that Keynes read Hobson and Mummery (1889) thoroughly. They are quoted in the midst of Keynes's discussion of Say's Law (*CW* VII: 19n) and then, in Chapter 23, a further seven pages are devoted to providing a discussion with extended quotations (ibid.: 364–70). Keynes agreed with Hobson that the constraint on

---

[1] But not all. There are detailed notes on Heckscher's *Mercantilism* in Keynes's handwriting in the Modern Archive at King's College, Cambridge (KP: Box GTE/3).

[2] Had Keynes discussed Say's Law with anyone, Sraffa would have been the most likely. Keynes and Sraffa were in regular contact during the latter half of 1932, as Keynes's letters to Bonar make clear. Sraffa would have had at least some knowledge of the issues surrounding Say's Law due to his researches into Ricardo, and he was therefore in a position to provide guidance to Keynes.

activity is due to demand deficiency. In fact, he wrote to Hobson immediately after the publication of the *General Theory* to say: 'I am ashamed how blind I was for many years to your essential contention as to the insufficiency of effective demand' (*CW* XXIX: 211, the letter is dated 14 February 1936).

Keynes also mentioned two other contemporary authors in his 'brave army of heretics': Silvio Gesell and Major Douglas. Keynes provided brief descriptions of their works, but they are unlikely to have provided the same kind of guidance as did Hobson. And, although not mentioned in the *General Theory* itself, Keynes was acquainted with the writings of two other authors who were identified with the under-consumption school during the 1930s, namely the American authors, Foster and Catchings. They had been discussed in the *Treatise* (*CW* V: 160) and were referred to in an early draft of the *General Theory* (*CW* XXIX: 82n).

UNDOCUMENTED INFLUENCES

There are, however, two additional writers whose influence on Keynes is worthy of note. These are the authors Fred Taylor and Harlan McCracken. Both wrote at some length on Say's Law. The influence of Taylor is more speculative and may have been indirect, but in the case of McCracken it is virtually certain that Keynes read what he had written and that those writings had an enormous influence on the *General Theory*.

Fred Taylor

In the literature on the *General Theory*, Fred Taylor[3] has not been previously cited as having influenced the development of Keynes's thought. Keynes never mentions Taylor in any of his writings nor were they associates. Yet there is a possible relationship between Keynes and Taylor which merits investigation, and that is their common interest in Say's Law. The possibility of a direct influence of Taylor on Keynes arises not just because of the similarity of their analysis, but also from the likelihood that it was Taylor who coined the term 'Say's Law' in the first place.[4]

Taylor's first recorded use of the phrase 'Say's Law' is found in a 1909 article on 'teaching elementary economics' published in the *Journal of Political Economy*. There he provided an utterly orthodox definition of the law of markets but referred to it as 'Say's Law'. The following single sentence comprised his entire discussion:

---

[3] Fred Taylor (1855–1932) was Professor of Economics at the University of Michigan (1894–1929). He is mostly remembered today for his reply to Mises on the practicability of socialism (Lange and Taylor [1938] 1964).

[4] There has been virtually no discussion on the origins of this term. Thweatt (1979: 80), for example, appears to assume the form of words originated with Keynes.

We set forth in definite form and with ample illustration *what I call Say's Law*; that is, the principle that products constitute at once the demand for goods and the supply of goods, and so, if we assume production to be directed in accord with individual wants, supply and demand must necessarily be equal. (Taylor 1909: 691, italics added)

Taylor had thus used the term 'Say's Law' to refer to the underlying conception of the law of markets at least as far back as 1909 and obviously had been using it as a teaching device for some time before that. That Taylor believed that he had coined the term is shown where he wrote that this conception is 'what I call Say's Law'.[5]

An article on undergraduate pedagogical techniques is hardly likely to have been the point of origin for the more general use of this term amongst economists. The source would almost certainly have been Taylor's introductory textbook, *Principles of Economics*, first published in 1921, in which his discussion of Say's Law plays a very significant role. Chapter XV is entitled 'Say's Law' and deals with a certain set of arguments which, Taylor writes, 'we shall designate Say's Law' (Taylor [1921] 1925: 196). He then commences his discussion of a series of economic propositions, prefacing his final conclusion with these words:

I shall therefore put the proposition we have discussed in the form of a principle. This principle, *I have taken the liberty to designate Say's Law*; because, though recognized by many earlier writers, it was particularly well brought out in the presentation of Say (1803). (Ibid.: 201)

Here, too, Taylor shows that he believed that, in using the words 'Say's Law', he was introducing a new term into the literature of economic theory.

Taylor, for the largest part of his discussion, takes an utterly orthodox position. As one of the general demand fallacies which he enumerates, he includes 'the fears of those who periodically prophesy universal overproduction – a universal glut' (ibid.: 197). In classical fashion, he argued that 'demand [is] coincident with product' (ibid.: 199). In saying this, he made the standard classical proviso, that producers must be 'producing something demanded and producing that something in the proper proportions to other goods produced' (ibid.). Taylor made the point

---

[5] Taylor also indicated that in regard to Say's Law his 'special aim [was] to restore to an important place in economic instruction certain elementary principles, almost truisms, on which the early economists laid much stress, but which have latterly fallen into the background' (Taylor 1909: 690–91). This observation was expanded upon in answer to a question on the readings used in his course: 'At present the readings largely consist of rather inaccessible materials on matters which are commonly neglected in current economic texts.... [There is a reading] from Say, discussing and explaining the principle that demand must in the end coincide with product' (Taylor 1909: 722). Taylor recognised both the crucial importance of the law of markets and the way that it had virtually disappeared from the forefront of economic discourse but without it having been discarded. It was precisely because the law of markets had fallen into the background in the way Taylor described that Keynes was able to overturn Say's Law without anyone noticing what had taken place.

that demand is constituted by supply by stating that 'the demand made by all society for market goods of all kinds can include nothing but goods which the same society has produced and offered on the market' (ibid.: 200). Moreover, demand 'must be as great as product' so long as 'producers have directed their production in true accord with one another's wants' (ibid.). Taylor emphasised that the goods produced must consist of what others wish to buy and that they must be produced in the proper proportions to each other:

> A particular product comes to constitute a part of the total demand for goods only in so far as it is a product for which there is a corresponding demand.... This implies, it should be noted, that the product in question is demanded in the proportion in which it is produced – when we produce a thing we do not add to demand in proportion to the volume for our product unless we are maintaining the proper proportion between our products and other products. (Ibid.: 201)

Taylor then enunciates the principle which he had 'taken the liberty to designate Say's Law':

> **Principle** - Say's Law. The Ultimate Identity of Demand and Product.
> In the last analysis, the demand for goods produced for the market consists of goods produced for the market, i.e., the same goods are at once the demand for goods and the supply of goods; so that, if we can assume that producers have directed production in true accord with one another's wants, total demand must in the long run coincide with the total product or output of goods produced for the market. (Ibid.: 201–2)

Following J.S. Mill ([1874] 1974b: 70), Taylor then draws attention to the separation in time between sale for money and the subsequent purchase of other goods using the money receipts. This separation permits the sale of one's own goods without the immediate purchase of another set of goods:

> Every exchange of product for product is broken into two parts – (1) exchanging one's own product for money or bank credits, and (2) exchanging the money or bank credits thus obtained for the product of the other man. Obviously, an interval of time can be put between these two operations; and, as a matter of fact, such an interval, short or long, almost always intervenes.
> It follows from the facts just brought out that it is possible for us to *postpone* for a long period, even indefinitely, the second part of the operation, thus *cutting down for the time being the general demand for goods, though we have not cut down the amount of production.* (Taylor [1921] 1925: 202)

The most important instance where such a discrepancy between production and demand occurs is during a 'depression which follows a business crisis' (ibid.: 203). This, too, follows Mill's argument, in which a fall in confidence leads to a desire for liquidity and a resulting fall in the demand for goods. Where Taylor takes a position perhaps different from Mill,[6] and at least superficially characteristic of Keynes, is where he supports the use of public expenditure to raise the level of demand during the depression. He argues that:

> If...the public authorities step in and undertake a large program of road-making or building construction or harbor improvements, this will really mean a considerable increase in total demand and so an increase in general prosperity. (Ibid.: 203)

The evidence that Keynes read Taylor's analysis is entirely circumstantial. Taylor was the first to use the term 'Say's Law' to describe what had previously been referred to as 'the law of markets' or the '*théorie des débouchés*'. The phrase must have come to Keynes's attention from somewhere, since he does not suggest he coined the term himself. And, with Keynes's likely interest in deepening his understanding of the concept after his first encounter in Malthus, it is possible that at some stage Keynes became acquainted with Taylor's discussion.

There are also similarities between Keynes and Taylor which are suggestive. The argument presented by Taylor was that Say's Law referred only to the long term, implying, to some extent, that it was irrelevant, or even dangerous, when applied to cyclical activity. Taylor highlighted the fact that the act of purchase and sale was divided into two separate operations, the second of which might occur a long time after the first. There was, therefore, no certainty in the shorter term that everything produced would be bought. Taylor was thus an advocate of public works during depression at least as early as 1921.[7]

On the other hand, Keynes never referred to Taylor in any of his published writings nor in any of his correspondence or drafts. There is thus no direct evidence linking Taylor with Keynes. Taylor also provided a more positive explanation of Say's Law than did Keynes and, more fundamentally, showed that there was no inconsistency between acceptance of Say's Law, recognition of the existence of depression and advocacy of public works. Keynes would thus not have found in Taylor support for his attack on classical economic theory. All things considered, it is unlikely that Keynes would have referred to Taylor's argument in support of his own, but reference to 'Say's Law' in the *General Theory* suggests that he may have read it.

---

[6] But only perhaps. Mill ([1871] 1921: 86) too had argued that unemployment could be reduced if the government were to 'lay on taxes, and employ the amount productively'. Whether Taylor believed that government spending should be deficit financed, as Keynes was to argue, or should be financed through higher taxation is left unstated.

[7] In light of his discussion of Say's Law, it is noteworthy that Taylor ([1921] 1925: iv–v) wrote in the introduction to his text that 'the body of doctrine herein contained is, on the whole, rather markedly orthodox.... I have been at some pains, however, to stress the point that the acceptance of orthodox economic doctrine is entirely compatible with giving support to whatever degree of interference with the working of the present economic order may prove on the whole conducive to the welfare of society'.

Taylor's Possible Influence Through Others

A stronger reason for believing that Keynes had another source for the term 'Say's Law' is that it is unlikely that he would have wanted to identify his own theory with that of someone else which was both similar to his own and also contradicted his own. It is certainly arguable that, had Keynes been aware that Taylor had coined the term 'Say's Law', he might have been reluctant to adopt it or use it in such an off-hand manner. Keynes may therefore have come across the term from elsewhere. Other possible sources may have been Arthur Adams's[8] *Economics of Business Cycles* (1925) or the works of Alvin Hansen.

Within four years of Taylor's coining the term, it seems that Say's Law had gone into general currency. Note the following statement by Adams in 1925:

> Many reputable economists have maintained that there can be no general oversupply of goods. They defend their position upon the proposition, *sometimes referred to as Say's Law*, that demand for goods is always equal to the quantity of goods produced. (Adams 1925: 95, italics added)

Here 'Say's Law' is just a term 'sometimes referred to', so it may be used wherever it applies. Had Keynes come across it in Adams, he would have been less concerned to use the term himself. Moreover, Adams is quite critical of this conception, and applies it in a similar manner to Keynes. Say's Law is, in Adams's view, the proposition that total demand is equal to total supply. It is put in a way which can be read in an aggregative sense:

> The ability to buy is always equal to the ability to sell, the ability to sell is, in general, equal to the cost of production (including profits). (Ibid.: 96)

Adams considered this a fallacy:

> Whatever may be the merits of Say's Law from the long-time point of view, it is undoubtedly fallacious as applied to the everyday business world. (Ibid.)

His intent is to demonstrate that demand can and does fall short of supply, and that this is a frequent cause of depression, thus invalidating Say's Law.

Hansen, who had been Taylor's student, also used the term 'Say's Law', writing that 'there may be a limited market in the sense that there is not a sufficient quantity of money offered by buyers to take the goods off the market at the existing level of prices. Say's law of markets failed to take into account the money economy' (Hansen 1927: 23–4). Hansen then immediately refers to Taylor's discussion, and quotes more than a page from Taylor's *Principles*. No mention is made that Taylor invented the term; the passage is quoted only to corroborate what Hansen is himself writing. Hansen also referred to Say's Law in his *Economic Stabilization in an Unbalanced World* ([1932] 1971: 162).

---

[8] Adams was Dean of the School of Business and Professor of Economics at the University of Oklahoma.

The term 'Say's Law' had thus entered the business cycle literature of the 1920s and 1930s. It is therefore possible that Keynes, in trying to deepen his understanding of what he had first come across in the Malthus–Ricardo correspondence, read either Taylor or other economists who had been influenced by Taylor, and it was this influence which was ultimately reflected in Keynes's use of the term 'Say's Law'.

Harlan McCracken

The one book it is certain that Keynes did consult was Harlan McCracken's *Value Theory and Business Cycles* (1933).[9] In a draft of Chapter 2, Keynes makes the following footnote statement in reference to a discussion of Marx:

> Cf. H.L. McCracken, *Value Theory and Business Cycles*, [New York, 1933] p. 46, where this part of Marx's theory is cited in relation to modern theory. (*CW* XXIX: 81n)

One would not be aware from the title that McCracken's book deals with Malthus, Ricardo and Say's Law. The book is a discussion of the difference between a Malthusian 'commanded value' theory of value and a Ricardian 'embodied theory of value'.[10] From his reading of the correspondence between Ricardo and Malthus, Keynes had established a deeply critical view of Ricardian theory. Reading McCracken would have emphasised to Keynes the continuing effects of the Ricardian influence on contemporary economic theory. McCracken described Ricardo in the following terms:

> *Could there be a General Overproduction?* To this question Ricardo's logic gives an emphatic 'NO!'... According to Ricardo the only source of *demand* for goods consisted of a *supply* of other goods. If everyone had an abundance of *supply*, then exchange would be easy, and society would revel in opulence.... A temporary maladjustment might be conceivable – a temporary shortage of *certain* goods – but never a general overproduction.... Ricardo could not conceive total demand and total supply out of proportion. In fact he took little notice of demand.... **A business cycle positively could not happen in Ricardo's assumed economic world**. (McCracken 1933: 10–11, bold added)

This is a powerfully stated polemic on Ricardian economic theory. The point made is not just that over-production could not occur in the Ricardian world, but that it was theoretically impossible even to generate a business cycle. The flaw in Ricardian economics was its virtual refusal even to acknowledge the demand side

---

[9] Harlan L. McCracken was lecturer in economics at the University of Minnesota at the time he wrote *Value Theory and Business Cycles*. He afterwards taught at Louisiana State University.

[10] Spiegel (1991: 294) notes that 'Smith had offered a number of variants of the labour theory of value, and among these Malthus preferred "labour commanded" as a measure of value, whereas Ricardo emphasised "labour embodied"'.

of the economy and, therefore, to recognise that failure of effective demand held down the level of economic activity. It is this argument, whatever may have been its origins, which provided the *General Theory* with much of its polemical power. McCracken contrasted Ricardo with Malthus in a manner which is today quite familiar, but which was very unusual for the early 1930s:[11]

> Ricardo assumed demand, stating that due to the insatiable nature of human wants, demand was always present when the individual possessed a supply.... Malthus, on the other hand, was careful to point out that such was not the case. Exchange value might decrease even though supply increased, due to a failure in demand. And demand might fail either because of a voluntary failure of demand on the part of the rich who might prefer saving to spending, or from an involuntary failure of demand on the part of the poor who had keen wants but no purchasing power. To create exchange value or increase wealth there must be an increase in effective demand as well as in supply. (Ibid.: 122)

The celebrated passages dealing with the damage done to economic theory by Ricardo's writings (*CW* VII: 32–4) restate McCracken's argument in an even more polemical fashion. Keynes's characterisation of economists as having a Candide-like attitude ought to have been something of a mystery in the face of a well-developed theory of the cycle which had existed since at least the middle of the nineteenth century, and which had reached a new pitch of interest during the Great Depression. Even if it had been true that Ricardo himself was little interested in the business cycle, this could not have been said of the economists who followed him. What Keynes appears to have done is to apply McCracken's judgement on Ricardo to the whole of the economics profession of his time. At the very start of the *General Theory*, Keynes specifies that he is opposed to the entire classical theory based, as he saw it, on Ricardian economics:

> 'The classical economists' was a name invented by Marx to cover Ricardo and James Mill and their *predecessors*, that is to say for the founders of the theory which culminated in the Ricardian economics. I have become accustomed, perhaps perpetrating a solecism, to include in 'the classical school' the *followers* of Ricardo, those, that is to say, who adopted and perfected the theory of the Ricardian economics, including (for example) J.S. Mill, Marshall, Edgeworth and Prof. Pigou. (*CW* VII: 3n)

The implication is that the flaws, as they existed in contemporary economic theory, were due to acceptance of a theoretical structure which began with Ricardo. The mere fact that Malthus had disputed Say's Law with Ricardo would not, of itself, have led to the conclusion that economists more than a century later

---

[11] In a later work, McCracken (1961: 26) points out 'that when *Value Theory and Business Cycles*...was published in 1933...one of the reviewers wrote that he had read a great deal about the Malthusian theory of population, but had never heard of his principles of political economy'.

were still following in a Ricardian tradition. It is here suggested that this conception may have come from Keynes's reading of McCracken.

There is another feature of McCracken which has its echo in the *General Theory*. It is that the very term 'classical' was used by McCracken in referring to the Ricardian tradition. In his discussion of Aftalion's attack on the law of markets, McCracken, on a number of occasions, contrasts Aftalion's theory with 'classical' predecessors. Note the following passages from McCracken (1933):

> Aftalion next directs his attention to the classic doctrine that goods exchange against goods. (146)

> Then Aftalion trains his argumentative artillery upon the last defense of the Ricardian Classicists, who are not yet ready to capitulate and grant the possibility of a crisis from general overproduction. (147)

> Just as the old classical economics pointed to market values fluctuating about normal values determined by cost of production, so the modern economics show how prices at the moment depend upon final utility but gravitate towards a point of equilibrium as determined by marginal cost. (150)

It was Keynes's use of the term 'classical' to characterise his contemporaries (especially Pigou) which added to the polemical force of the *General Theory*.[12] McCracken would also have alerted Keynes to the significance of providing a refutation of the law of markets. In a footnote dealing with Aftalion, McCracken emphasised how revolutionary such a refutation would be:

> If Aftalion has succeeded in establishing the possibility of a voluntary failure of demand by those who have purchasing power but insufficient keenness of desire when facing expanded production under the influence of the principle of diminishing utility, then it constitutes one of the greatest contributions to economic theory in a generation. Say's *Law of Markets*, according to which production financed consumption and supply generated adequate demand is in serious need of modification. (Ibid.: 149n)

To achieve 'one of the greatest contributions to economic theory in a generation' would have been a powerful incentive to Keynes. That he felt that he was about to achieve exactly that is shown in his famous letter to George Bernard Shaw (*CW* XIII: 492–3).

It is perhaps also noteworthy that McCracken uses the phrase 'Say's Law of Markets'. It is possible that the reason Keynes uses the term Say's Law in so

---

[12] Sowell (1972: 211) wrote that 'the "classical" economist was an interesting expository device, which undoubtedly sped the acceptance of Keynesian analysis as an intellectually revolutionary doctrine'. Similarly, Meek ([1951] 1967a: 180) wrote that 'no better word than "classical" could possibly have been discovered – given Keynes's basic purpose – with which to stigmatize his predecessors and to highlight what he regarded as his own essentially new contribution. It immediately focussed attention upon Keynes's rejection of "Say's Law"'.

natural a fashion is that he had come across it in the midst of his reading of McCracken.[13] Keynes may merely have truncated the phrase for brevity.

Lastly, Keynes would have been sympathetic to McCracken because of the manner in which McCracken had treated Keynes's previous writings. In an eponymous chapter devoted to discussing Keynes's work, McCracken (1933: 193) described Keynes as 'one of the most outstanding exponents of a managed currency'. And in a passage of extraordinary insight, McCracken, in 1933, opened the chapter with these words:

> Keynes is a true descendant of Malthus with respect to the importance of the 'short-run forces'.... Keynes joins the swelling ranks of those economists who insist that major attention, in the face of business instability, should be given to those short-run forces which Malthus alluded to a century ago. (Ibid.: 193)

This passage is likely to have encouraged Keynes in the direction in which he was already in the process of moving. He had already recognised a kinship with Malthus from his reading of the correspondence. McCracken's comment would have helped solidify these impressions, and assisted Keynes to understand the nature of the conflict between Malthus and Ricardo.

The parallels between McCracken's *Value Theory and Business Cycles* and the *General Theory* are more than coincidence. Keynes read McCracken during the period in which he was writing the early drafts. The reference to McCracken, in fact, occurs just after Keynes's first discussion of Say's Law. There is a page missing from the draft, and in Keynes's *Collected Writings* the last paragraph before the missing page reads:

> The doctrine that supply creates its own demand has dominated classical theory during the century since Ricardo established it. Malthus's powerful arguments against this theory were completely forgotten, partly –
> ...[A page of manuscript is missing at this point] (*CW* XXIX: 81)

This statement, partial though it may be, was fully consistent with the position taken by McCracken. The missing page may have demonstrated an even closer relationship between Keynes and McCracken, but it would not add much to what we can already discern. If one seeks an explanation for Keynes's very harsh criticism of Ricardo, and of those who were his alleged descendants, then McCracken provides that explanation. It is through McCracken that Keynes may have conceived of the notion that his contemporary economists were Candides, attempting to explain the business cycle while always assuming full employment. McCracken provides an important link between Keynes's personal discovery of Say's Law and the attitude that he ultimately took to classical economics. McCracken is likely to have shaped the final polemical style of the *General Theory*, and in this way helped to create the intellectual environment which facilitated the Keynesian Revolution. McCracken, in writing a text on Keynesian

---

[13] McCracken, being himself American, would have taken the term either directly or indirectly from Taylor.

economics twenty-eight years later, recognises just how similar his ideas had been to those of Keynes (McCracken 1961: 27). What McCracken could not have known was that he may have had a significant influence in shaping the way in which Keynes thought about the issues raised in the *General Theory*.

9. The Early Post-*General Theory* Evolution of Say's Law

This chapter deals with the development of the conceptual issues surrounding Say's Law from the *General Theory* to the publication of Becker's and Baumol's classic article in 1952. There were two separate streams in this development. There was, first, the stream which led from the *General Theory*, based on clarifying what was meant by 'supply creates its own demand'. The second stream developed out of a 1942 article by Oskar Lange, 'Say's Law: A Restatement and Criticism'. This led to a controversy which was brought to an end a decade later by Becker and Baumol with the development of the concepts of 'Walras' Law', 'Say's Identity' and 'Say's Equality'. It was not until the beginning of the 1950s that the Keynes and Lange streams began to converge.

Keynes was in some respects quite straightforward about the importance of Say's Law in terms of the structure of the *General Theory*. He devoted several pages in the introductory chapters to dealing with it, stressing that it was a latent acceptance of Say's Law that made classical economists incapable of understanding involuntary unemployment. He made it clear that his book was an attempt to overturn contemporary economic thought, which in his view was based on an acceptance of Ricardian economics, and therefore Say's Law. He raised the question of Say's Law in the conclusion to his *Quarterly Journal of Economics* article in the following year (*CW* XIV: 122–3). He described Say's Law as a fallacy in the introduction to the French edition of the *General Theory* (CW VII: xxxv), and wrote to Abba Lerner to stress the importance of Say's Law in the development of his ideas (*CW* XXIX: 215). In many ways it was not for want of trying that Say's Law itself never became an issue.

For all that, one cannot say that Keynes was as candid as he might have been. He never once used the words which would have alerted contemporary economists to his intent. He did not discuss deficient aggregate demand in terms of the possibility of a 'general glut'. He did not suggest that 'over-production' was a potential problem. His chosen form of words, 'supply creates its own demand', was entirely his own. It was all there and yet it was not. And, as matters turned out, this lack of clarity may have been one of the most important elements in permitting the *General Theory* to gain acceptance, since the discussion turned on the detail rather than the broad conception. Whatever else the debate following the publication of the *General Theory* was, it was not a rerun of the general glut debates of a century before. No one took up the issue as to whether failure of effective demand could occur. That it could was accepted from the very start by all, both by those who agreed with Keynes and by those who opposed him. The validity of the law of markets did not at any stage become an issue and the Keynesian Revolution occurred without anyone even noticing what had taken place.

THE KEYNESIAN STREAM: 'SUPPLY CREATES ITS OWN DEMAND'

The *General Theory,* while clearly intended as an attack on Say's Law, started no debate on Say's Law. While an enormous controversy surrounded the *General Theory* itself, that controversy, at least that part of it carried out in English, was notable for the absence of any discussion of Say's Law. No reviewer discussed it. No commentator at the time remarked on the relationship between the *General Theory* and Say's Law. The attack on Say's Law in the *General Theory* was comprehensively ignored.[1]

Possibly the most remarkable of the reviews, with regard to the absence of discussion on Say's Law, was that of Hans Neisser.[2] Neisser had himself published a major article on Say's Law only two years before (1934), in which he was critical of its implications. Yet, in his review of the *General Theory*, there is not so much as a passing glance at Say's Law and its role. Hansen is in a similar position. In his review of the *General Theory* (1936) he made no mention of Say's Law, yet he had previously presented his own views on its limitations.

Two references to Say's Law occur in the English language reviews of the *General Theory*. One was in Brian Reddaway's review in the *Economic Record*. In his opening paragraph, Reddaway ([1936] 1964: 99) wrote that 'Mr Keynes attacks one of the fundamental assumptions which has underlain orthodox theory since the days of Ricardo. This is the doctrine which used to be expressed categorically in the phrase "Supply creates its own demand"'. That having been said, there is no further reference to Say's Law. The other reference occurs in Dennis Robertson's discussions of monetary theory. Robertson ([1936] 1983: 101) merely adopts Keynes's distinction between the economics of the *General Theory* and something called classical economics, positing increased entrepreneurial expenditure on the assumption that business people have recently read J.-B. Say. It is nothing more than a touch of humour. These references to Say

---

[1] See Wood (1983, vol. 2), which contains virtually all the most important English language reviews of the *General Theory*. No discussion of Keynes's views on Say's Law is contained in any of them.

[2] Hans Neisser was a refugee to the United States who taught economics at the University of Pennsylvania from 1933 to 1940, when he went to the Graduate School of the New School of Social Research where he remained until he retired in 1970. Schumpeter described him as 'one of the most brilliant economic minds of his generation' (Rutkoff and Scott 1986: 95).

or Say's Law could have been removed without the slightest disturbance to their line of argument.[3]

The attack on Say's Law was thus a non-controversial part of the Keynesian Revolution.[4] It was non-controversial, in part, because the significance of Say's Law in the *General Theory* went unrecognised. While debate raged over virtually every other aspect of the *General Theory*, Keynes's 'supply creates its own demand' slipped by unnoticed, to become the generally accepted definition of the law of markets, just as Say's Law became the standard form of words to refer to it.

It was also uncontroversial because the significance of the law of markets in orthodox economic theory was itself unrecognised. Economists had not been explicitly taught the law of markets since the end of the nineteenth century. Even those who applied the law of markets were often not conscious they were doing so. They were frequently unaware of the tradition which lay behind the judgements they were making. Even where they were aware they were applying the law of markets, they would have been unlikely to say so explicitly.[5] Other than as part of a course in the history of economic thought, by 1936 most economists would never have come across the law of markets and would have felt it to be part of the ancient history of the subject. The early pages in the *General Theory* dealing with Say's Law would, therefore, have been seen as irrelevant to the theoretical issues. But whatever may have been the reason, the plain fact is that none of Keynes's critics based his criticisms on a defence of Say's Law.[6]

Even had it been recognised that Keynes had misunderstood Say's Law, unless the crucial significance of Say's Law were understood, it would have been peculiar to have attempted to attack the *General Theory* by demonstrating that Keynes was wrong in his history of economic theory.[7] Keynes was writing a book

---

[3] Say's Law did receive detailed attention in a review of the *General Theory* in French by Étienne Mantoux ([1937] 1960).

[4] Cf. Kohn (1986: 1191–2) where he wrote: 'Contrary to what one might have expected from reading the first few chapters of the *General Theory*, no "classical" economist stepped forward to debate with Keynes the validity of Say's law. Instead, the debate raged over the instantaneous multiplier, the role of expectations, liquidity preference versus loanable funds, and, in general, over the nature and the validity of Keynes's concept of equilibrium'.

[5] In apologising for previously using 'the Say Law' rather than 'Say's Law', Hutt (1979: 7n) wrote in explanation, 'I think my old teacher Edwin Cannan must have used those words in his teaching. He never mentioned the law in writing, although he often referred to J.B. Say'. It is interesting that even Hutt, who had made a study and defence of the law of markets, was unaware of how great the Keynesian legacy has been.

[6] Even Marget, who wrote two massive volumes attacking Keynes and defending pre-Keynesian economics, did so without serious discussion of Say's Law, mentioning the law of markets only in passing. While he accepted its validity (see [1942] 1966b: 355), in no sense is a defence of Say's Law the basis of his critique of Keynesian economics.

[7] Heckscher's example provides an interesting case study. Keynes had used the first edition of Heckscher's *Mercantilism* to demonstrate the wisdom of much Mercantilist thought (*CW* VII: 340–51). In Heckscher's second edition (1955) an appendix was added

of contemporary significance. To show that he had misunderstood Say's Law would not have affected the perceived validity of Keynes's analysis of how economies actually work. Therefore, while the key to what Keynes was actually saying was right before their eyes, explicitly stated in the opening chapters of his book, no one appreciated just how significant this issue was, and therefore no one took up directly the issue of Say's Law. Had the significance of Say's Law been understood, the course of the debates over the *General Theory* might have taken a very different course.[8]

As it was, at the start of the most widely read economics book of its time was a discussion of Say's Law which went uncontested. Without actually being aware of it, the entire economics profession was being instructed in an entirely new view of the meaning of Say's Law.

CHANGING INTERPRETATIONS OF SAY'S LAW IN HISTORY OF ECONOMICS TEXTS

An appreciation of the change within the economics profession can be gauged from a narrow survey of the discussion of Say's Law in history of economics texts published before and after the publication of the *General Theory*. In 1931, Alexander Gray's *The Development of Economic Doctrine* was published, containing a three-page discussion of the law of markets in which the core ideas were discussed, together with their implications ([1931] 1944: 268–70). This is in a chapter entitled, 'The Classical Tradition: Say, Senior, J.S. Mill and Cairnes'; Say's Law is discussed in isolation from Malthus.

Gray notes that the law of markets was 'long regarded as Say's passport into the company of the immortals' but that it 'perhaps does not come to much' (ibid.: 268). He describes it as the theory 'that goods and services are only superficially bought with money; they are, in fact, bought with other goods and services' (ibid.). He notes that 'it is likewise an integral part of the theory that a product, when created, offers from that very moment a market for other products. General over-production is thus an impossibility' (ibid.: 268–9). The cure for over-production is the production of other goods which will offer an outlet for this excess. Gray's attitude is that Say's Law is valid, but uninteresting. There is no

---

which severely criticises Keynes's interpretation of mercantilist theory. This criticism has had no impact on the development of Keynesian economic theory, nor would one expect it to. A discussion of the history of economic thought is a mere sidelight in a discussion of economic theory.

[8] Sowell (1972: 3) is right and wrong when he writes that there were two great debates over Say's Law, one at the start of the nineteenth century and one following the publication of the *General Theory*. He is right that following the publication of the *General Theory* a debate ensued which was, to its core, about the validity of Say's Law. Where he is wrong is that no one, aside from Keynes, understood the extent to which the validity of Say's Law was the fundamental issue.

suggestion that, in rejecting the possibility of over-production, Say was ruling out the possibility of prolonged recessions and high rates of unemployment.

A further example of the pre-Keynesian attitude to Say's Law was that provided in the influential *History of Economic Doctrines* by Gide and Rist ([1915] 1925). In their view, Say's Law had been overrated in the past, and that what had once appeared as a profound truth was in fact not particularly deep at all. The essence of Say's Law was that goods paid for goods, while money was merely an intermediary in the exchange of one good against another (ibid.: 115). They discuss how Say's Law was used to analyse 'over-production crises' (ibid.) in which there was a fear that a general glut of markets was possible. They recognise that Say, in employing his own law of markets, was perfectly clear that crises could occur, but that they were not due to the existence of over-production (ibid.: 116–17).

Three years after the publication of the *General Theory* a very different perspective on Say's Law is found in Erich Roll's *A History of Economic Thought* (1939). Now it is interpreted to mean that disequilibrium is impossible. In discussing Ricardo, he wrote:

> Having put the causes of economic fluctuations outside the economic system, it is natural that Ricardo should also claim that that system had no inherent tendencies to disequilibrium. In this respect he was accepting the theory which he attributed to the French economist, Jean Baptiste Say, that there could never be any general over-production or glut of capital in a country. (Ibid.: 191)

Most of the discussion of Say's Law comes in the chapter on Malthus, whose differences with Ricardo and Say are the central issue. Roll writes, following Keynes, that Say's Law meant that every product put up for sale 'creates its own demand' (ibid.: 200). If the law is valid, a glut of commodities in general is impossible, as is an excess accumulation of capital (ibid.: 201). The consequence of the refusal to accept that capital accumulation could be excessive was that:

> it buttressed the case for capital accumulation by destroying any objection to it; it denied the possibility of economic dislocations for reasons inherent in the capitalist system, since that system was shown to be self-adjusting. (Ibid.: 203)

Keynes's influence is obvious. For Roll, Say's Law is about supply creating demand. It has shifted from being a valid, though perhaps trivial, concept to being a major impediment to understanding the nature of the capitalist system. It is the basis for *laissez-faire*, underpinning the view that an economy is fundamentally self-adjusting.

Keynes's influence is also evident in Edmund Whittaker's *A History of Economic Ideas,* published in 1940. Whittaker echoes Keynes:

> The answer of Classical economics to the problems of commercial depressions was to be found in Say's *law of markets*, which, in effect, denied their possibility altogether, other than as a temporary or frictional condition. (Whittaker 1940: 705)

Whittaker is somewhat dismayed at what he has himself written, adding later in his discussion that 'it is difficult to believe that the Classical economists shut their eyes to the obvious truth of the trade depression' (ibid.: 713). He is able to believe it in the end by arguing that classical economists were only interested in long-run tendencies.

Lerner (1939)

An early depiction of Say's Law from a Keynesian perspective is provided by Abba Lerner. He had written a review of the *General Theory* for the *International Labour Review* (1936). Prior to publication, Lerner sent Keynes a draft. In his reply, dated 15 June 1936, Keynes wrote: 'there are two points which played a considerable part in my own mental development, which you scarcely touch on. The first of these concerns the breaking away from the assumption in some shape or form of Say's Law' (*CW* XXIX: 215).

In spite of Keynes's comment, Lerner's review contained no mention of Say's Law. In 1939, however, Lerner published an article on 'The Relation of Wage Policies and Price Policies' ([1939] 1951) which, in spite of what the title might have suggested, contained a good deal of material on Say's Law. In doing so, Keynes's influence on the meaning Lerner attaches to Say's Law is clearly evident. Lerner firstly defines Say's Law in the following way:

> Very roughly speaking, Say's Law points out that the demand for the output of any industry (or firm or individual) comes from the supplies of all the other industries (or firms or individuals). This is because these supplies translated into money constitute the demand for the output of the first industry (as well as for each other's output). A general restriction of supply would bring about a general restriction of demand, and, therefore, could not be depended upon to increase prosperity. Total demand is not independent of total supply. (Ibid.: 315)

This is a very sensible definition, and indeed it is this definition which Schumpeter ([1954] 1986: 617) accepts as his own. Demand is constituted by supply through the mediating role of money, and therefore variations in supply will lead to variations in demand. But Lerner then goes on to provide a further definition, which is more consistent with that of the *General Theory*:

> Say's Law is usually found in a more rigid form than the rule given above. It declares not merely interdependence but equality between total supply and total demand. (Lerner [1939] 1951: 316–17)

Yet Lerner has been brought up within the classical tradition and is not fully satisfied, because he goes on to provide examples where, even on this definition, there is value in the concept:

> If this means that the total quantity of each good actually demanded is equal to the total quantity of it that is actually supplied, it is a true but not very useful identity, since the two phrases represent the same quantity of goods that changes hands in a

given period. If it means that a general increase in output in the 'right' proportions will increase total money expenditures by exactly as much as the increase in the selling price of the total output, this is again true, but not much more useful. (Ibid.: 317)

Lerner has to this point claimed that Say's Law is true but of little economic value. On the presentation thus far, there is no reason to see in it a concept which would have led economists always to assume the existence of full employment. Lerner, therefore, begins to move closer to the definition of Say's Law in the *General Theory*:

> Such interpretations of Say's Law in terms of tautological identities will not do. They prevent the law from being used for the purpose for which it was designed. This was to show that although a section of the economy may get into trouble by producing too much relatively to the rest of the economy, a general overproduction is impossible since it creates its own demand. (Ibid.)

Lerner has now dropped the qualification he had noted earlier, where the goods had to be produced in the right proportions, and has adopted the concept of supply creating its own demand. He takes up this Keynesian theme and argues that the sum of the marginal propensity to consume and the marginal propensity to invest are generally less than unity (ibid.: 319), so that the proportion of income saved keeps increasing as the economy expands. This leads to his identifying a further concept underpinning Say's Law, namely that all savings are invested:

> What is really implied in Say's Law is that every individual desire to save is in the nature of a desire to buy a newly manufactured asset.... But in any modern economy where individuals can save and use their savings to demand not only new investment goods but already existing assets, the whole scheme breaks down and – what so many economic theorists still find so surprising – an equilibrium with unemployment is possible where an expansion of output would lead to losses and a return to the previous equilibrium level of employment. (Ibid.)

Thus, from a reasonable definition of Say's Law, Lerner ended up endorsing Keynes's perspective. But what is important about this article is that it is one of the few dealing explicitly with Say's Law written in the first few years after the publication of the *General Theory*. Lerner was undoubtedly led to discuss Say's Law because of the letter he had received from Keynes, but his relatively accurate rendering of the law of markets also suggests that he had undertaken some further research. Be that as it may, Lerner's discussion provided support for the Keynesian definition of Say's Law.

Spengler (1945)

An important and early example of the adoption of Keynes's version of Say's Law occurs in Joseph Spengler's two-part article on 'The Physiocrats and Say's

Law of Markets' in the *Journal of Political Economy* (1945a, 1945b).[9] This article took up fifty pages in what was arguably the most prestigious journal in the United States at the time. Spengler's aim was to demonstrate the relationship between elements of Physiocratic theory and the development of Say's Law as a response to it, but in his discussion he fully adopted the Keynesian version of Say's Law. Spengler (1945a: 193) notes that this 'so-called' law gave a particular direction to economic analysis, 'one unintended outcome of which was Lord Keynes's "general theory"'. In discussing Say's criticisms of the physiocrats, Spengler made it clear that he thought Keynes was right in his judgement of Say and the law of markets:

> Say directed against [the physiocrats] his law of markets, a law which must have been suggested to him by their analysis of circulation and the role of money in a healthy economy. Say, however, unlike the physiocrats, supposed this law to hold under nearly all conditions. His law, despite its inherent defectiveness and its failure to correspond with the facts, gave a direction to economic thought regarding consumption and expenditure out of which the Keynesian theory evolved as a kind of antithesis. (Spengler 1945b: 327)

Spengler's concluding paragraph picks up the notion of the circular flow of output and expenditure, and the possibility of an unemployment equilibrium. These are directly related to Keynesian analysis and Keynes's discussion of Say's Law. In Spengler's view:

> The physiocratic contribution to the formulation of this law was forgotten at a time when it was directed against...[those] who asserted that the circular flow of goods, services, and money is susceptible of interruption. Forgotten too...was the more important discovery...that economic relations are resolvable into a circular flow, whose continuity is contingent upon the presence of certain conditions. To these conditions...the Keynesian analysis drew attention at the same time that it revealed...that an economy may come to rest at a prosperity level, or at a depression level, or at some intermediate level. (Ibid.: 347)

In discussing Turgot, Spengler endorses Keynes's view of the effect on the theory of employment if one accepts Say's Law. Spengler wrote that 'Turgot, in an earlier work, had implicitly denied that unemployment would persist so long as interoccupational movement was possible, thus anticipating Say's law' (ibid.: 319). It is thus clear that Spengler accepts the view that Say's Law guarantees full employment.

Spengler attributed to Say's Law the focus of economic theory on resource allocation rather than the level of activity. In spite of the existence of an enormous literature on the business cycle, he endorsed Keynes's argument that:

---

[9] Spengler was Professor of Economics at Duke University from 1934 to 1972, specialising in population issues and the history of economics.

The nineteenth and early twentieth century writers, in consequence of their subscription to Say's law of markets, practically removed...the level of activity from consideration and concentrated attention upon...resource allocation and pricing. (Ibid.: 345)

In the end Spengler, in spite of his tremendous erudition, merely added his authority to the Keynesian thesis that acceptance of Say's Law meant that economists assumed full employment and left aside considerations of employment and involuntary unemployment. Although he provided a few examples of the actual writings of Say and James Mill, they are only straw men to be knocked down.

The *New Economics* (1947)

Further indication of the extent to which the economics profession had adopted the Keynesian interpretation of Say's Law may be obtained from a survey of the articles in Seymour Harris's *The New Economics*. First published in 1947 and reprinted a number of times, this book contained forty-six articles written by twenty-six authors between 1936 and 1946, and presented 'Keynesian economics, written mainly [though not entirely] by Keynes' followers' (Harris [1947] 1960: 3). Eight different economists refer to Say's Law. All reinforce what had by then become the orthodox interpretation.

Sweezy, for example, stated that Keynes 'was able to demonstrate that his fellow economists, by their unthinking acceptance of Say's Law, were in effect asserting the impossibility of the kind of economic catastrophe through which the world was indubitably passing' (Sweezey [1947] 1960: 106). He made the highly insightful point that 'the Keynesian attacks, though they appear to be directed against a variety of specific theories, all fall to the ground if the validity of Say's Law is assumed' (ibid.: 105).

In another article Samuelson described Say's Law as a 'latent belief...according to which only "frictions" could give rise to unemployment or over-production' (Samuelson [1947] 1960: 147). Metzler specifically adopts 'supply creates its own demand' as the definition of Say's Law, and states that, since this was 'generally accepted, it was difficult to see how producers' expectations, in the aggregate, could be disappointed' (Metzler [1947] 1960: 439).

Haberler's contribution is the most striking, since it is written by someone who could not be described as sympathetic to Keynesian economics. In his article Haberler states that 'apart from policy recommendations, no revolution had taken place; the *General Theory*...[is] not a break or a new beginning in the development of economic theory' (Haberler [1947] 1960: 176). Yet, even as he was making this statement, he was unknowingly reinforcing the very core of what made Keynesian economics revolutionary by including his own attack on Say's Law. Haberler argued that there was nothing theoretically new about Keynesian economics because economists had already abandoned Say's Law long before the *General Theory* was written (ibid.: 175). Haberler accepted all of Keynes's criticisms of Say's Law, and thus we find a critic of Keynesian economics accepting in full Keynes's attack on Say's Law.[10]

Student Guides to the *General Theory*

The impact of the *General Theory*, combined with its difficulty for the undergraduate reader, led to the publication of student guides to make Keynes's theories more accessible. The two most important, by Dudley Dillard (1948) and Alvin Hansen (1953), contained full discussions of Say's Law, adopting in their entirety Keynes's definitions.

Dillard ([1948] 1960: 14) provides an early chapter in which he states that his concern is to provide the reader with 'the classical theory as background and not with what Keynes said it was'. Yet the contours of Keynes's discussion of Say's Law are unmistakable. Dillard wrote a short summary of classical economic theory along Keynesian lines. His discussion of Say's Law was in the form which was to become the generally accepted view amongst economists:

> Acceptance of full employment as the normal condition of an exchange economy is justified in classical economics by the assumption that supply creates its own demand. This assumption or 'principle' is called Say's law of markets, after J.B. Say, an early nineteenth-century French economist who was one of the first to state the 'law' in a dogmatic form....
>
> In an exchange economy, Say's law means there will always be a sufficient rate of spending to maintain full employment. The classical justification of full employment as 'normal' rests on the assumption that income is spent automatically at a rate which will keep all resources employed.... Since saving is just another form of spending, according to the classical theory, all income is spent, partly for consumption goods and partly for investment (producers goods). There is no reason to expect a break in the flow of the income stream and therefore supply creates its own demand. (Ibid.: 18–19)

The Keynesian version of Say's Law as the classical linchpin for *laissez-faire* was presented by Dillard without his apparently recognising that this argument had originated in the *General Theory*.

Hansen's *A Guide to Keynes* (1953) provided a more sophisticated discussion of classical economics and Say's Law. Hansen was himself an historian of economic thought, and, as noted in the previous chapter, had written on Say's Law prior to the publication of the *General Theory*. In his *Business-Cycle Theory: Its Development and Present Status*, published in 1927, he had discussed Say's Law, accepting it as a valid long-run principle, and agreeing that on the question of general gluts, Say, Ricardo and Mill had the better of the argument with Malthus (1927: 19). This did not imply that Hansen fully accepted Say's Law. He saw it failing, firstly, because rapid accumulation would lead to a fall in prices leading to 'price maladjustments' (ibid.: 22) and, secondly, because it

---

[10] Hazlitt's criticisms of Haberler in regard to his treatment of Say's Law are discussed in Chapter 11.

failed to take into account the separation in time between sale and subsequent purchase (ibid.: 23–4). But what he did not do was to suggest that acceptance of Say's Law meant that recession was impossible, or that there was no obstacle to full employment. Nor did he indicate that Say's Law meant that supply creates its own demand, or that it was the fundamental premise of *laissez-faire* economic theory. In fact, when he came to discuss the issue at stake in the general glut debates, Hansen was unequivocal in stating that 'Say, Ricardo and Mill were quite right in their insistence that overproduction is inconceivable' (ibid.: 101).

Thus, by the time he wrote his guide to the *General Theory*, Hansen had a considered view of the classical meaning of Say's Law. And, to some extent, this showed in his first statements on Say's Law:

> Say's law, in a very broad way, is a description of a free-exchange economy. So conceived, it illuminates the truth that the main source of demand is the flow of factor income generated from the process of production itself. (Hansen 1953: 3)

But while seeing merit in Say's Law, he argued that a valid principle can often be used to solve 'highly complex problems for which it is unsuited' (ibid.: 4). Hansen discusses the dissatisfaction with economic theory amongst economists during the period 1900 to 1936. As part of this, Say's Law 'in particular' (ibid.: 6) was subjected to serious questioning. Yet the only specific example Hansen cites was Aftalion, and this, he notes, 'was laughed out of court by reviewers both in England and America' (ibid.: 7).

Hansen states that the 'basic premise' of Say's Law is 'that the price system tended automatically to produce full employment' (ibid.: 6, 14). The acceptance of *laissez-faire* is attributed to the prior acceptance of Say's Law. Any indication that an economist accepted the existence of automatic forces which move an economy out of recession is similarly attributed. Pigou is Hansen's major example of an economist who built his macroeconomic theory on Say's Law. He devotes a number of pages to discussing Pigou's theory of wages to show that it is premised on Say's Law. Yet, Hansen admits, he has no evidence for this. He acknowledges that 'Pigou never specifically mentioned Say's law' (ibid.: 17). For all that, Hansen can confidently state that Pigou's failure to mention Say's Law is due:

> not to any doubts about its fundamental validity, but rather, *it may be inferred*, to the fact that the older formulation of the law...was cast in terms of a society that has largely passed away. (Ibid.: 17, italics added)

Hansen adopted the Keynesian definition of Say's Law. This was in spite of his deeper previous knowledge of the surrounding issues and of pre-Keynesian business cycle theory. As an authority, he was able to transmit this Keynesian version of the flaws in classical economic theory, complete with their assumed basis in Say's Law, to a succeeding generation, which, if it learned anything at all in introductory courses on Keynesian economics, would have learned that Say's

Law was something which economists had once believed but which Keynes had since shown to be fallacious.

Keynes's attack on Say's Law thus slipped by without controversy, and the original conception of the law of markets was replaced by Keynes's 'supply creates its own demand'. While controversy raged over virtually every aspect of the *General Theory*, the central issue raised by Say and Mill – whether demand failure provided a realistic theory of recession – was entirely ignored.

THE SECOND STREAM: WALRAS' LAW, SAY'S IDENTITY AND SAY'S EQUALITY

There was no explicit academic controversy within the journals over Say's Law for the first six years after the publication of the *General Theory*. In 1942, Oskar Lange ([1942] 1970) published an article entitled 'Say's Law: A Restatement and Criticism'. In it Lange set out to provide a rigorous understanding of Say's Law. He, however, does not refer to the *General Theory* to set the stage for his discussion. While Keynes and the *General Theory* are mentioned in passing, no specific connection is made between Lange's discussion of Say's Law and the *General Theory*. It is an article that, to all appearances, could have been written whether the *General Theory* had been published or not.

There are only two references to Keynes and the *General Theory* in the article, and both are in footnotes. The first (ibid.: 155n) occurs six pages into the article and deals with Keynes's distinction between user costs and supplementary costs. Seven pages later, Lange distinguishes the excess supply of primary factors from the Keynesian definition of involuntary unemployment. One would not know from this article that Keynes had ever employed Say's Law in any of his written work, still less that he had devoted his *magnum opus* to its refutation. It is, however, impossible to believe that Lange was not deeply influenced by what Keynes had written in the *General Theory*.

Keynes had defined Say's Law as 'supply creates its own demand', meaning that every addition to supply would be bought: total demand would equal total supply so that there could be no unemployment. It is from this standpoint that Lange also begins. His opening words are: 'Say's law is the proposition that there can be no excess of total supply of commodities (general oversupply) because the total supply of all commodities is *identically* equal to the total demand for all commodities' (ibid.: 149). In other words, everything produced will be sold. To this there is an associated proposition: 'there cannot be such a shortage of total entrepreneurial receipts relative to total entrepreneurial cost as to cause losses throughout the whole economy (general over-production)' (ibid.).

This proposition is a restatement of Keynes's definition of Say's Law – 'aggregate demand price of output as a whole is equivalent to its aggregate supply price for all volumes of output' – and leads to similar conclusions. Both Keynes and Lange agree that recession and unemployment are ruled out by Say's Law because total demand is always equal to total supply.

Lange begins his analysis by isolating what he defines as 'Walras' Law', the proposition that 'total demand and total supply are identically equal' (ibid.: 150). This is true for all *n* commodities; the *nth* commodity being money, this is indeed true by definition. But now Lange moves to consider commodities and money separately. With this distinction between commodities and money in place, Lange notes that the total demand for commodities is equal to the total supply of commodities *only* when the demand for money is equal to the supply of money. So far Lange has done no more than define a series of aggregate relationships.

Lange states that the demand for and supply of money have been defined in a particular sense. The former has been defined as the demand for money in exchange for commodities and the latter has been defined as the supply of money offered in exchange for commodities. Lange now notes that he has been describing a world in which money is never demanded for itself, but only in exchange for commodities. There never exists, in this world, 'a desire to change the total sum of cash balances relative to the quantity of money'. He specifies that the total demand for commodities is equal to the total supply of commodities only in such a state of *monetary equilibrium* (ibid.: 152).

Lange then defines Say's Law as the condition in which 'the total demand for commodities (exclusive of money) is *identically* equal to their total supply' (ibid.: 153). That is, Say's Law is the proposition that the demand for commodities is always equal to the supply of commodities. If the total demand for and supply of commodities is always equal, then by definition, the demand for money is always equal to the supply of money. And this is equivalent to the proposition that there is never a desire to change cash balances. From this, Lange asserts:

> Say's law implies a peculiar nature of the demand for money, namely, that the individuals in our system, taken together, are always satisfied with the existing amount of money and never wish to hold either more or less. There is never a desire to change the total cash balances otherwise than to adapt them to changes in the amount of money available. Under these circumstances, purchases of commodities are never financed from cash balances nor do sales of commodities serve to increase cash balances. (Ibid.)

From this Lange infers that money, as a store of value, was ignored by the classical economists. This classical view 'excludes the use of cash balances for financing purchases of commodities' (ibid.).

Lange then states that Say's Law has been associated with the proposition that there can be 'no "universal glut" or "general overproduction"' (ibid.: 154). He defines a universal glut as a condition in which 'all entrepreneurs [are] suffering losses' (ibid.) and notes that classical economists accepted that a partial glut could occur when more was produced than could be sold at cost-covering prices. Over-production could only be partial, 'each partial over-production being accompanied somewhere by a partial under-production somewhere else in the economic system' (ibid.).

Lange draws a series of conclusions from his postulate that Say's Law means that individuals' demand for money is identically equal to the supply of money.

He shows that, if money demand and supply are identically equal, then, for the economy in aggregate, there are $n-2$ independent equations, while the number of equilibrium prices to be determined is $n-1$. 'Thus, when Say's Law holds, the equilibrium prices are indeterminate' (ibid.: 163).

But Lange takes note of the 'peculiar' nature of the demand for money function implied by his version of Say's Law. From this, he asserts:

> Say's Law precludes substitution between money and commodities because it implies that purchases of commodities cannot be financed from cash balances and that cash balances cannot be increased out of the receipts from the sale of commodities. (Ibid.: 164)

The supply and demand functions for commodities alone are therefore homogeneous of degree zero, so that a proportional change in all prices will not affect the relative demand and supply of individual commodities. Therefore, relative prices can be determined, but the price level itself remains indeterminate. Indeed, Lange goes further. He states:

> By precluding the substitution of money for commodities or vice versa, Say's Law constructs a system which is equivalent to a barter economy. Money in such a system is merely a worthless medium of exchange and a standard of value. (Ibid.: 165)

The classical economists had introduced the quantity theory of money to permit them to determine the price level. But Lange shows that the quantity equation is self-contradictory if it is assumed that no one ever wants to alter their holdings of money, since Say's Law then 'implies an indeterminate velocity of circulation $(1/k)$ and the money prices are indeterminate' (ibid.: 167). From this he concludes:

> We have seen that Say's Law precludes any monetary theory. The theory of money must, therefore, start with a rejection of Say's Law. (Ibid.)

Lange thus concluded that an economy in which Say's Law operated applied only to a barter economy. Money had no role other than as a worthless medium of exchange, which was never held for its own sake, and the price level was therefore indeterminate, although relative prices could be determined. An acceptance of Say's Law meant that a coherent monetary theory was logically impossible. This was to be the foundation from which the modern interpretation of Say's Law was to evolve.

Modigliani (1944)

This 'classical dichotomy' was taken up by Franco Modigliani in a 1944 *Econometrica* paper entitled 'Liquidity Preference and the Theory of Interest and Money' ([1944] 1960). This was a landmark paper which did much to forge the neoclassical synthesis between the Keynesian and classical models. It provided a formidable challenge to the Keynesian theoretical model, with Hutt (1960: 397) going so far as to say that the 'article quietly caused more harm to the Keynesian thesis than any other single contribution'.

Modigliani's discussion demonstrates just how separate the two Say's Law streams were. His article is a critique of the economics of Keynes, yet when he comes to discuss Say's Law, his frame of reference is Lange. There is no reference to Keynes's discussion of Say's Law, and there is thus no indication that Modigliani appreciated the significance of Say's Law in the structure of the *General Theory*.

In his article, Modigliani sought to defend classical monetary theory, and in particular the quantity theory of money with its 'traditional dichotomy' between the real and monetary sectors of the economy. But, in doing so, he accepted Lange's definition of Say's Law without reservation: 'Lange's criticism of Say's law cannot be questioned' ([1944] 1960: 160). He repeated Lange's conclusion by accepting that, 'if...Say's law holds, the demand and supply of money are identically equal' (ibid.: 161) and added that 'one of Lange's conclusions, namely that 'Say's law precludes any monetary theory,' is perfectly justified' (ibid.: 162). Modigliani's way round this problem is merely to state that 'the traditional theory of money is not based on Say's law' (ibid.), which not only left Lange's definition of Say's Law unchallenged, but went further by giving it explicit acceptance. Of course, all Modigliani had done was deny the validity of Say's Law in the sense of Lange, and therefore his statement that Say's Law in this sense had not been the basis for monetary theory was perfectly valid. But by failing to challenge Lange's definition, the actual meaning of Say's Law, or to be more precise, the actual meaning of the law of markets, became even more remote.

Patinkin

In 1948 and 1949, Don Patinkin published two articles which dealt with the classical monetary theory of the Walras–Pareto school. Both papers seem to have been written at more or less the same time,[11] although their publication dates are some eight months apart. Both accept Lange's definition of Say's Law as part of an argument intended to demonstrate the inconsistency of classical general equilibrium analysis; Say' Law is, however, only a side issue.

The first of these papers is entitled 'Relative Prices, Say's Law, and the Demand for Money' (1948). It is basically a discussion of the monetary implications of the microeconomic theories of Walras, Pareto and Divisia.[12] Patinkin commences his argument with the statement that:

---

[11] Each of the articles refers to the other, indicating that they were in preparation at the same time.
[12] Divisia (1889–1964) was a French monetary economist and critic of the *General Theory*.

The basic postulate of the classical monetary theory is that people do not derive any utility from holding money, and consequently it does not enter the utility function.... The classical theory deals with money only as a counting unit. There is no treatment of its far more important functions as a medium of exchange or store of value. Furthermore, it will be shown that the Walrasian–Paretian system does not determine absolute prices. (Patinkin 1948: 135)

Following Lange, Patinkin claims that 'in a monetary economy, it is impossible for Say's Law to hold'. He argues that:

If Say's law holds, people will retain the same amount of cash balances regardless of the absolute price level. But if money plays a real role in the economy, then the desire to hold cash must depend to some extent on the price of money (i.e., the absolute price level).... It will be shown that Say's law and the dependence of demand functions on relative prices only are equivalent properties: if one holds, the other must hold; if one does not hold, the other cannot hold. (Ibid.: 136)

In dealing with Say's Law, Patinkin asserts that the proposition that 'the individual will decide (regardless of the price level) to maintain his initial stock of money constant' is equivalent to the assumption of Say's Law (ibid.: 144). But if money enters the utility function, then Say's Law defined in this way cannot hold (ibid.: 151).

In the second of his two articles, Patinkin (1949) dealt with the indeterminacy of the absolute price level in classical economics; that is, with the 'classical dichotomy'. Patinkin opens his article by stating:

Classical economic theory postulates two parallel dichotomies: the real and monetary sectors of the economy on the one hand, and relative and absolute prices on the other. (Ibid.: 1)

Relative prices are determined in the real sector, while absolute prices are determined in the monetary sector. But, as Patinkin points out, decisions in these two sectors cannot be made independently of each other. People can only obtain money by selling goods, so that the demand for money is equivalent to the supply of goods. From this it follows that:

When people determine how much to supply of every good, they simultaneously determine how much money to demand.... [Therefore] if the supply of all goods depends only on relative prices, then, of necessity, the demand for money can depend only on relative prices. Thus absolute prices appear nowhere in the system, and hence obviously cannot be 'determined' by it. (Ibid.)

Patinkin concludes that the 'classical dichotomy is self-contradictory' (ibid.) since the monetary system, according to classical theory, is dependent on both absolute and relative prices. At this point he introduces Say's Law, arguing that it removes a number of contradictions from the classical system but, in doing so, renders the determination of all prices impossible. He explains his reasoning while defining Say's Law in the same way as Lange:

> The meaning of Say's law is that people spend all they receive, regardless of prices. Another way of saying the same thing is that people maintain their money stocks constant regardless of prices. (Ibid.: 2)

If this is what Say's Law means, then:

> prices play no role in the monetary sector; consequently the monetary sector can have no influence on the determination of prices.... The assumption of Say's law renders the system incomplete. (Ibid.)

In 1951, Patinkin replied to three critics of his earlier views, and also discussed an article by Karl Brunner (1951) which appeared in the same issue. Brunner's article was on 'Inconsistency and Indeterminacy in Classical Economics'. In his article, Brunner (ibid.: 162) adopted and employed the Lange–Patinkin definition of Say's Law.

In the second of the articles to which Patinkin replied, Hickman (1950: 9) argued that 'it is quite possible to set up a consistent classical system in which relative prices are determined in the real sector independently of absolute prices in the monetary sector'. With regard to Say's Law itself, Hickman accepted the Lange–Patinkin definition that held Say's Law to mean that the total demand for commodities is identically equal to the total supply. It was noted that 'this condition occurs in any barter economy, in any primitive monetary economy having only a money of account, and in a full monetary economy in which goods are sold only for the purchase of other goods' (ibid.: 18). Thus Say's Law may be consistent with the operation of a full monetary economy, but only where individuals never desire a change in their holdings of money.

Two other shorter notes followed (Leontief 1950; Phipps 1950). Although both were critical of Patinkin's views on classical monetary theory, neither dealt explicitly with Say's Law. Nevertheless, Leontief clearly accepted the Lange–Patinkin definition, since he incorporated the following into his own model:

> Since money does not enter in his utility, i.e., preference, function, an individual according to the classical theory of economic behaviour offers real commodities and services for sale only in order to be able to purchase other real goods and services. (Leontief 1950: 23)

This is Say's Law as described by Lange and Patinkin.

Patinkin's reply to his critics is concerned with the broader issues of classical monetary theory; Say's Law is only a stepping stone along the way. What is important here is that Patinkin specifically notes that he has employed Lange's 1942 definition of Say's Law (Patinkin 1951: 138–9n13; 139n15; 150–51n33). It is notable that, throughout the entire debate, the Lange definition of Say's Law has been accepted without reservation or discussion. Moreover, entirely absent from this subsequent post-Lange debate are references to the writings of classical economists and references to Keynes's statements on Say's Law.

Becker and Baumol (1952)

In 1952, Gary S. Becker and William J. Baumol summed up the previous debate in a landmark article in which specific reference is made to the writings of the classical economists and to Keynes. But the context of the original debate is made clear from the opening sentence:

> Recently a number of economists have shown a revived interest in the monetary theory of the classicists and of the members of the Lausanne School and their successors. (Becker and Baumol 1952: 355)

The unimportance of Keynes and the *General Theory* in generating this debate is unmistakable. Becker and Baumol state that they 'consider the attack on the earlier writers to have been opened by Lange' (ibid.), that is, in 1942, although 'the immediate centre of contention is Patinkin's restatement and refinement of the Lange position' (ibid.), that is, at the end of the 1940s and the start of the 1950s. The views of Keynes are not given even passing mention as a stimulus to the debate.

Of crucial importance, Becker and Baumol deny the validity of the Lange–Patinkin characterisation of classical theory. Their conclusion, stated in the introductory section, is that:

> It will be argued through re-examination of some of the classical writings that most of the group probably never held views like those ascribed to them.... Many of the members of that group, among them some of those specifically accused, have passages in their writings which explicitly contradict the charges against them.... In most cases where the problem was considered *explicitly*, it was analysed in a manner which is at least formally valid. (Ibid.: 355–6)

Becker and Baumol commence by making three distinctions: these are between 'Walras' Law', 'Say's Identity' and 'Say's Equality'. Walras' Law states that the total value of all goods and services demanded (including money) is identically equal to the total value of all goods and services supplied (again including money) (ibid.: 356). Say's Identity is defined in a way equivalent to what Lange and Patinkin refer to as Say's Law. This is the proposition that the total money demand for commodities is identically equal to the money value of the total supply of commodities (ibid.: 356–7). Finally, Say's Equality is defined as the proposition that '"supply will create its own demand", not despite the behaviour of the price level but because of it' (ibid.: 360–61). The process is described by Becker and Baumol as follows:

> An excess supply of goods, obtained by disturbing a market equilibrium situation by a cash reduction, will cause the price level to fall to just that point where the excess

demand for money is eliminated, since the price level will fall so long as and only so long as there is an excess demand for (insufficient supply of) cash. (Ibid.: 361)

Becker and Baumol note that 'the foregoing is, in effect, the reasoning behind the cash balance forms of the quantity theory of money and, incidentally, the Pigou effect' (ibid.). They explicitly accept that Say's Equality is compatible with simultaneous determinacy of both relative prices and the absolute price level. They thus reject the classical dichotomy, at least for this form of Say's Law (ibid.).

It is noteworthy that Becker and Baumol cast the Say's Equality version of Say's Law in terms of Keynes's 'supply creates its own demand'. This is Keynes's definition, but they do not say so. This is a further example of the extent to which the definition found in the *General Theory* had, by the early 1950s, simply become part of the vernacular of economic discourse.

Becker and Baumol then sum up the three 'allegations' made against classical economists by Lange and Patinkin: firstly, that 'cash has no utility on its own' (ibid.: 363); secondly, that 'supplies of and demands for all commodities are homogeneous of degree zero in prices alone and so cannot be affected even momentarily by the quantity of money, and that [classical economists] sought thus to dichotomise the pricing process' (ibid.); and thirdly, that 'by Say's Law [classical economists] meant Say's Identity, which states that the *supply of commodities will create its own demand* irrespective of the behaviour of the stock of cash and the price level' (ibid.: 364, italics added).

Becker and Baumol then demonstrate, through reference to the writings of classical economists, that none of these propositions is true. It is significant that, in denying the validity of the third proposition, they are also denying the validity of the Keynesian proposition, 'supply creates its own demand'. Indeed, as they demonstrate, variations in the behaviour of the stock of cash and of the price level mean that, in the real world of classical theory, supply will not necessarily create its own demand at all.

In regard to the first allegation against classical theory, Becker and Baumol show, by quoting from Say, Ricardo, Senior, Jevons, Wicksteed, Marshall, Walras, Pareto and John Stuart Mill, that classical economists clearly understood that cash had an intrinsic value whose utility was greater than zero (ibid.: 364–7).

As to the second allegation, they reject the claim that, in classical theory, the supply of and demand for commodities cannot be affected by changes in the quantity of money (ibid.: 367–71). They cite Pigou and the 'Pigou effect', which dispenses with the allegation that the demand for commodities is unaffected by a fall in the absolute price level. But they go on to deal with the homogeneity allegation in far more detail. Again, a large number of classical economists is cited: Cantillon, Hume, Malthus, Ricardo, McCulloch, Walras, J.S. Mill, Marshall and Wicksell. Becker and Baumol conclude that 'there seems to be considerable ground for doubt about the validity of the attack on the classical system' (ibid.: 370).

Finally, they deal with the third of the allegations, that Say's Law meant Say's Identity (ibid.: 371–5). In looking at the writings of Say, they find his meaning to be ambiguous. But, after quoting from McCulloch, Becker and Baumol ask: 'could there be a more forceful rejection of the identity?' (ibid.: 374). And, finally, J.S. Mill is quoted, including the very passage cited by Keynes in the *General Theory*. But reference is then made to 'the clearest statement on the point', in Mill's second essay in his *Unsettled Questions*.[13] About this essay they state:

> It is all there and explicitly – Walras' Law, Say's Identity which Mill points out holds only for a barter economy, the 'utility of money' which consists in permitting purchases to be made when convenient, the possibility of (temporary) oversupply of commodities when money is in excess demand, and Say's Equality which makes this only a temporary possibility. Indeed, in reading it one is led to wonder why so much of the subsequent literature (this paper included) had to be written at all.[14] (Ibid.)

The article was subsequently updated with 'several minor changes' (Baumol 1976: 612). But, in a postscript, the authors state that their basic position remains unchanged:

1. The classics never really concerned themselves in detail with the issues under discussion and were therefore not in error with respect to them....
2. The classical and neoclassical analyses of problems of comparative statics are essentially valid, and the Lange–Patinkin discussion is not directly relevant to them. (Ibid.)

In the view of Becker and Baumol, Lange and Patinkin got it wrong. In reaching this conclusion they do not take the next step and recognise that, in their rejection of the Lange–Patinkin definition of Say's Law, they were also rejecting Keynes's definition. Since Keynes had been trying to show that classical economists had been unable to understand the true nature of unemployment because of their belief in Say's Law, to demonstrate that Keynes had himself not properly understood Say's Law would have put a very different complexion on the nature of Keynes's attack on his predecessors.

Becker and Baumol do, however, refer to Keynes, both by name and, obliquely, through references to 'supply creates its own demand'. Two of these references are noteworthy. The first comes where Becker and Baumol are summing up on the issue of homogeneity:

> Somehow the impression seems to have arisen (and to have gotten into teaching) that this was indeed the nature of the classical system.... Keynes' polemics may have contributed considerably. (Becker and Baumol 1952: 370–71)

Here Becker and Baumol acknowledge that Keynes had an influence on the direction of the debate over classical monetary theory. But Keynes's views in this debate are not treated as a serious attempt to provide a proper understanding of

---

[13] This passage is also quoted in Chapter 4.

[14] Corry (1978: 23), in citing the same passage, comes to exactly the same conclusion.

the issues. His views are seen, rather, as having served a polemical purpose, the effect of which was to misrepresent classical economic thought.

Even more notable, perhaps, is their attempt to capture Say's own definition of Say's Law, which they consider vague and subject to shifting interpretations over time. Say himself, according to Becker and Baumol, confused his own Law with the following 'assertion':

> The second [possible interpretation of Say's Law] is the *almost Keynesian view* that demand will not exist without production since production creates the income with which goods can be bought. (Ibid.: 372, italics added)

Given that Keynes expressly states that he is trying to refute Say's Law, it is deeply interesting that Becker and Baumol should actually suggest that one of the ways Say may have conceived the law which today bears his name happens to coincide with Keynes's view of the nature of demand.[15] Keynes writes his *magnum opus* to refute Say's Law. The *General Theory* is specifically about demand. Becker and Baumol describe as 'almost Keynesian' the view that 'demand will not exist without production since production creates the income with which goods can be bought', which they accept as one of the ways in which Say described Say's Law. Thus, without saying so explicitly, they demonstrate that Keynes may not have refuted Say's Law, as he had supposed, but may have actually adopted it.

The most curious result of the Becker and Baumol paper is that, even as it absolved classical economics of almost all the charges levelled at it by Keynes, Lange and Patinkin, the distinctions they made between Walras' Law, Say's Identity and Say's Equality have entered the economic literature as the correct meaning and interpretation of the classical theory of Say's Law.

Further, even though 'supply creates its own demand' was seen as equivalent to Say's Identity, and even though Say's Identity was recognised as an invalid explanation of the true meaning of Say's Law, none of the criticisms was aimed at Keynes himself. The issue was whether Lange was right, not whether Keynes was. The entire discussion left the issues of the *General Theory* untouched. The debate merely carried the understanding of Say's Law farther and farther away from the meaning the law of markets had held for classical economists.

What had been, only two decades before, one of the central pillars of economic theory had by the early 1950s all but disappeared from the conceptual framework of economics. Classical economic theory was replaced by Keynesian economics, which was premised on the exact antithesis of Say's Law. Economic theory, instead of denying the possibility of deficient aggregate demand, became preoccupied with it. Over-production, in the sense of more being produced than would be bought, became a general concern of economists and policy makers.

---

[15] In a separate work, Baumol (1959: 101n) was even more explicit. In discussing Keynesian income analysis he wrote: 'this view, that production creates the income with which goods can be bought is, incidentally, one of the several somewhat contradictory versions of Say's law, which can be read into Say's writings'.

The central question of economic theory and policy became 'how a market can be created for produce' (Mill [1871] 1921: 562), that is, how to stimulate demand. Say's Law, as an operational concept amongst economists, was stone-cold dead.

10. Modern Interpretations of Say's Law

This chapter deals with academic discussions of the meaning of Say's Law from the publication of Becker's and Baumol's article in the early 1950s through until the discussion in the *New Palgrave* (Eatwell *et al.*: 1987). This chapter will show that while there have been some variations between commentators, in general the interpretation of Say's Law has remained remarkably stable.

FROM THE 1950s TO THE PRESENT

A survey of the literature following Keynes's and Lange's discussions provides a wealth of examples of the interpretations of Say's Law which they helped to create. Moreover, following Becker and Baumol, few of these writers accepted the Keynes–Lange interpretation wholeheartedly. There were, instead, further attempts to return to the original meaning by a reading of the classical literature. Yet, even then, the distorting lens of the Keynes–Lange discussions is clearly evident. Also evident is that after Becker and Baumol, most writers who comment on Say's Law recognise both the Keynesian and Lange streams. And, while there are varying interpretations, only very occasionally is it suggested that there are implications for modern macroeconomic theory should Say's Law be valid.

Schumpeter (1954)

Schumpeter's discussion in his posthumously published *History of Economic Analysis* provides one of the first examples of the interweaving of the Keynes and Lange versions of Say's Law (but not Becker and Baumol, as Schumpeter had died in 1950). He draws on both streams for his discussion, yet accepts neither as valid. Schumpeter's exposition is noteworthy, not only for indicating (as did Becker and Baumol) that much of the modern interpretation of Say's Law is wrong, but for making the unusually favourable judgement that 'Say's Law is obviously true.... It is neither trivial nor unimportant' (Schumpeter [1954] 1986: 617). Schumpeter interprets Say's fundamental meaning as follows:

Aggregate demand and aggregate supply are not independent of each other, because the component demands 'for the output of any industry (or firm or individual) comes from the supplies of all the other industries (or firms or individuals)'[1] and therefore will in most cases increase (in real terms) if these supplies increase and decrease if these supplies decrease. (Ibid.)

The demand curve for any individual product is derived from the incomes earned from the supply of all other products. Schumpeter notes that there are a number of important implications, among these being the impossibility of a 'general glut'. He states that Say's Law 'avers correctly that crises can never be *causally explained* solely by everybody's having produced too much' (ibid.: 618). Indeed, in his discussion of the business cycle, he wrote:

> So far as the subject of crises is concerned, the main merit of [Say's] law was a negative one. Say showed successfully that, however large the phenomenon of overproduction may loom in the historical picture of individual crises, no causal explanation can be derived from it: there is no sense in saying that there is a crisis *because* 'too much' has been produced all round. Though negative, this contribution was very important. It may be said to stand at the fountainhead of the scientific analysis of cycles and to mark the point at which the latter broke away from pre-analytic thought. (Ibid.: 739)

In terms of the modern interpretation, Schumpeter attributes to Say himself 'the battle cry, Supply creates its own Demand', which, adds Schumpeter, 'was made to mean much more than it can possibly mean when properly interpreted' (ibid.: 618). Yet, while attributing Keynes's words to Say, Schumpeter also notes that 'Say's Law is not an identity' (ibid.). The reason it has been so interpreted is, according to Schumpeter, Say's 'blundering exposition' (ibid.). In this regard, Schumpeter was able to write, combining both streams into one:

> Still another interpretation of Say's law as an identity has been adopted by Lord Keynes and will be presented in the more exact form that O. Lange has given to it. (Ibid.: 619)

Schumpeter completely misunderstood the importance of Say's Law to Keynes. Because Schumpeter believed Keynes came upon Malthus after formulating his own theory of effective demand, he wrote that he 'cannot help thinking that Lord Keynes should not have approved of Malthus' every word so sweepingly' (ibid.: 623). Schumpeter wrongly states that 'Keynes, of course, never meant to contradict the proposition that has been called Say's law above' (ibid.). Schumpeter ends up by arguing that, when all is said and done, it would have been best if Keynes had not bothered to mention Say's Law in the first place.[2]

---

[1] Schumpeter's quotation is from Lerner ([1939] 1951: 315).

[2] Schumpeter repeated this at another stage in his discussion. He argued that the proposition which Keynes really meant to object to was that 'competition between firms always *tends* to lead to an expansion of output up to the point of full utilisation of

Of Lange's interpretation, he wrote:

> There is nothing to stop us from developing as a useful exercise in pure theory, the consequences of the hypothesis, Dn ≡ Sn. But it should not be called Say's law, because Say, though he did not consider the problem of hoarding, did consider the problem of increasing the effective quantity of money in case increase in transactions should require it. (Ibid.: 619)

Schumpeter's discussion was written before the publication of the Becker and Baumol article, yet he reinterprets Say's Law in terms of what was later to become known as Say's Equality. Schumpeter's version is styled on Keynes's wording:

> The law asserts that the aggregate demand price of output as a whole is *capable of being equal* to its aggregate supply price for all volumes of total output.[3] (Ibid.: 624)

Schumpeter's discussion provides an interesting synthesis which draws on both Keynes and Lange. He explicitly accepts neither, yet ends up opting for an interpretation entirely consistent with the equilibrium version, now known as Say's Equality. Moreover, while Schumpeter denies the validity of Keynes's interpretation, he attributes Keynes's form of words to Say himself. Thus, even while stating that Say's Law is true and non-trivial, he helped to establish the Keynesian version; and even while denying the validity of Lange's version, he provides support for Say's Equality. Schumpeter's discussion, rather than providing guidance as to the classical meaning of Say's Law, is in fact part of the process of reinterpretation commenced by Keynes and Lange.[4]

Patinkin (1956)

As already discussed, Patinkin was an important influence on the course of the debate following Lange's initial paper which led ultimately to Becker's and Baumol's formulation of the Say's Identity–Say's Equality versions of Say's Law. Yet, in his *Money, Interest and Prices*, first published in 1956, Patinkin (1965: 193) states: 'my sympathies are with those who deny that this identity is a basic component of the classical and neoclassical position', and concedes that 'Say's identity is not a logically necessary component of the classical position' (ibid.: 645). He had, by this stage, obviously been influenced by Becker and Baumol and had largely changed his position. Patinkin agrees there are passages

---

resources' ([1954] 1986: 624). Of this proposition, too, 'it would have been more natural not to object...but to say simply that the operation of Say's law, though it states a tendency correctly, is impeded by certain facts which Keynes believed important enough to be inserted into a theoretical model of his own' (ibid.).

[3] Winch (1987b: 80) provides the same definition.

[4] See Mehta (1978: 17–19) for a criticism of Schumpeter for disregarding what Say actually said in arriving at his own interpretation.

in Say and James Mill from which one might conclude that they had endorsed Say's Identity, but with regard to John Stuart Mill, Patinkin states: 'the standard passage from J.S. Mill which Keynes cites in support of his identity interpretation definitely does *not* carry the meaning that Keynes – and later writers – have attached to it' (ibid.: 646).

Patinkin notes that the term 'Say's Identity' was chosen by Becker and Baumol 'to emphasise that it may not really represent "Say's Law" in its classical and neoclassical meaning' (ibid.: 193n). He believes the evidence that Say's Law referred to secular stagnation is 'convincing' (ibid.: 649), and provides examples showing that classical economists did not dismiss the possibility of recession (ibid.: 648). Indeed, Patinkin goes farther in his criticism of Becker and Baumol, suggesting that Say's Equality does not properly represent the views of classical economists, and that though there are 'hints here and there of an equilibrating mechanism...these are never developed into a systematic theory' (ibid.: 649n). Patinkin states that 'Becker's and Baumol's attempt to give a classical connotation to the concept they call "Say's Equality" can only mislead' (ibid.: 193).

Patinkin begins his introduction with the words: 'Money buys goods, but goods do not buy money' (ibid.: xxiii).[5] This is an apparent rejection of the position taken by Say himself, where he states that a good once produced must then be turned into money before that money is converted back into other goods. In the conceptual world of Say's Law, goods do buy money. Clower ([1967] 1984b: 84n), in fact, described these words as Patinkin's 'nonsensical opening statement'. And in a famous aphorism, Clower wrote, contradicting Patinkin, 'money buys goods and goods buy money; but goods do not buy goods' (ibid.: 86).

Blaug (1958)

In Blaug's text on Ricardian economics is found one of the most sophisticated discussions of the issues which surround Say's Law. Blaug recognises the essence of Say's Law as the proposition that demand failure is not a cause of recession. In discussing Ricardo's views on full employment, he writes:

> Whatever the many interpretations which later came to be attached to Say's Law the essential meaning of the doctrine stands out clearly in Mill's *Commerce Defended*: unlimited industrial expansion is possible without breakdown through barriers set on the side of demand. (Blaug 1958: 65)

This insight must then be supplemented with a recognition that economic breakdown can occur due to barriers set on the supply side. But it is the lack of condescension which sets Blaug apart. At no stage does he dismiss past

---

[5] Cf. Adam Smith ([1776] 1976: I. 459): 'The merchant finds it generally more easy to buy goods with money, than to buy money with goods', which is perhaps Patinkin's message.

economists for being superficial, but in fact casts their views into forms which show genuine depth. Blaug quite correctly notes that even in holding Say's Law, 'there was no attempt to deny the obvious fact of recurring distress and unemployment. The matter in dispute was...not cyclical depression' (ibid.: 92–3).

Blaug also recognises that Say was fully aware that not all savings would be utilised.[6] He does not view this as a contradiction but rather 'as an expression of the long-run tendency of the economy to full employment equilibrium' (ibid.: 90). He interprets the practical message in a way which shows an appreciation of the issues at stake, writing that 'the cure for overproduction is not to encourage wasteful luxury spending but to furnish such conditions as will stimulate the over-all expansion of industry' (ibid.).

Further, Blaug recognises the important issue of the structure of demand in Ricardo's reply to Say when he notes that 'Ricardo objected to the manner in which Say tended to brush aside the problem of the correct composition of output with respect to consumers' demands' (ibid.). Blaug, however, believes that the underlying issue of Say's Law was the possibility of secular stagnation. In using strongly positive wording, very similar to that employed by Schumpeter, he writes:

> Say's Law is neither a truism nor a trivial proposition: it asserts that there are no inherent obstacles in a capitalist economy that would prevent the absorption of a constantly expanding output. (Ibid.: 93)

Blaug is quite explicit on this point. In dealing with 'the outcome of the debate' he notes that some authors 'drew a sharp distinction between business cycles and secular stagnation' (ibid.: 100). John Stuart Mill is his prime example. Blaug recognises that Mill could accept the existence of recession and also simultaneously accept the validity of Say's Law:

> As Mill observed correctly: 'The permanent decline in the circumstances of producers, for want of markets, which those writers contemplate, is a conception to which the nature of a commercial crisis gives no support.' (Ibid.: 101)

Blaug points out that Mill did not contemplate a fall in demand to explain the loss of markets. He takes two quotations from Mill to demonstrate that Mill gave no credence to the speed of capital accumulation or over-production as causes of unsold goods in all markets at once (ibid.: 100). Blaug acknowledges that 'in general, the meaning of Say's Law is preserved' (ibid.) in Mill's discussion of the causes of recession. It is indeed, but to reconcile these propositions Blaug argues that Mill was merely trying to deny the possibility of secular stagnation.

In Mill, as Blaug clearly recognises, there is both an acceptance of Say's Law and an explanation of recession not built on a failure of effective demand. Blaug believes that once classical economists had realised that cyclical downturns could

---

[6] Blaug (1958: 90) quotes Say's criticism of Ricardo, in which Say points out that, even as he writes, 'capitals sleep at the bottom of the coffers of capitalists'.

occur, Say's Law was from then on used merely 'to emphasise the fallacy...that the "unproductive expenditure of the rich" is necessary to prevent stagnation and breakdown' (ibid.: 221). This does not go far enough. The initial insight, that no obstacle exists on the demand side, had unfortunately been lost sight of. Had Blaug appreciated that this was the central issue which Say's Law was intended to demonstrate, he would have seen the consistency that Mill brought to the argument in an entirely different way. Indeed, in discussing Ricardo, he asks rhetorically:

> If Ricardo did not deny the possibility of something like 'cyclical' under-employment of labour and at the same time emphasized the incidence of technological unemployment, what is the meaning of his espousal of Say's Law? (Ibid.: 74)

Ricardo's meaning was that demand deficiency did not cause recession and unemployment, but this still left open the possibility of economic downturns and technological redundancy. Although Blaug recognised many of the critically important implications of Say's Law, he did not tie structural issues into the basic framework. It is the distorting lens of the Becker and Baumol analysis which may have deflected him from grasping the final piece in the puzzle.

Skinner (1967)

Skinner (1967) provides a sophisticated and insightful look at the meaning of Say's Law. Although he says he is attempting to understand Say's Law by using an historian's techniques (ibid.: 153) rather than by accepting the received opinion of his own time, he makes the Keynesian interpretation his point of departure:

> There appears to persist a somewhat hazy (although not entirely inaccurate) notion that the law involves two propositions which are by no means the same, namely, that supply creates demand, and that there must be, at any given point in time, a tendency to full employment equilibrium. (Ibid.)

Although Skinner is right about the distinction he makes, Keynes, in fact, treated the two propositions as theoretically equivalent in that the first implied the second. Nevertheless, it is a reasonable paraphrase of Keynes's depiction of the Law in the *General Theory*. And, after his historical exegesis, Skinner reaches the same conclusion:

> We find the *explicit* assumption that savings once made will be *used,* and the *implicit* assumption that at any given point in time there will be no tendency to contraction in the level of activity. (Ibid.: 157)

Skinner enumerates four rather more concrete conclusions about the nature of Say's Law (ibid.: 162):

1. In a strict sense the Law only states that there is a necessary relationship between the level of production and the level of purchasing power.
2. It was, however, also *assumed* that the level of effective demand would be co-extensive with the level of purchasing power.
3. Therefore, since effective demand would by assumption rise with production, there would be no tendency for a fall in the level of activity.
4. But since it was only an assumption that effective demand would rise with production, it was necessary to recognise that situations might occur in which effective demand did not rise to the same extent as production. The possibility of a fall in the level of activity could occur when effective demand failed to rise along with production.

Although based on an analysis of the original texts, this is a Keynesian reading of the literature. The aggregate level of production is compared with the aggregate level of demand. The third point in particular assumes that that array of goods and services produced matches the array of goods and services that is sought. The difference between the totality of production and demand is conceived only in its aggregated sense rather than as a consequence of disharmony between demand and supply. But, as the fourth point shows, Skinner acknowledges that classical economists accepted the possibility of a fall in the level of economic activity, which Skinner sees only in terms of 'a divergence between the level of purchasing power and the level of effective demand' (ibid.: 163). From his reading of Mill's *Unsettled Questions*, he saw that this could occur as a result of 'the general problem of commercial confidence' (ibid.), or there might be a divergence 'arising from the use of money' (ibid.: 164), or it might arise 'from the fact that money is itself a commodity' (ibid.). But, in Keynesian fashion, the level of demand is seen as the single factor determining the level of activity.

Skinner's is a penetrating analysis which identifies a number of the strands which go into the matrix of arguments collectively known as Say's Law. And although he followed the Keynesian approach, he was capable of seeing that classical economists did not seem to need a theory of over-production to explain the existence of recession and unemployment. Skinner recognised that there were other reasons, aside from a failure of effective demand, which were used to explain why all goods produced might not be purchased. But, in the end, Skinner merely confirmed Keynes's basic conceptions of Say's Law rather than challenging them in any fundamental way.

Sowell (1972)

Thomas Sowell is the modern writer most closely associated with Say's Law. He has written one of only two books devoted to Say's Law since the publication of the *General Theory* (Sowell 1972).[7] He provided the entries in the *New Palgrave* (Eatwell *et al.* 1987) on both J.B. Say and Say's Law and included a long discussion of Say's Law in his *Classical Economics Reconsidered* ([1974] 1994).

---

[7] The other was by Hutt (1974) who is discussed in the next chapter.

While it is a narrow field of interest, Sowell's imprint on the meaning of Say's Law carries an important measure of authority.

In the very first line of his *Say's Law: An Historical Analysis*, Sowell (1972: 3) alerts his reader to his basic frame of reference by defining Say's Law in Keynesian terms as 'the idea that supply creates its own demand'. He states that the basic idea is 'both simple and important' (ibid.: 4). Yet his presentation of the meaning of Say's Law is scattered throughout the chapter, with many separate strands discussed at different times. While on the one hand he seems to have understood more than most the actual arguments of the classical economists with regard to Say's Law, and is perfectly well aware that the modern meaning of Say's Law is a caricature, he nevertheless spends many pages trying to reconcile the modern post-*General Theory* meaning with the classical meaning. This leads him into a series of contradictions, his way out of which is to argue that 'Say's Law has both lost and acquired meanings in the long process of theoretical refinement' (ibid.: 5). Sowell, in the end, treats the modern meaning as just as valid an interpretation as the classical. There is indeed a modern meaning, but this is the interpretation held by those who had never accepted the validity of the law of markets. The only valid meaning is the meaning held by those classical economists who argued on its behalf. And it is this meaning that continuously and frustratingly eludes Sowell.

Sowell explains 'the basic idea behind Say's Law' (ibid.: 4) as the process by which production generates the income with which everything produced can be purchased. More supply meant more income with which to demand. In explaining Say's Law in this way, he not only adopts Keynes's form of words, 'supply creates its own demand', but he also conceives the process in aggregative terms, adopting the Keynesian concept of an aggregate supply price (ibid.).

Sowell argues that there was 'a solid core of propositions on which the whole orthodox tradition was agreed' (ibid.: 12), along with a number of associated concepts which some writers adopted while others did not. There was thus a 'basic practical meaning of Say's Law' which was 'the proposition that there was no secular limit to the expansion of aggregate output' (ibid.: 13). Yet, in saying this, he added that it was not a point of disagreement between Say and Ricardo on the one hand, and Sismondi and Malthus on the other (ibid.), implying that on this interpretation of Say's Law no disagreement existed. Nor, adds Sowell, did they differ over whether there could be partial gluts. Where he says they did differ was over 'whether there could be a *general* glut' (ibid.). And this, in turn, pointed to what Sowell considers the fundamental issue:

> Implicit in this issue is the more basic question, whether there is such a thing as an equilibrium level of aggregate real income. (Ibid.: 13–14)

This issue is 'implicit', never actually stated. Yet, even in arguing that this is what the controversy is about, Sowell also states that 'the concept of an equilibrium national income does not contradict the essential logic of Say's Law' (ibid.: 14). In Sowell's view, this concept of an equilibrium level of income was attacked because 'it was perceived as a threat by the defenders of Say's Law' (ibid.). What was opposed, according to Sowell, was Sismondi's proposition 'that it was possible to have an "above-equilibrium" level of output, even as a temporary phenomenon' (ibid.: 51).

Sowell provides what he sees as the 'key propositions in the classical version of Say's Law' (ibid.: 15) by showing how the concept developed in the classical literature. He begins with Adam Smith, who is credited with providing three important features. These were, firstly, that money merely facilitates exchange without changing the real results (ibid.); secondly, that 'savings are always invested and spent' (ibid.: 17); and, thirdly, that 'saving rather than consumption promotes growth' (ibid.). J.B. Say then added two further points. These were, firstly, that 'a country offers *increased* markets in proportion to its increased output' (ibid.: 19) and, secondly:

> For every case of excess production in the economy, there was simultaneously a corresponding deficiency elsewhere in the economy – and therefore no aggregate overproduction, even temporarily. (Ibid.: 20)

That is, an economy could not produce too much although it might produce the wrong things. To these ideas, James Mill was said to have added two others. The first was that the concept 'output necessarily equals purchasing power was made plainer and more insistent' (ibid.: 23), and the second was that an individual's addition to supply was proportional to the additional demands he wished to make. Therefore, supply and demand were always equal (ibid.). This then led to two conclusions:

> that (1) the disequilibrium implied by an uncleared market cannot *persist*, and that (2) adjustments to equilibrium take place not in aggregate production...but in its internal composition. (Ibid.: 25)

According to Sowell, 'Say and Mill postulated a constancy of aggregate output...even though its internal proportions may vary through miscalculation' (ibid.: 26). Sowell added that 'miscalculations which affect internal proportions can also affect aggregate output' (ibid.: 27), which was a point accepted throughout the classical period. This is, in fact, stated by Sowell in his discussion of Sismondi:

> The classical economists were never guilty of the absurdity sometimes attributed to them of denying the *existence* of depressions, unsold goods, and unemployment, but their *explanation* was not the modern one of deficient aggregate demand, even in the short run. These phenomena were a result of internally disproportionate production (relative to the consumers' preferred mix), not excessive aggregate output, even temporarily. (Ibid.: 51)

Here Sowell sets out the difference between those who supported Say's Law and those who opposed it.[8] It is stated in passing without fanfare. It is one of the

---

[8] He makes the same point in his *Classical Economics Reconsidered* ([1974] 1994: 41).

curiosities of Sowell's work that, while he does not capture the issue of demand deficiency as the fundamental point at issue, he does recognise the different theory of recession to which an acceptance of Say's Law leads.

But what he cannot understand is why Say's Law should have been so large an issue, creating the firestorm of debate which raged for thirty years.[9] Since he is perfectly well aware that classical economists recognised the existence of recession, and also that the question at hand was not the possibility of secular stagnation (ibid.: 5, 64), he is at a loss in understanding what it was they were arguing about. His conclusion is that the issue was the possibility of an equilibrium level of aggregate output (ibid.: 53), a very unsatisfactory answer since he was also well aware that there was no fundamental inconsistency between accepting such a possibility and endorsing Say's Law.[10] Sowell simply did not recognise that the issue was demand deficiency. He understands that classical economists did not use deficient demand as an explanation for recession, and instead employed the concept of disproportionality. But what he does not see is that the very issue underlying Say's Law was the conclusion that demand deficiency is not a valid explanation of recession. And this is so even though he quotes Ricardo, in the midst of this very discussion, saying: 'Men err in their productions, there is no deficiency of demand' (ibid.: 52).

Thus, in summing up what he considers to be the seven major propositions contained in the classical understanding of Say's Law (ibid.: 32–3), Sowell can repeat what he had gleaned from reading Adam Smith, J.B. Say and James Mill, but cannot provide a compelling reason why classical economists should have cared as passionately as they did about these issues.

Sowell then turns to discuss the modern interpretations of Say's Law which he classifies, in the now traditional way, as Walras' Law, Say's Identity and Say's Equality.[11] This modernisation, he wrote, 'produced greater clarity and precision by revealing the essential logic running through the often loose, ambiguous, or even contradictory statements of the classical economists' (ibid.: 5). Sowell, in fact, accepts Say's Identity as the correct interpretation of Say's Law, writing:

> The classical economists *(and their 'general glut' opponents as well)* went beyond Walras' Law to assert Say's Identity, that there is no excess demand for money holdings – and/or that such excess demand for money as may develop in unusual

---

[9] Sowell (1972: 14) argues that the general glut debate commenced with the publication of Sismondi's *Nouveaux Principes* in 1819 and ended with the publication of Mill's *Principles* in 1848. Yet, as discussed in the chapter on Ricardo, no genuine debate began until after the publication of Malthus's *Principles*. Virtually all of the subsequent debate in English, including Say's *Letters to Mr Malthus*, were directed towards Malthus and not Sismondi.

[10] In the very passage he quotes (1972: 53) to show Sismondi's use of equilibrium income, both sides of the general glut debate are shown to accept the existence of an equilibrium. The only difference is the path back to equilibrium, not whether it exists.

[11] In this discussion, Sowell makes no reference either to Lange or to Becker and Baumol.

circumstances is a consequence rather than a cause of disequilibrium. Say's Identity was of course flatly denied by Keynes and the Keynesians. (Ibid.: 37, italics added)

The first point to note is that Sowell states that not only the advocates of Say's Law accepted Say's Identity, but so too did their opponents. There is thus, according to Sowell, no insight into the differences between the sides provided by this concept.[12]

It is also clear that Sowell accepts the Keynes–Lange interpretation of Say's Law – everything produced is bought, and excess demand for money has no effect on economic outcomes. He says this in spite of his having recognised in Ricardo an autonomous role of changes for money and credit in causing recession:

Ricardo recognized that a sharp contraction of money or credit would have 'the most disastrous consequences to the trade and commerce of the country', causing 'much ruin and distress' in the economy. This did not prevent his denying, in the same writing, the possibility of a general glut – which was a different phenomenon, both in his eyes and in the eyes of the general glut theorists. (Ibid.: 31–2)

And finally, though he accepted the Say's Identity interpretation of Say's Law, and argues that this was rejected by Keynes, in the chapter on the Keynesian Revolution Sowell is sharply critical of Keynes's attack on Say's Law:

Say's Law...meant for Keynes not only a coincidence of supply and demand functions but also the automatic maintenance or restoration of full employment. No such doctrine was expressed by the classical economists. (Ibid.: 210)

He added, 'the "classical" economist described in Keynes' *General Theory* was a straw man' (ibid.: 211). The final irony is that Sowell, in a book devoted to Say's Law, seems unable to relate Keynes's attack on it to the actual change in the direction of economic theory or policy which followed the publication of the *General Theory*. No one who had properly understood the nature of Say's Law and the manner in which Keynes overturned the conclusions derived from it – conclusions which had been upheld for more than a century – could have written:

The recognition of Keynes' originality and his role in inaugurating a new era in economic thinking does not depend upon the dubious claim that he contradicted a fallacious orthodoxy with an unprecedented theory. (Ibid.: 214)

Leaving aside the issue of whether the orthodoxy had been 'fallacious', the changes wrought within economic theory by the *General Theory* were the result of Keynes's attack on Say's Law. The orthodoxy had, until 1936, accepted its conclusion that demand deficiency (i.e. over-production or a general glut) would

---

[12] Sowell (1972: 37) also states that 'no economist of the classical or modern period ever denied Say's Equality', so that this concept is also, in his view, of no help in distinguishing the different points of view.

not cause recession. With the publication of the *General Theory*, this settled conclusion was overturned and replaced by the opposite conclusion which Say's Law had originally been devised to deny. Sowell is oblivious to all of this because he does not understand the nature of the debate over the law of markets. Therefore, while he is able to discuss intelligently many of the surrounding issues, and to refute many of the incorrect collateral statements made about Say's Law, he is not able to provide an account of what the Law meant to classical economists or why they considered it as important as they obviously did.

Baumol (1977)

Twenty-five years after the initial appearance of the Becker and Baumol article, Baumol returned to the issue in an important article entitled 'Say's (at Least) Eight Laws, or What Say and James Mill May Really Have Meant' (1977). Baumol had obviously continued to dwell on the issues associated with Say's Law and in this paper attempted to demonstrate that classical economists had had a wider understanding of Say's Law than is captured in the phrase 'supply creates its own demand':

> J.B. Say and his contemporary James Mill...really seem to have had in mind a set of ideas rather more complex than [supply creates its own demand] and, moreover, that the main policy implications they drew from their discussion went well beyond the comforting thought that fears of universal glut are baseless. (Baumol 1977: 145)

However, before launching into his extended meanings of Say's Law, Baumol repeats his definitions of Say's Identity and Say's Equality, about which he states:

> When discussing Say's Law, the literature since Ricardo seems generally to refer to one of two propositions – a strong assertion, which Becker and I have referred to elsewhere as 'Say's Identity', and a weaker variant, which we labelled 'Say's Equality'. (Ibid.: 146)

Baumol seems, on the face of it, to accept that these two interpretations of Say's Law exhaust the field. If it is 'the literature since Ricardo', then it must refer to all of the classical economists since 1817 through to the publication of the *General Theory*.[13] However, Baumol indicates that he wishes to move beyond the

---

[13] In a personal communication on 2 October 1997, Professor Baumol stated that he had not meant to write that it was 'the literature since Ricardo' which had discussed Say's Law in terms of Say's Identity and Say's Equality but rather that it was 'the literature since Keynes'. Thus, in an article in which Professor Baumol had intended to demonstrate that the modern Say's Law is different from the classical law of markets, he instead reinforced the belief that they were one and the same. Seldom can an inadvertent slip have left so wrong an impression on the reader. Substituting Keynes for Ricardo is obviously consistent with the remainder of the article and with Professor Baumol's subsequently stated views (see Baumol 1997).

Say's Identity–Say's Equality definition of Say's Law to show that, while Say's Law means either Say's Identity or Say's Equality, J.B. Say had other 'associated propositions' (ibid.: 146) which he was trying to establish, but these were not themselves what classical economists were trying to argue. His point is that what we call Say's Law today is an entity entirely different from the law of markets. Say's Law is a construct which merely grew out of the controversy which followed Lange's original 1942 paper. It is not to be confused with the law of markets itself. This was made clear in a personal letter dated 1 April 1992 in which Baumol wrote that he accepts neither Say's Identity nor Say's Equality as a correct interpretation of the classical meaning of the law of markets:

> The basic problem arises out of 'Say's identity' and 'Say's equality', both of which I believe, as you do, are a gross distortion of what Say and Mill really had in mind. Both the identity and the equality are figments of the imagination of economists since Keynes who had not studied the earlier works. Thus, when I write to the effect that neither Say nor Mill provided in their writings what today is called 'Say's Law' (note the quotation marks) that is not intended as a criticism of either of them, but as further evidence that they have been misunderstood by modern writers. Thus, when I say that Say does not really get around to anything like 'Say's Law' until his second edition I mean only that the second edition does give us something a bit like 'Say's identity' or 'Say's equality,' but that there is no reason for Say to have done so even then, since neither the identity nor the equality is equivalent to what he meant in the law of markets.

This statement puts an entirely different perspective on the textbook meaning of Say's Law and on Baumol's 1977 paper. Superficially it may appear that Baumol associates the meaning of the law of markets amongst classical economists with what he had termed Say's Equality. At the end of his article, in presenting the eighth and last meaning of Say's Law, he wrote:

> Thus the eighth (and for our purposes the last) of Say's eight propositions is Say's Law itself. Apparently this takes the form of a type of Say's equality, i.e., supply and demand are always equated by a rapid and powerful equilibration mechanism. (Baumol 1977: 159)

This is Say's Law but it is not the law of markets. This is what economists since Keynes have generally meant but it is not what classical economists had meant. It is Say's Identity and Say's Equality which have become the textbook interpretations of the law of markets although, as Baumol himself clearly states, 'both the identity and the equality are figments of the imagination of economists since Keynes who had not studied the earlier works', adding that 'neither the identity nor the equality is equivalent to what [Say] meant in the law of markets'. This was clarified to an even greater extent in a second letter from Baumol in which he wrote:

> All of the writers, Say, Mill, Ricardo, etc., said some things that sound like either 'Say's identity' or 'Say's equality', and mean something related to one or another of

them. However, my test of whether a particular author meant something that is attributed to him or her is the following imaginary experiment: Consider a James Mill brought back to life, and read to him what Keynes attributed to him, and also the Becker–Baumol passages defining the identity or the equality. Give Mill a choice of the following comments (a) 'This is just what I meant.' (b) 'This is certainly not what I meant.' and (c) 'Did I say that? – I'm not even sure I understand what you are talking about.' I am reasonably confident that Mill and the others would not select either (a) or (b) and that they would very likely choose (c). This is in contrast, say, with Marx, who would unambiguously select (b) (with some expletives) if told he believed in 'the iron law of wages', while Dupuit would surely say that modern interpreters have his views on consumer's surplus right. (Personal letter to the author, 19 September 1997)

The unfortunate fact is, however, that it is Becker's and Baumol's Say's Identity and Say's Equality, gross distortions though they are, which have become established as the modern interpretation of the law of markets. Indeed, as Baumol (1972: 369) has himself noted elsewhere, it is Say's Identity which is the form of the law of markets 'found in most modern references'. And what is found there is a straw man caricature of the actual meaning of the law of markets. As Baumol makes clear, it is not what classical economists meant. He was to make this even more apparent in an article which was part of a symposium on Say's Law and which is discussed in the following chapter.

Hollander (1987)

Samuel Hollander deals with Say's Law comprehensively and with great insight in his classic studies of David Ricardo (1979: 67–97, 500–539) and John Stuart Mill (1985: 467–513).[14] These views are summarised in his text on classical economics (1987). And, like others before him, Hollander notes that Keynes misunderstood the implications of Say's Law:

> J.M. Keynes cited Mill to illustrate an extreme 'classical' position on the law of markets. But he did so selectively, failing entirely to note the strong qualifications, and therefore seriously distorted the historical record. (Hollander ibid.: 260)

Hollander discusses Say's Law entirely within the Becker–Baumol framework of Say's Identity and Say's Equality. His main discussion commences in his chapter on 'Money and Banking', and he states from the outset that the law of markets was the 'key classical monetary concept' (ibid.: 241). He conceives Say's Identity in terms of the general unwillingness to hold money for any length of time, which implies that, if there were any money in the system, the price level would, of necessity, be driven up to infinity. Therefore Say's Identity must imply a system of barter exchange and is inconsistent with the quantity theory of money (ibid.: 242). Say's Equality, however, allows for variations in the supply of money to affect the price level, so that 'supply creates its own demand' through

---

[14] See Chapters 3 and 4.

movements in prices (ibid.). The essence of the matter, according to Hollander, is in the community's desire to hold a certain proportion of their command over goods and services in the form of money. A doubling of the money supply would lead to a doubling of the price level but leave relative prices unaffected.

In Hollander's discussion of Say's Law in relation to Say, James Mill, Ricardo and John Stuart Mill, there is no suggestion that demand failure is the issue they are addressing. In this he follows the modern reading of Say's Law. But, as a presentation of the arguments put by classical economists, Hollander's judgements are sound and provide a useful antidote to the usual interpretations. He notices that Say was unconcerned with the effects of capital accumulation, and also recognises that Say was aware that recessions occurred (ibid.: 243). Say appeared to hold the Equality version of Say's Law while James Mill adopted the Identity version (ibid.: 247). With Ricardo, Hollander feels that there is evidence that he held the Identity form of Say's Law, but suggests that the evidence is 'mixed' (ibid.: 248), ultimately opting to place Ricardo in the Say's Equality camp (ibid.: 249). In regard to J.S. Mill, he makes the following observation:

> The law of markets stands sentinel as firmly as ever, if by the term is meant the impossibility of overproduction as such, for *secular* expansion of output can never be checked by lack of purchasing power. On this matter Mill stood shoulder to shoulder with Ricardo. (Ibid.: 258)

Hollander seems to define the central issue of the law of markets as whether demand can be slowed by a lack of purchasing power. Since the existence of the power to buy had not been contested, Hollander finds himself off the track. And with this in mind, it is therefore not surprising that Hollander seems to disassociate the notion of aggregate demand from the issues surrounding Say's Law. The section of the chapter on Say and the law of markets is separated from the section on John Stuart Mill and the law of markets by a section in which Hollander states he must 'digress somewhat' (ibid.: 242). In this digression, Hollander discusses 'Malthus and Aggregate Demand' (ibid.: 250–55). This digression is a discussion of 'effective demand' and contains no explicit reference to Say's Law, indicating that Hollander saw these issues as distinct.

The New Palgrave: Sowell Again (1987)

Thomas Sowell, having written the one major treatise on Say's Law since the publication of the *General Theory*, also wrote the entry on Say's Law in *The New Palgrave Dictionary of Economics* (Sowell 1987). The *Palgrave* entry represents an important first (and often last) acquaintance with Say's Law for many with only a casual interest in the subject. And the definition provided is a confirmation of the Lange–Patinkin version of Say's Law, although with some additional subtlety. The opening sentence of the entry harkens back to Keynes, and also opens the possibility of a variety of valid interpretations:

Say's Law, the apparently simple proposition that supply creates its own demand, has had many different meanings and many sets of reasoning underlying each meaning – not all of those by Jean-Baptiste Say. (Ibid.: 249)

Sowell goes through the historical development of Say's Law during the nineteenth century, relating it to the proposition 'that there was no long-run limit to the growth of output, or to the demand for it' (ibid.: 250). By this stage, Sowell was no longer discussing Say's Law in terms of an equilibrium level of aggregate incomes as he had in his book. He notes the importance attached to the proposition that over-production was an impossibility, although '*short-run* derangement of the economy could take place' (ibid.). Because he fails to recognise the role that Say's Law played in classical business cycle theory, he argues that after John Stuart Mill wrote on Say's Law in the 1840s, and aside from Wicksell's discussion of it in the early twentieth century (see Wicksell [1935] 1967: 159-60), 'Say's Law did not become a major concern again until the appearance of John Maynard Keynes's *General Theory of Employment, Interest and Money* in 1936' (ibid.: 251). Sowell then goes on to endorse the modern interpretation:

Modern, and especially Post-Keynesian[15] discussions of Say's Law have revealed it to be not one, but a number of related propositions. (Ibid.)

Sowell then provides a summary of the related propositions, which are the familiar Walras' Law, Say's Identity and Say's Equality, all defined in the normal way. Sowell finally discusses Say's Law in the context of the Keynesian Revolution. Although the disappearance of Say's Law is of critical importance to the changes in the thinking of economists which occurred in the aftermath of the publication of the *General Theory*, Sowell gives no indication that there is an important relationship between Say's Law and Keynes. He notes only in passing, in one brief paragraph, that Keynes's interpretation of Say's Law was a 'distortion' of the meaning of Say's Law to the classical economists. This is his entire discussion of Keynes's relationship with Say's Law:

The Keynesian revolution not only produced a more sophisticated theory of aggregate equilibrium, but also contributed to the distortion of Say's Law, which Keynes reduced to Say's Identity. According to Keynes, Say's Law 'is equivalent to the proposition that there is no obstacle to full employment'. Only the cruder statements of the Ricardians said that. (Ibid.: 250)

Although Sowell recognises that Keynes seriously misunderstood Say's Law, he sees it as just one of those things, with no relevance to the theories presented in the *General Theory*.

---

15 'Post-Keynesian' is here used in a chronological, not a doctrinal sense.

CONCLUSION

A reasonably coherent understanding of the nature of Say's Law has grown out of the synthesis between the Keynesian stream on the one hand and the Lange stream on the other. The foundation of this synthesis is the further development provided by Becker and Baumol in their classic 1952 article. It is now generally accepted that Keynes's position may be identified with Say's Identity, while the classical meaning is more closely represented by Say's Equality. It is also now generally accepted that Keynes misinterpreted Say's Law, but no wider implications are drawn from this. Certainly, it is seldom suggested that the validity of the arguments raised in the *General Theory* can be questioned on the basis of Keynes's distortion of the meaning of Say's Law.

What is also shown by this discussion is that there is now only a very hazy understanding of why the law of markets was important to classical economists. When Keynes's interpretation was first accepted, the denial of general gluts was taken in the Keynesian way to mean a denial that recessions could ever occur. Over the years, it has become increasingly recognised that classical economists were very much aware of the possibility of recession. J.S. Mill's *Some Unsettled Questions* made it very difficult to accept the Keynesian version of Say's Law. The Say's Identity version was therefore shown to be false, while the Say's Equality version came to be accepted as a reasonable approximation of the classical argument. This version merely stated that recessions, when they occurred, would be brief. Not only did it allow recessions, unemployment and monetary instability to occur, just as classical economists had recognised, but it also provided some explanation for the intensity of the debate which had continued for nearly three decades. This also allowed the version of Say's Law presented in the *General Theory* to appear somewhat more restrictive than the correct explanation, but not fundamentally wrong. What was not recognised was that Say's Law, if properly understood, represented a direct challenge to Keynesian economic theory. Only occasionally were the issues raised by Say, James Mill, Ricardo and J.S. Mill understood and, as the next chapter shows, only very rarely was the significance appreciated. The next chapter deals with those who attempted to show that there was more to the classical position than is generally stated, and that, if Say's Law were correct, then this has implications for economic theory even today.

11. Critics of the Modern Interpretation

While there have been scattered criticisms of the modern interpretation of Say's Law, major critiques are rare. More rare still are indications that a proper understanding of the issues attached to the original meaning of the law of markets is relevant to modern economic theory. This chapter presents the arguments of various economists who have stood outside the generally accepted position.

A RETURN TOWARDS THE LAW OF MARKETS

Clower

The most trenchant, while at the same time lucid, criticism of the standard interpretation of Say's Law is provided in the works of Robert Clower and Axel Leijonhufvud. It may at first appear paradoxical that two writers normally associated with Keynesian analysis should be included amongst the critics of Keynes's position on the fundamental issue of the Keynesian Revolution. Yet it is Clower and Leijonhufvud who have come closest to fostering a revival of Say's Law as the means by which the underlying reality of an economy can best be understood.

Indeed, in turning to the works of Robert Clower, we have come full circle. Keynes's aim was to overturn Say's Law. Clower, in invoking the name of John Maynard Keynes, now interprets Keynes as meaning what classical economists themselves meant.[1] That this is so is seen in Clower's praise for Lavington's *The Trade Cycle* (1922) which, Clower (1989: 26) argues, represents what Keynes was trying to get at. As shown in Chapter 6, Lavington presented a theory of the cycle embedded in Say's Law. Yet, according to Clower, it is Lavington's theory which contains the central message of the *General Theory*! Clower is, of course, right about the acuteness of a theory of the cycle built on Say's Law foundations. He is, however, wrong about this being the message that Keynes wished to

---

[1] It has also been argued that Keynes, rather than denying the validity of Say's Law, might instead have argued its importance (see Kaldor 1989: 75; Macgregor 1949: 111–13).

convey. Therefore, the kinds of statements Clower has made over the years in explaining what Keynes really meant can and should be seen in a very different light. Most famously, Clower wrote ([1962] 1984a: 52): 'Keynes either had a dual-decision hypothesis at the back of his mind, or most of the *General Theory* is theoretical nonsense'. He also added:

> It is another question whether Keynes can reasonably be considered to have had a dual-decision theory of household behaviour at the back of his mind when he wrote the *General Theory*. For my part, I do not think there can be any serious doubt that he did, *although I can find no direct evidence in any of his writings to show that he thought explicitly in these terms*. (Ibid.: 51, italics added)

Clower, rather than properly interpreting Keynes, has instead rediscovered the law of markets. The basic operating principle of Say's Law is that demand is constituted by supply: one makes purchases with the receipts from one's sales. The Clower variant of this process is what he terms 'Say's Principle':

> No transactor consciously *plans* to purchase units of any commodity without at the same time *planning* to finance the purchase either from profit receipts or from the sale units of some other commodity.[2] (Ibid.: 47)

But the essence of the process, in which goods buy goods, is what Clower has in mind. Clower was undoubtedly aware of his parallels with classical economic theory when he wrote:

> *Money buys goods and goods buy money; but goods do not buy goods.*[3] This restriction is – or ought to be – the central theme of the theory of a money economy. (Clower [1967] 1984b: 86)

What Clower ([1962] 1984a: 48) has done is impose an equilibrium condition in which everyone is able to finance all of their planned purchases and then consider the implications when reality differs from expectation. He finds that such miscalculations lead to involuntary under-consumption, which is his counterpart to involuntary unemployment (ibid.: 51). We shall return to Clower after a brief discussion of his most famous student, Axel Leijonhufvud.

Leijonhufvud

Leijonhufvud's *On Keynesian Economics and the Economics of Keynes* (1968) is an attempt to demonstrate that the message of the *General Theory* is different from the presentations found in the standard income–expenditure model (ibid.: 8). It is also written by someone who describes himself as 'partial to Keynes' (ibid.:

---

[2] Leijonhufvud (1969: 34) has elsewhere defined Say's Principle to mean that 'every individual transactor draws up his plan so as to make sources and uses of funds equal'.

[3] Clower ([1967] 1984b: 84n) may have been referring to the opening to Patinkin's *Money, Interest and Prices* which he cites in the same article.

10n) and thus, while critical of many aspects of Keynesian economics (see, for example, ibid.: 33n), sees himself following in a Keynesian tradition. Leijonhufvud interpreted the revolution commenced by Keynes 'as an attack upon the foundation of the received Theory of Markets as a tool for the analysis of short-run problems' (ibid.: 24). The manner in which Leijonhufvud proceeds is to assume that what Keynes meant to say was that quantity adjustment occurred more rapidly during disequilibrium than price adjustment, reversing the typical judgements of classical economists (ibid.: 67).

Leijonhufvud reluctantly accepts Lange's definition of Say's Law because it has entered into the economist's jargon. He nevertheless adds that 'the terminological thicket is a bother' (ibid.: 91). More importantly, he rejects what he calls the standard interpretation of the *General Theory* in which 'Keynes accused the Classical economists of being addicted to Say's Law in the sense of Lange' (ibid.: 100). He rejects this interpretation because:

> However many statements suggestive of the 'invalid dichotomy', etc., may be found in pre-Keynesian writings, it is absurd to suggest that summing over $n-1$ excess demands was an accepted convention 'underlying the whole classical theory'. And, even had this been true, of course, the discoverer of such a monumental blunder could never have argued that the theory 'would collapse without it'. Obviously, elimination of the error could only have strengthened received doctrine. (Ibid.: 101)

This is a devastating criticism of Lange's position, but less of Lange than of Keynes himself. If Keynes and Lange held the same criticism of Say's Law, then the criticism of Lange applies with equal force to Keynes. Therefore, to preserve Keynes's argument, Leijonhufvud argues that Keynes and Lange did not hold the same view. Leijonhufvud includes Say's Law 'in the sense of Lange' as one of a 'motley assortment of outlandish propositions' (ibid.) which he refuses to accept as Keynes's meaning. He is therefore compelled to argue that Keynes's theory was 'obscurely expressed and doubtlessly not all that clear even in his own mind' (ibid.: 102), and claims that he and Clower are able to provide the proper interpretation. The fact remains, however, that if Keynes did mean Say's Law in the sense provided by Lange, then Leijonhufvud, in spite of his best endeavours, has provided one of the most devastating criticisms of Keynes's interpretation of Say's Law.[4]

Clower and Leijonhufvud

But a more important statement than that provided by Leijonhufvud alone is found in a joint paper by Clower and Leijonhufvud which has been published in the collected works of both (see Clower and Leijonhufvud 1973). It originated in a set of class notes handed out by Leijonhufvud which 'have been extensively rewritten and extended' (Clower [1973] 1984c: 145n). The paper is entitled

---

[4] Not that he would think it matters. Leijonhufvud (1969: 19–20) wrote, 'Keynes's all-out attack on Say's Law of Markets turns out to have been as irrelevant as the rest of his critique of the "classical" theory' (see also Clower 1971: 20).

'Say's Principle, What it Means and Doesn't Mean'. The page numbers in Clower (ibid.) will be referred to throughout the following discussion.

Clower's and Leijonhufvud's aim is to deal with the proper meaning of Say's Law and how it has been misinterpreted over the years. They note that 'textbook discussions of SL [Say's Law] are seldom fair to pre-Keynesian writers' and that 'the extensive literature since Keynes...has failed to address squarely the main issues in dispute and so has got bogged down in a mire of conceptual and semantic confusions' (145). But, curiously, at no stage is reference made to Becker and Baumol nor to any of the discussions which preceded their summation. There is no mention of Say's Identity or Say's Equality. What is discussed is 'Say's Principle' (SP), which Clower and Leijonhufvud believe to be of extreme importance to economic thinking:

> This principle, though elementary and outwardly trivial, is crucial for clear understanding of macro-theory. Indeed, there is hardly a single problem in macro-theory (or, for that matter, micro-theory) that can be consistently analyzed without it. (146)

Clower and Leijonhufvud derive what they describe as the 'aggregate version' of Say's Principle: the aggregate excess demand for every good or service sold in every market, including the money market, is zero. This is not just the excess demand for final goods and services, in the modern sense of aggregate demand as it has developed as part of Keynesian economics. This is excess demand for everything bought and sold, including all intermediate goods, which are netted out in Keynesian aggregate analysis.[5] Within this definition, which they term 'the aggregative version of SP', aggregate demand is identically equal to aggregate supply.

From this they note a number of features, one of which is important in its implications. This is that 'no general statement can be made about the sum of the money values of any proper subset of the aggregate EDs' (153). To choose any subset of all of the exchange transactions in an economy (such as the final demand for goods and services taken on their own) means that no assumption can

---

[5] This is set out where they write as follows about Say's Principle (SP): 'In macroeconomics texts, SP (aggregative version) is sometimes said to imply that aggregate demand always equals aggregate supply. If one's definitions of aggregate demand and aggregate supply are, respectively, the summed money value of all commodities in aggregate ED and the summed money value of all commodities in aggregate ES, then, naturally, this is what SP means. (It is not an implication of the Principle, but simply a restatement.) However, the accepted, conventional definitions of aggregate demand and aggregate supply are quite different. The coinage of both terms is associated with the development of Keynesian macroeconomics, and it is the usage within that body of doctrine that must be decisive. In macroeconomics, aggregate demand is defined as the summed value of the demands for all final goods and services; similarly, aggregate supply is defined as the summed value of supplies of all final goods and services' (158).

be made as to the sign or magnitudes involved. This will become important when they discuss modern national income analysis.

With their definition of Say's Principle in place, they turn 'to discuss certain interpretations of SP that appear frequently in the literature' (153). It is important here to appreciate that the authors, from this point in their paper onwards, use their own Say's Principle interchangeably with Say's Law. Although they distinguish their own 'aggregative' principle from the disaggregative principle which they consider to be the essence of the classical meaning of Say's Law (152n), their discussion makes no sense if Say's Principle cannot be used interchangeably with Say's Law. The interpretations they discuss, which 'appear frequently in the literature', are interpretations of Say's Law, since it is, of course, Say's Law which has appeared in the literature, not Say's Principle. Unless it is understood that Clower and Leijonhufvud are discussing Say's Law itself, and not some invention of their own, then it is not possible to understand the critical points they are trying to make.[6]

Their discussion covers a number of areas in which they systematically dispose of the modern myths which have surrounded the classical teachings on Say's Law.

Old familiar phrases

The first of the 'old familiar phrases' they discuss is 'a general glut of commodities is impossible'. They are unequivocal on this; the statement is true (153). A glut means excess supply (or negative excess demand).[7] They write: 'If general glut is interpreted to mean notional ES prevailing for all commodities simultaneously, then such a situation is flatly inconsistent with SP in any of its variants' (153).

The second phrase discussed is 'supply creates its own demand'. They describe this as the 'most ambiguous statement that students of economics are ever asked to ponder' (153). They then discuss four possible interpretations. The first is that the 'supply of a commodity at some price gives rise to an equal demand for the same commodity at that price' (153). The statement is false, but they note, it is a version of Say's Law that has wrongly been attributed to classical economists.

The second interpretation is that 'no one plans to supply anything of value without also planning some use for the proceeds from the sale, which may include simply planning to hold money until a later decision is made to purchase other commodities' (153–4). This they agree would be correct and sensible.

---

[6] Cf. Jonsson (1995: 154n1): 'Clower and Leijonhufvud use the term *Say's principle* for the concept that *ex ante facto* the net value of an individual's trading plan is zero. In the aggregate this suggests that the planned demand for all goods people intend to buy is equal to the planned supply of the things people intend to sell (including money). If we assume that all individuals expect *quid pro quo* in their trades then Say's principle is a logical corollary to the law of vent'.

[7] They explicitly recognise that over-production and demand deficiency are two sides of the same coin: a glut may be seen as excess supply (i.e. over-production) or negative excess demand (i.e. demand deficiency).

The third interpretation is that 'confronted with given prices, each transactor must plan to supply commodities of sufficient value to finance all his planned net demands' (154). They agree this is correct.

The final interpretation they provide is one which they state is false. It is that 'if prices are given, each transactor's planned sales will create the means to finance his planned purchase' (ibid.). The emphasis here is on the individual transactor. Not all transactors find reality living up to how they had imagined it would be.

Without saying so, what they have done is to demonstrate that the interpretations which are false are also not what was meant by the classical economists when they applied Say's Law. In contrast, the two interpretations which they accept as true are consistent with the classical meaning of the law of markets.

General equilibrium

Clower and Leijonhufvud then discuss the equilibrium conditions of a general equilibrium model. The conclusion they reach is that in general equilibrium the sum of all excess demands is identically equal to zero. About this condition they say: 'this fatuous proposition should never be confused with Say's Principle' (156).

They discuss the economic implications where this equilibrium condition is not met, where the aggregate excess demands for two or more commodities are not zero. Moreover, some of the commodities in excess supply may well be labour services. Of this condition, they observe:

It follows that SP is entirely consistent with the existence of large-scale unemployment. SP is also consistent with indefinite persistence of unemployment on a large scale, for it involves no assumptions and yields no implications about the dynamic adjustment behaviour of the economic system. (Ibid.)

They note that to say 'that a general glut is impossible is not an empty statement' (157). This conclusion is an implicit criticism of Keynes. Note how in the following passage the reference to Say's Law is converted to Say's Principle from one sentence to the next:

Quite a few otherwise reputable economists have put in print the proposition that Classical economists were unable to provide a meaningful and useful theory of large-scale unemployment because they believed in Say's Law. This is simply inane: SP, by itself, could not possibly pose a mental block to the development of unemployment theory. On the contrary, correct and systematic application of it is necessary for the construction of a consistent theory of any disequilibrium (or equilibrium) phenomenon. (Ibid.)

They deny any role to Say's Principle in determining the stability conditions of an economy. From this they conclude:

Many pre-Keynesian writers, who simply believed in the existence of general equilibrium, assumed 'flexible prices'; they also assumed or argued that flexible prices would tend to move in such a manner as to reduce aggregate EDs to zero. Some of them may have been unable to conceive of persistent mass unemployment as a realistic possibility; however, it was clearly these sundry beliefs and assumptions – *not* SP – that constituted mental blocks for them. (158)

National income analysis

In this section, Clower and Leijonhufvud discuss the criticism that Say's Law means that aggregate demand equals aggregate supply. In terms of the summed money values of aggregate excess supplies and excess demands, they note that this is precisely what Say's Principle means. But, in modern macroeconomics, aggregate demand refers only to 'the summed value of the demands for all final goods and services' (ibid.). It is thus a subset of all of the transactions which take place within an economy during a period of time. Given the modern definition of aggregate demand and aggregate supply, Clower and Leijonhufvud conclude that the proposition that Say's Principle implies equality between aggregate demand and aggregate supply is untrue.

General deflation

Clower and Leijonhufvud then discuss the situation where the sum of the value of all commodities is in excess supply, and is equal to the excess demand for money:

> This means, on balance, that the entire business sector is under general deflationary pressure. The typical industry will be laying off workers. If there are some industries hiring, they won't hire enough; unemployment will be widespread. (159)

They discuss the policy dilemma posed by a recessionary economy. They note that classical economists were perfectly aware of this class of disequilibria, and that John Stuart Mill 'diagnosed general depressions of trade in precisely these terms' (160). They capture completely the relationship between the classical acceptance of the law of markets and the recognition of the existence and severity of recessions:

> The Classical economists were not unaware of this class of disequilibria or of their seriousness.... Naive *laissez-faire* notions do not figure at all in the theory of economic policy of the British Classical school. Nor was Classical thinking on this subject in any way inhibited by prevailing views about 'Say's Law of Markets'. SP is entirely consistent with confirmed disbelief in the possibility of general gluts and, simultaneously, with clear recognition of the actuality of frequent and prolonged bouts of general deflation. John Stuart Mill's *Principles*, the 'Bible of Economics' during the later Classical period, is the perfect illustration. (Ibid.)

Lange's laws: a restatement and criticism

Clower and Leijonhufvud subject Lange's analysis of Say's Law to detailed and scathing criticism. They point out that Lange reached his conclusion by beginning with a money economy wherein the sum of excess demands is equal to zero. This, they note, is termed 'Walras' Law' by Lange. Lange then removes money and asks the question: what are the implications if we define Say's Law as an equilibrium where the sum of the excess demands of n-1 commodities is identically equal to zero? 'Not very surprisingly, [Lange] discovers that his condition will be satisfied if and only if the ED for money is zero, a state of affairs he calls "monetary equilibrium"' (161). Say's Law is then defined by Lange as a proposition in which Walras' Law and monetary equilibrium both occur in all possible states of a monetary economy. They then make a number of observations about Lange's version of Say's Law (SL) and classical economics:

> Attributing a belief in SL (in his sense) to Classical economists, Lange also argues that pre-Keynesian theories of employment, interest and money are (a) logically false, and (b) economically nonsensical because they rest on the assumption that SL is valid for a monetary economy. In this part of his argument, Lange is guilty not only of repeated sins of verbal sophistry but also of gross historical inaccuracy. As argued earlier, the statement that the summed values of aggregate EDs over a subset of tradable commodities is identically zero involves a most elementary error.[8]
>
> So what remains of Lange's analysis when all is said and done? Our answer is, quite bluntly: nothing of value. Nonetheless, Lange's terminological innovations – including, in particular, the entirely superfluous term Walras' Law – somehow have taken root in macroeconomics; and his associated criticisms of Classical economics are now part of the mythology of the subject. (162–3)

'The mythology of the subject' they are referring to is the modern interpretation of Say's Law. Their aim is to draw attention to Lange's economic errors and distortions of doctrinal history. That they have had limited success is testimony to the entrenched nature of the distortions which have been introduced into economics because of the nature of the Keynes–Lange attack on Say's Law.

Clower and Leijonhufvud have provided an invaluable antidote to the continuous misunderstanding of the meaning and implications of Say's Law. They state that their construct, 'Say's Principle', is of fundamental importance to a proper understanding of the operation of an economy. They also show that what is today understood as Say's Law bears little relation to its original meaning. Yet they do not achieve their end since they invent the concept Say's Principle and use it in place of Say's Law. In their initial discussion of the formal derivation of Say's Principle, this is acceptable since they are attempting to clarify issues. But when they turn to the historical record, they refuse to state unequivocally what they clearly imply, that modern criticisms of Say's Law are wrong because Say's Principle is true. Continuous use of their term 'Say's Principle', where Say's Law would have sharpened their meaning, makes their criticisms less effective than they might have been.

Moreover, their paper is, in the end, no more than an attempt to show that classical economists did not believe the absurd notions that economists since the

---

[8] In a footnote, Clower and Leijonhufvud add: 'As far as we know, no major Classical economist has ever been shown to commit this error outright' (163).

publication of the *General Theory* have attributed to them. It shows that an acceptance of Say's Law did not prevent economists from having sensible views on the deep-seated and prolonged nature of recessions. They show that the modern textbook versions of Say's Law are largely mythology. But what they do not do is explain the implications for economic theory and policy if Say's Law is valid.[9] Their article makes it appear that the importance of Say's Law is that it is an *n*-commodity version of the income constraint provided by a budget line in the basic two-good model. While they are excellent at explaining what Say's Law did not mean, they fail to indicate why classical economists held it in such high regard, and certainly there is no indication why acceptance of the validity of Say's Law is fundamentally inconsistent with Keynesian economic theory.

Anderson, von Mises, Hazlitt

Attempts to undermine the validity of Keynesian economics by attacking Keynes's interpretation of Say's Law are extremely rare, and none occurred in the crucial first years after publication of the *General Theory*. Indeed, the first such attempt may not have occurred until 1949. In a digression in his work on the financial history of the United States, Benjamin M. Anderson[10] included a discussion of Keynes in which he focused on Keynes's attack on Say's Law. As will be discussed below, Anderson is likely to have been the inspiration for subsequent criticisms of Keynes on Say's Law by Ludwig von Mises and Henry Hazlitt. Their criticisms should therefore be seen as related rather than independent. It was Anderson, however, who presented the deepest argument, and, although flawed in his interpretation of Keynes, Anderson understood the essence of Say's Law and its significance in classical theory.

Keynes, Anderson ([1949] 1979: 384) wrote, was 'the leading advocate of the purchasing power doctrine' which is that 'purchasing power must be kept above production if production is to expand' (ibid.: 383). In contrast to the Keynesian view:

> The prevailing view among economists, on the other hand, has long been that purchasing power grows out of production. The great producing countries are the great consuming countries.... Supply and demand in the aggregate are thus not merely equal, but they are identical, since every commodity may be looked upon either as supply of its own kind or as demand for other things. But this doctrine is subject to the great qualification that the proportions must be right; that there must be equilibrium. (Ibid.)

---

[9] Coddington (1983: 33) points out that there is nothing in the Clower approach which would explain how an economy gets into disequilibrium in the first place.

[10] Benjamin Anderson (1886–1949) served as Assistant Professor at Harvard from 1914 to 1918 when he became economist for the National Bank of Commerce in New York. In 1920 he was made Chief Economist for the Chase National Bank. He returned to academia in 1939, becoming Professor of Economics at UCLA, where he remained until his death.

Anderson notes that disequilibrium generally follows an economic upturn and therefore periods of active trade are almost inevitably followed by periods of contraction and readjustment. There is thus no implication that Say's Law means downturns are impossible or that unemployment cannot in principle occur.

With regard to Anderson a number of points may be made. Firstly, Keynes never argued that purchasing power needed to keep ahead of production. The issue was whether purchasing power would be employed. Thus, however accurately Anderson may have captured the meaning of Say's Law, this fundamental mistake in interpreting Keynes's meaning would have reduced the impact of his arguments. Secondly, Anderson used the Keynesian form of words, 'supply creates its own demand', no less than five times in three pages (ibid.: 384–6). Thus, even while attempting to deny the validity of Keynes's interpretation of Say's Law, he was inadvertently reinforcing it. For all that, Anderson understood quite clearly that the flaw in the *General Theory*, from a classical perspective, lay in a proper understanding of Say's Law. He fully understood that from the Say's Law perspective, demand is supply. Recessions are not due to too little demand, but are a consequence of disharmonies in demand and supply. Anderson's discussion of Keynes is thus one of the very few which highlight the importance of Say's Law in classical theory and which show an appreciation of the difference to economic theory and policy that a proper understanding of Say's Law makes.

In the introduction to his book, Anderson had acknowledged the help he had received from Dr Ludwig von Mises 'who had been good enough to give a critical reading to...[the] "Digression on Keynes"' (ibid.: 15) which is the chapter in which Anderson dealt with Say's Law. A year later, and almost certainly due to the influence of Anderson, Mises ([1950] 1980a) himself wrote a brief article on Say's Law attacking the Keynesian interpretation.[11] Mises recognised that Say's Law does not represent a denial of the possibility of recession and unemployment, but denied only one particular explanation of recession. As he states, 'attempts to explain the general depression of trade by referring to an allegedly general over-production are...fallacious' (ibid.: 65). That is, recessions do occur but general overproduction does not. Mises further noted that, following the general glut debates, 'during the whole of the rest of the nineteenth century, the acknowledgement of the truth contained in Say's Law was the distinctive mark of an economist' (ibid.: 67). He added that 'Keynes did not refute Say's Law' (ibid.: 70).

Mises captures essential aspects of Say's Law, but does not see it as having a particularly significant role in pre-Keynesian economic theory. One would not appreciate the critical importance of Say's Law in classical economics from what Mises wrote. In the article, he was too concerned with the issue of sound money to see Say's Law as much more than just background. He saw Say's Law as serving a negative purpose in exposing certain fallacies. Indeed, he wrote that

---

[11] In the same collection of essays is an article on Benjamin Anderson (Mises [1950] 1980b: 94–107). Although the article contains no discussion of Say's Law, it is clear from it that Mises held Anderson in high regard.

Say's Law 'was not an integral part of the new science of economics as taught by the Classical economists' (ibid.: 64). Much as he was an opponent of Keynesian economics, Mises did not think of Say's Law as an important battleground for his differences with Keynes.

This attitude is more strongly shown by Henry Hazlitt in his *The Failure of the 'New Economics'* (1959).[12] Hazlitt took his position from Anderson[13] and Mises, whom he quotes extensively. Following Mises, Hazlitt wrote: 'Say's Law was not originally designed as an integral part of classical economics...but as a refutation of a fallacy' (ibid.: 32–3). He accepted, following Anderson, the validity of the phrase 'supply creates its own demand' (ibid.: 35). And when he summed up his argument, he stated that 'Say's Law was **merely** the denial of the possibility of a *general* overproduction' (ibid.: 36, bold added), hardly a form of words one would use to demonstrate the importance of an argument. Hazlitt does, however, make a number of important points seldom found elsewhere. He states that:

No important economist, to my knowledge, ever made the absurd assumption (of which Keynes by implication accuses the whole classical school) that thanks to Say's Law depressions and unemployment were impossible, and that everything produced would automatically find a ready market at a profitable price. (Ibid.: 35)

He added that 'Keynes "refuted" Say's Law only in a sense in which no important economist ever held it' (ibid.: 42).

Hazlitt is also scathing about Haberler's rejection of Say's Law (discussed in Chapter 9). He notes that Haberler makes use of a truncated quotation from Ricardo (see Haberler [1947] 1960: 173), about which he writes:

Now the meaning of Ricardo's formulation of Say's Law is already quite clear, particularly when it is given in full. It does not require any exegesis by Haberler or anyone else and certainly no paraphrase that quite changes its meaning. Not only did Ricardo never explicitly assert the proposition that Haberler attributes to him; there is every reason to suppose that he would have repudiated it. (Hazlitt 1959: 40)

So, where Haberler had argued that there is 'no place and need for Say's Law in modern economic theory' ([1947] 1960: 174), Hazlitt can reply 'there is still need and place to assert Say's Law whenever anybody is foolish enough to deny it' (Hazlitt 1959: 41).

In the end, given how important Say's Law was to Keynes and to a proper understanding of the structure of the *General Theory*, the attempts by Anderson, Mises and Hazlitt to undermine the Keynesian interpretation of Say's Law lacked penetration. Partly through their misunderstanding of the *General Theory*, and

---

[12] Henry Hazlitt was an economic journalist whose career began on the *Wall Street Journal* in 1913. He joined the *New York Times* in 1934 where he wrote most of the financial and business editorials. From 1946 to 1966 he wrote the 'Business Tides' column for *Newsweek*. He was a relentless critic of Keynes and the *General Theory*.

[13] Hazlitt included part of Anderson's discussion of Keynes in his *The Critics of Keynesian Economics* (1960).

partly through their misunderstanding of the role of Say's Law in classical economics, they never really came to grips with the issues which were thrown up by the Keynesian Revolution.

W.H. Hutt

W.H. Hutt's *A Rehabilitation of Say's Law* (1974) is the only full-scale post-*General Theory* defence of the law of markets in the economic literature. While there has been some controversy over whether Keynes accurately portrayed Say's Law, and over the role and importance of Say's Law in classical and Keynesian economics, no one, other than Hutt, has attempted to return Say's Law to the mainstream of economic discourse. Hutt is unequivocal in his views:

> In defending the pre-Keynesian 'classical economists,' and 'Say's law', I shall insist that this law dominated the prevailing orthodoxy of the 1930s so naturally that it was seldom if ever stated explicitly and (prior to the 'Keynesian revolution') virtually never challenged.... I shall suggest that, fairly interpreted, 'Say's law of markets' survives as the most fundamental 'economic law' in all economic theory. It enunciates the principle that 'demands in general' *are* 'supplies in general' – different aspects of one phenomenon. (ibid.: 2–3)

Moreover, in a statement very similar to the statement made by Clower and Leijonhufvud, he wrote:

> A grasp of [Say's Law] is indispensable for an understanding of the true genesis of depression and of prosperity without inflation; that attempts at dynamic treatment of the economic system which ignore it are worthless. (Ibid.: 5)

Blaug (1985: 178) captures just how unique Hutt is in his survey of the literature on Say's Law by singling him out as presenting the most outrageous possible position:

> If the reader is now persuaded that he understands the meaning of Say's Law, at least in modern terms, he should take a look at W.H. Hutt...[who] argues that Say's Law is true then and now and, paradox of paradoxes, that it offers a complete and satisfactory explanation of the inherent tendency to depression in modern industrial society!

For all that, Hutt has a firm grasp of the classical meaning of Say's Law and of its implications. He recognises that it is a statement of the fundamental nature of demand which is constituted by supply. Demand in a Say's Law world is understood as embedded in supply. This is how Hutt first explains the meaning of Say's Law, in rejecting Keynes's 'supply creates its own demand':

> But the supply of plums does not create the demand for plums. And the word 'creates' is injudicious. What the law really asserts is that the supply of plums *constitutes* demand for whatever the supplier is destined to acquire in exchange for

the plums under barter, or with the money proceeds in a money economy. (Hutt 1974: 3)

In other words, the sales revenue from selling plums constitutes the demand for apples and oranges. Hutt explains Say's Law more formally as follows:

The *source of demand* for any particular input or output produced is the flow of inputs and outputs of all the things which do not compete with it; for some part of that flow is destined to be exchanged for it. (Ibid.: 5–6)

Hutt, for all his awareness of the issues, does a poor job of getting his message across. Even for a sympathetic reader, it is a testing exercise to follow his meaning.[14] Yet once the code is cracked, Hutt's meaning is reasonably straightforward.[15] Hutt is trying to explain the dynamics of an exchange economy where individuals have a reserve price for the goods and services they offer for sale. If they have miscalculated in their production decisions, so that the goods and services they have produced cannot be sold at prices they had originally expected, there is a general reluctance to sell. The miscalculation in production decisions, together with the refusal of producers to sell what they have produced for what they can realise in the marketplace, leads to a consequent fall in income. This reduction in the income stream is perpetuated so long as this refusal to sell continues.[16] Since one makes purchases with the receipts from one's sales, that is, since under Say's Law demand is constituted by supply, the refusal to sell leads to a fall in demand throughout the economic system as sales expectations are not realised. Recessions are thus fully consistent with Say's Law, and are, in fact, entirely explicable, in an internally consistent manner, by Say's Law.[17] The way out of recession is then to permit the price realignments to run their course as stocks are liquidated at prices below those which were expected when production

---

[14] See, for example, Horwood (1990: 271–2), Samuels (1990: 4) and Skousen (1992: 25) for discussions of Hutt's difficult writing style.

[15] The remainder of this paragraph is a paraphrase of pages 8–9 of his *Rehabilitation of Say's Law* which contain the essence of his argument.

[16] In a discussion of 'search behaviour and consumption demand', which is strikingly similar to Hutt's analysis of Say's Law, Leijonhufvud (1969: 31) remarks that 'I would like to make retribution for the worst sin of omission that I have so far found myself guilty of: Professor W.H. Hutt's *The Theory of Idle Resources*...ought to have been my *locus classicus* in this connection'. Leijonhufvud has found a kindred spirit, but is apparently unaware of what that similarity of viewpoint is based on. Cf. Rothbard (1992: 196), who writes of Clower and Leijonhufvud that they maintain 'absurdly...that [Keynes] was a prophet of the idea that search costs were highly important in the labour market'. This is, in fact, the argument presented by Hutt, which is itself based on Say's Law.

[17] Cf. Jonsson (1995: 149): 'Say fully recognized how coordination failures, even those created by productivity increases due to technical innovation...could lead to epidemic gluts'.

occurred.[18] It is instructive to compare Hutt with Ricardo, who also saw in the refusal to sell the prolongation of recession and unemployment:

> The duration of the intervals between marked changes are often much longer than is generally supposed.... The unwillingness that every man feels to sell his goods at a reduced price, induces him to borrow at high interest and to have recourse to other shifts to postpone the necessity of selling. The effect is however certain at last, but the duration of the resistance depends on the degree of information, or the strength of the prejudices of those who offer it, and therefore it cannot be the subject of any thing like accurate calculation. (Ricardo 1951–73: VII. 67).

It is, however, disappointing that Hutt, having recognised that Say's Law had dominated the economic orthodoxy of the 1930s, then fails to demonstrate this. His references to pre-Keynesian economists are to Say and James Mill, with only minor references to others. He does not embed Say's Law in the general conceptual apparatus of all economic thinking from the time of Say to the publication of the *General Theory*. It would have been a telling point had he been able to show, chapter and verse, how Say's Law had been integrated into the economic theories of pre-Keynesian writers. His failure to do so leaves his argument without sufficient documentary support.

Curiously, even while understanding the critical issue of Say's Law as a fundamental flaw in Keynesian economics, Hutt consistently pushed it into the background. In his *Keynesianism: Retrospect and Prospect* (1963), it is not until Chapter XVII (commencing on page 387) that he actually turns to deal with Say's Law. He then states, as the first point of his chapter summary, that 'the principal thesis of *The General Theory* falls or stands according to the validity or otherwise of the Say Law which, it can be shown, Keynes never understood' (ibid.: 387). For a book which is intended as a critique of Keynesian economics, one would have thought a point as fundamental as this ought to have been placed in a more prominent position. Even worse, when he then came to update *Keynesianism*, the revised edition, entitled *The Keynesian Episode* (1979), was substantially rewritten. Amongst the changes made was the omission of the entire chapter on

---

[18] Hutt explains all this in a shockingly convoluted way which makes access to his meaning exceedingly difficult. The key statement on the process of withholding almost certainly requires a prior grasp of what he is saying to make sense of it: 'If Say's Law holds, then any unemployment of *valuable* (i.e., potentially demanded) factors of production must be due to the supply of their services being *withheld*. And if supplies of non-competing productive services, which in the aggregate form *the source of* demands for *particular factors*, such as (say) for those used to make footwear, are being withheld, then the incentive may be enhanced to withhold also from production some part of the labor and assets which produce footwear. Such withholdings, *whether initiatory or induced*, may occur (i) through the direct holding off of potentially demanded supplies from the market, or (ii) (the same thing in practice) through *the price asked* being (a) higher than potential purchasers of the product *can afford* out of uninflated capital and income, or (b) higher than *they regard as profitable*, or (c) (a special case of [b]) higher than is consistent with *the cost and price expectations* of the community as a whole or with their predictions of the future of the market rate of interest' (1974: 8).

Say's Law. He explained this (ibid.: 7) as due to his having recently written a better explanation of Say's Law in his *Rehabilitation of Say's Law*. One can only wonder at this judgement. If the point is as crucial to a critique of Keynesian economics as Hutt indicated, then to omit the one chapter dealing with it is extremely odd.

In the final analysis, Hutt's critique of Keynesian economics, and his insight into the essential nature of Say's Law, misfires. Its exposition is too obscure and eccentric. He does not outline Say's Law as it was outlined by those who first developed and then defended it. He recognises that Say's Law had been an important part of economic theory right up to the publication of the *General Theory*, but then does not back this up with evidence. However right he may or may not have been in many of his insights, he would have made few converts. His critique of Keynesian economics, and defence of Say's Law, has ultimately sunk without trace.

SYMPOSIUM ON SAY'S LAW

In 1995, the *Eastern Economic Journal* published an article by Petur Jonsson, 'On the Economics of Say and Keynes' Interpretation of Say's Law' (Jonsson 1995). Jonsson's argument was that Say had not only had a theory of recession but that this theory was in its essentials the modern theory of recession based on co-ordination failure. Jonsson, however, went beyond this observation to write that Say not only did not deny the possibility of gluts, but '[went] on to attribute such gluts to a failure of effective demand' (ibid.: 148). John Stuart Mill, too, was deemed by Jonsson to have accepted the possibility of deficient aggregate demand during recession (ibid.: 153). This led to an exchange of correspondence with the *Journal* editor which led to the decision to conduct a symposium on Say's Law within the pages of the *EEJ*.[19] The symposium was published in the journal's Spring 1997 issue.

The participants were the present author, Petur Jonsson, William Baumol and Mark Blaug. Although each started from a different premise there was a remarkable degree of agreement over the major issues involved. Most significant was the manner in which the symposium cleared away large parts of the mythology which has surrounded Say's Law since the publication of the *General Theory*. It showed that what is today referred to as Say's Law is fundamentally different from the classical meaning associated with the law of markets. All of the participants agreed that Keynes misstated the actual meaning of the law of markets in classical theory and left behind, as Blaug (1997: 231) put it: 'hopeless confusion about the history of economic thought'. It was jointly agreed that whatever else the law of markets may or may not have meant, it did not mean that

---

[19] Enormous credit is due to the editor of the *Eastern Economic Journal*, Professor Hal Hochman, for recognising the significance of the issues at stake and for fostering the symposium and allowing it to take place within the *EEJ*. The present discussion is an edited version of the symposium summary (see Kates 1997a).

recessions and involuntary unemployment are impossible. What was made clear was that classical economists understood perfectly well that prolonged recessions and involuntary unemployment are a fact of economic life. If nothing else, the symposium showed that Keynes was wrong in his interpretation of Say's Law and, more importantly, that he was wrong about its economic implications. Say's Law did not rule out the possibility of recession and unemployment.

But if Say's Law did not rule out recession and unemployment, then what did it do? Here too there was general agreement. Each participant in his own way demonstrated that what the law of markets did was deny the possibility of demand deficiency or over-production. Each participant pointed out that the law of markets permitted recessions to occur for any number of other reasons while ruling out only one potential generative cause: demand deficiency or over-production. This was succinctly stated by Baumol:

> It is clear that [classical economists] did not use the Law of Markets to deny the occurrence of unemployment, and that the notion of a theory of unemployment would have been anathema to them only if it were based on a model requiring the occurrence of a universal glut of commodities. (Baumol 1997: 227)

This should not, of course, be taken to mean that Baumol endorsed the classical view, only that this is how he interpreted one part of what he believes classical economists meant when invoking the law of markets. Baumol's position is a further extension of his earlier view that the law of markets meant a good deal more to classical economists than just Say's Identity or Say's Equality.[20] The only theory of recession ruled out by the law of markets was exactly the one to emerge from the Keynesian Revolution, but it is this theory which has dominated macroeconomics ever since.

Blaug put the matter somewhat differently. To him the issue at hand was: 'could the capitalist system absorb the constant increases in productive capacity without breakdown from limits inherent in the system?'. That is, were there any demand-side limits to the rate of growth? As he recognised, classical economists denied that any such limits existed but by putting the issue in terms of secular stagnation their focus was more long term in nature. Blaug, however, also argued that the classics were right to deny the possibility of demand deficiency in their own time. What was good policy at the start of the nineteenth century, when capital shortage was the central problem in creating growth, would not be an appropriate basis for policy today.

Finally, Jonsson noted that classical economists did not have a theory of the cycle based on a Keynesian aggregate demand function but instead explained the

---

[20] There is far more to Baumol's paper than is provided by this summary. The paper is titled 'J.B. Say on Unemployment and Public Works' and contains a discussion of the attitudes of the early classical economists to unemployment and public policy in the context of their full acceptance of Say's Law. This paper marks Baumol's third foray since 1952 into the issues surrounding Say's Law. His three papers should be read together to appreciate both the depth of his analysis and the direction in which his own interpretation has progressed.

genesis of recessions in terms of co-ordination failures. As he showed, the cause of recession in classical theory was not deficient demand but was structural in nature. Classical theories of recession were 'quite different from those grounded in notions of inherent limits to the willingness to consume' (Jonsson 1997: 206).

In concluding the symposium, the emphasis was placed on the contemporary importance of this debate:

> In closing, I do not wish to overemphasise the level of agreement or pretend there is agreement in areas where none exists. Nor do I wish to suggest that the four papers presented represent the full range of views on Say's Law. As Baumol has shown, the meaning and validity of Say's Law has been a focus for discussion for more than two centuries. There is likely to be no last chapter in this ongoing debate. But as the symposium has also shown, the issues are of immense importance. How one answers the questions raised by Say's Law will make the largest imaginable difference to the theories accepted by economists and to the policies eventually adopted by governments to deal with recession and unemployment. The issues raised thus cannot become any more important than that. (Kates 1997a: 238–9)

SUMMING UP

To the extent that there is informed opinion on the law of markets, it can be said that the general conclusion is that Keynes failed to convey what classical economists had meant. Most of those who have looked into the matter have concluded that Keynes did not properly understand the law of markets. There has therefore been some effort made to put the matter right and there is a relatively large literature on what Say's Law really meant. But there has been little recognition that the law of markets, if properly interpreted, is valid and has something important to contribute to modern economics.

As things stand, since the publication of the *General Theory*, only Anderson in 1949 and Hutt in 1974 have attempted to demonstrate the enduring importance of Say's Law. Hutt has been the more important of the two, but even his *A Rehabilitation of Say's Law* went absolutely nowhere in raising the slightest interest in the classical meaning of the law of markets.

Clower and Leijonhufvud, although nominally Keynesian, have attempted to bring their own version of Say's Law into mainstream discourse. They have introduced a concept they term 'Say's Principle' which is their surrogate for the law of markets. They have argued that the standard interpretation of Keynes, if an accurate reflection of what he meant, is theoretical nonsense. Their preference has been to argue that Keynes was right and that it is the standard interpretation that is wrong. The irony is, however, that the very theory they have attributed to Keynes is based on Say's Law, which the *General Theory* was written to refute.

To point out that pre-Keynesian economists had a theory of recession does not demonstrate that their theory of the cycle is valid. To show that the law of markets denied the possibility of demand deficiency does not prove that demand deficiency cannot happen. But what it does do is show, firstly, that the history of economic theory, to the extent that it accepts Keynes's allegations against his predecessors, is wrong. Pre-Keynesian economists did have a theory of recession and this theory made deep sense of the world as it actually exists. It explained why recessions occur and it provided policy guidance. And this theory of recession was based on the law of markets.

But what is infinitely more important is that it highlights Keynes's most enduring legacy. To this day, macroeconomics is based on fluctuations in demand. It is a theory which classical economists denied with a consistency rarely seen in economic discourse. By the time John Stuart Mill came to write his *Principles* in 1848 the question had been utterly resolved, and it remained resolved for the succeeding ninety years. As Mill wrote in regard to the validity of the law of markets:

> The point is fundamental; any difference of opinion in it involves radically different conceptions of Political Economy, especially in its practical aspect. On the one view, we have only to consider how a sufficient production may be combined with the best possible distribution; but, on the other, there is a third thing to be considered – how a market can be created for produce, or how production can be limited to the capabilities of the market. (Mill [1871] 1921: 562)

And as noted in Chapter 2 on Mill, this passage continues with a statement on the consequences for economic theory if one adds demand deficiency to its concerns:

> A theory so essentially self-contradictory cannot intrude itself without carrying confusion into the very heart of the subject, and making it impossible even to conceive with any distinctness many of the more complicated economical workings of society. (Ibid.)

Mill was not writing about the *General Theory*, but could have been. The conclusion he reached was accepted by every economist of consequence through until the 1930s: demand deficiency does not cause recession and to believe otherwise will fatally cloud the judgement of any economist who believes that it does. Across the great divide of the Keynesian Revolution economists have lost touch with what was once regarded as amongst the most important economic principles ever developed. As this chapter has shown, there have been some who have seen what pre-Keynesian economists were trying to say, but they have been very few in number and they have been very far between.

12. Conclusion

This has been the story of the evolution of a concept. It first emerged during the latter half of the eighteenth century, but was not fully formulated until the beginning of the nineteenth. The essential meaning of the concept was that demand failure and over-production are not valid explanations for recession. Recessions are instead caused by structural disharmonies between independent economic agents. And, reduced to its bare essentials, the same theory was provided by Say and James Mill in the first decade of the nineteenth century as by business cycle theorists in the 1930s. Virtually every mainstream economist during the intervening period took the same view.

With the publication of Keynes's *General Theory* in 1936 the law of markets disappeared. As was made absolutely clear at the start of the *General Theory*, Keynes specifically set out to refute what he referred to as Say's Law. His objective was to demonstrate that failure of effective demand is the single most important cause of recession and unemployment. In this he was wildly successful. Within a decade, demand failure was the almost universally accepted explanation for fluctuations in economic activity. As to the law of markets, not only its message but even its meaning disappeared from economic discourse. There was a rapid reconstruction of what the law of markets was supposed to have meant by those who did not accept it as a valid economic principle. Through the writings of Keynes in 1936, Lange in 1942 and Becker and Baumol in 1952, a generally accepted meaning of Say's Law emerged, a meaning far different from the concept recognised and accepted by classical economists.

Under this modern interpretation, the Keynesian 'supply creates its own demand' became associated with Say's Identity while, in the more sophisticated versions, and following the lead of Becker and Baumol, the classical meaning of Say's Law was usually identified with Say's Equality. The Lange interpretation of Say's Law was integrated into monetary theory, and was used as the key example of the superiority of the New Economics of Keynes in comparison with the classical theory it had replaced. In more penetrating discussions, reference tended to be made both to the Keynesian 'supply creates its own demand' and to Say's Identity/Equality. And while there was often recognition that Say's Law contained elements of truth, such as an appreciation of the circular flow of income, it was seen as irrelevant to a more sophisticated understanding of the operation of a modern economy, if not actually false.

215

In essence, the themes which became bundled under the heading of Say's Law were these. Firstly, and of fundamental importance, it was argued that Say's Law implied the assumption of full employment, or at the very least, a rapid return to full employment if recession struck. Secondly, discussions of Say's Law were conducted under three headings: Walras' Law, Say's Identity and Say's Equality. These distinctions revolved around the issue of the demand for money. Acceptance of Say's Law in the form of Say's Identity meant that one assumed the demand for money was identically equal to the supply of money and therefore that everything produced would be sold. This led further to the identification of what was termed the 'classical dichotomy', which stated that, in classical economic theory, relative prices were determined in the real economy while the price level was determined in the money economy through variations in the quantity of money. The classical dichotomy, however, involved a logical contradiction. Once it was assumed that the demand for money and the supply of money were identically equal, there was one equation too few to determine the economic system. If one accepted Say's Law as interpreted by Lange, then the price level became indeterminate.

But as there was a mass of evidence that classical economists had recognised that recessions occurred and that there were variations in demand for money over the cycle, Say's Equality was taken to be the classical meaning of Say's Law. According to Say's Equality, there could be short-run deviations from full employment and variations in the demand for money, but, in the long run, the economy was self-adjusting and would return to a fully employed equilibrium position. This was undoubtedly consistent with the writings of classical economists, but it left one central question unanswered: why had there been so intense a debate over the validity of Say's Law?

The answer given by some was that the key issue was not whether recessions occurred but how long they would last. It was argued that the debates about the law of markets were over whether recessions would be brief and more or less self-correcting. It has been argued that the law of markets was a response to those who were concerned about the possibility of secular stagnation. This plausible argument has the merit of at least explaining why the debate was as fierce as it was, but it does not come to terms with what the protagonists actually said to each other.

Almost entirely lost in the modern discussion is the original meaning of Say's Law, that is, the meaning held by those who had originally constructed and then defended what was known as the law of markets or *théorie des débouchés*. In accepting the law of markets, they had not denied the occurrence of recession, or that recessions have endogenous causes, or that monetary instability can lead to recession. It would have been extraordinary beyond words if they had. But what they had done was to deny flatly that failure of effective demand was a cause of recessions and unemployment. The denial of the possibility of demand failure (a general glut) was the essential point of the law of markets and, from James Mill onwards, the surrounding arguments in the early literature were attempts to establish that conclusion.

What also emerges is the problem for post-*General Theory* commentators on Say's Law caused by John Stuart Mill's discussion in *Some Unsettled Questions in Political Economy*. It is apparent that the accusations made by Keynes against the law of markets cannot bear comparison with Mill's essay. This is one of the fundamental points established by Becker and Baumol, and since the publication of their paper it has become increasingly difficult for anyone who cares to examine the issue closely to adopt wholeheartedly the Keynesian version of Say's Law. Mill, moreover, was summarising what others had already concluded and would thereafter accept. Mill was thus not unique in his views, but merely represented the conclusions accepted by virtually the entire classical school.

Nevertheless, to the extent that Say's Law is taught today, it is in the form that has been bequeathed through a combination of the positions taken by Keynes, Lange and Becker and Baumol. There would be very few economists indeed, who would consider it worth their while to understand correctly the classical meaning of Say's Law. In their view, it would be irrelevant to today's concerns if it should turn out that classical economic theory had deeper insights than Keynes had given it credit for. Yet the significance for economic theory in the disappearance of Say's Law lies in the fact that for more than a century the law of markets had been used to deny absolutely the argument developed by Keynes in the *General Theory*.

This is more than a matter of the history of economics. The validity of Say's Law runs to the very core of economic theory. A line of descent running from Smith through Say, James Mill, Ricardo, John Stuart Mill, Marshall and just about every major economist prior to the publication of the *General Theory* denied the possibility of demand failure in the sense that production might outrun the willingness to buy. Modern economic theory, to the extent that it still admits the possibility of demand failure as an important cause of recession and unemployment, follows in a second tradition established by Sismondi, Malthus, Hobson and Keynes. Keynes described Say's Law as fallacious. The law of markets was devised to demonstrate that theories based on failure of effective demand were themselves fallacious. Between the polemical skills of Keynes, the obfuscations of Lange and the penetrating summary statement by Becker and Baumol, the actual meaning and significance of the law of markets disappeared from economic theory. The Keynesian Revolution was a revolution indeed, but the full significance and nature of that revolution have not yet been understood.

Appendix A: Say's Law in the *General Theory*

Keynes's polemical skills were never better shown than in his attack on Say's Law. In creating a straw-man version of the law of markets, he changed the terms of the argument just enough to ensure that he did not clearly reveal what the issues at stake were. Keynes had to discredit the law of markets which denied the possibility of over-production and general gluts, but he had to do so in a way which would not alert his contemporaries to the full nature of what he was trying to do. He thus could not argue in a straightforward way that he had realised that *over-production* was a problem and a *general glut* could occur. These words do not appear anywhere in the *General Theory*. He instead focused on the form of the classic demonstration rather than on the conclusion to which it led. Moreover, in so doing, he left out the crucial qualification to supply creating its own demand, that being that supply would create demand only if the goods that would be demanded were the ones which were produced. In this qualification was the basis for a powerful and penetrating theory of recession which had by then been the basis for business cycle analysis for more than a century.

Keynes's discussion on Say's Law is broken into two sections: the first from pages 18 to 22 of Chapter 2; the second on pages 25 and 26 of Chapter 3 (in *CW* VII). Chapter 2 deals with 'The Postulates of the Classical Economics'. Towards the end of the chapter Keynes introduces his definition of Say's Law. There is no explicit mention of 'Say's Law', but J.-B. Say is referred to along with Ricardo. It is not until page 26 that Say's Law is referred to by name.

In beginning his discussion of Say's Law Keynes wrote: 'from the time of Say and Ricardo the classical economists have taught that supply creates its own demand' (*CW* VII: 18), by which they implied 'in some significant, but not clearly defined, sense' (ibid.) that all incomes earned from being involved in the production process would necessarily be spent on purchasing what has been produced (ibid.). That is, according to Say's Law, income earners will spend everything they earn.

At this point Keynes provides a quotation from J.S. Mill. This quotation is Keynes's first example of classical reasoning. It is provided to demonstrate that classical economists, when invoking Say's Law, did indeed use this Law to argue that all incomes will be spent. Keynes states that this doctrine – that supply creates its own demand – 'is expressly set forth' (ibid.) in the passage from Mill.[1] His objection to the view that all incomes are spent, as he will elaborate later in the chapter, is that it ignores the existence of money. The reality, according to Keynes, is that what constitutes the payment for commodities is money. Keynes argued that, because classical economists tended to ignore the implications of economies being monetary economies, they were led to make grievous errors in analysing economic aggregates.

Keynes then takes a step away from his definition of Say's Law by turning to what he believes is implied by it. He argues that there is a 'corollary' (ibid.: 19) to Say's Law as he has defined it. This is the classical economists' belief that whether or not one spends one's income on consumption is irrelevant to whether all incomes received are spent. What is not spent on consumer goods is just as certainly spent on investment. Thus, from the proposition that all income is spent, it follows that what is not spent on consumption is spent on investment. To save is automatically to invest. As a representative example from an economist nearer to his own time than Mill, Keynes selects a passage from Marshall's *Pure Theory of Domestic Values* (ibid.).[2] The issues highlighted in the quotation are that all income is spent and that saving is equivalent to spending. Keynes suggests that it would be difficult to find an equivalent passage amongst his own contemporaries[3] because:

> the doctrine is never stated to-day in this crude form. Nevertheless it still underlies the whole classical theory, which would collapse without it. Contemporary economists, who might hesitate to agree with Mill, do not hesitate to accept conclusions which require Mill's doctrine as their premiss. (Ibid.)

Keynes then turns to examine the implications of a capitalist economy being a monetary economy, entirely different in Keynes's view from the world conceived by Mill:

> The conviction...that money makes no real difference except frictionally and that the theory of production and employment can be worked out (like Mill's) as being based on 'real' exchanges with money introduced perfunctorily in a later chapter, is the modern version of the classical tradition. Contemporary thought is still deeply

---

[1] In fact, Keynes misunderstood Mill's intent in this paragraph which is actually directed at the question of whether purchasing power is sufficient to buy what has been produced, not whether all income will be spent. That this is the point Mill is making is noted by Hobson and Mummery (1889: 102n) who had cited the same passage to show that this had 'become mere commonplaces of economics' (ibid.: 102). See also Patinkin (1965: 646–8 and 1976: 89n).

[2] This had been printed for private circulation in 1879 (Kahn 1984: 12).

[3] But cf. Wesley Mitchell writing in 1927 (151): 'We commonly think of spending money and saving money as activities the opposite of each other. But every kind of saving except actual hoarding involves spending. In the business economy, indeed, the process of saving is one current in the flow of money payments'. And far from this preventing the development of theories of recession, Mitchell then immediately added: 'This process...has been made to yield theories of the business cycle' (ibid.).

steeped in the notion that if people do not spend their money in one way they will spend it in another. (Ibid.: 19–20)

The existence of money affects the operation of an economy because it enables individuals to hoard. Invalid conclusions about the operation of an economy will be drawn from theories which do not recognise this salient fact. For Keynes, what he calls the 'modern' version of classical theory is built on the invalid assumption that a theory of employment and production can be constructed on the basis of real variables, with money introduced at a later stage in the argument more or less as a side issue.

The question has moved from whether all *income* will be spent to whether all the *money* in one's possession will be spent.[4] This is Keynes's own distinction, and it is of critical significance. It is an issue which will figure prominently in the rest of the *General Theory*. Liquidity preference, the holding and hoarding of money, represents a vital element in the logic of the *General Theory*.

Keynes then offers two explanations as to why economists have maintained this 'real' approach. It is, firstly, because of the false analogy from a 'Robinson Crusoe economy' in which the income from what is retained in production is of itself the output of that productive activity. But there is, according to Keynes, a second reason why the argument of the classical economists has maintained so strong a grip. And this is because an untrue proposition, that the total revenue received by business is equal to the total costs incurred in production, is given credence by a similar but true proposition, which is that the total of all incomes received (including normal profits) is identical to the total cost of production (ibid.: 20). In other words, while total incomes received during the production process always equal the total costs of production, the total costs of production are not always covered by total business receipts. This is because not all incomes earned are necessarily spent.

The position Keynes attributes to classical economists runs as follows. Individuals make themselves better off by increasing their own level of savings. Increases in saving must automatically lead to an increase in investment. Hence, the entire community becomes better off because the increased savings have automatically led to increased investment.

Keynes argues that economists are wrong to think as they have. Decisions to save are made by different individuals and for different reasons from those who make the decisions to invest. And because decisions to save are made by one group and decisions to invest are made by another (admittedly with some overlap between the two), there is no simple economic mechanism which co-ordinates each set of decisions with the other. Because the motivations of savers and investors are different, so too may be the magnitude and timing of their decisions. The implication is that there can be no certainty that all savings will be invested.

---

[4] 'If they do not spend their money in one way they will spend it in another' (*CW* VII: 20).

From this Keynes concludes that the assumption that total revenue is equal to total costs of production is the fundamental flaw in classical economic theory.

Thus the entire edifice of classical theory is said to stand or fall on Say's Law as Keynes has defined it. The fundamental flaw in classical theory follows from assuming that total revenue is equal to total costs for the economy in aggregate, irrespective of the level of production. If this assumption were true, Keynes argues, then the entire structure of classical theory would also be true. But since in his view it is false, large parts of the classical theory are open to serious question. The error is the assumption that 'supply creates its own demand in the sense that the aggregate demand price is equal to the aggregate supply price for all levels of output and employment' (ibid.: 21–2). With this Chapter 2 comes to an end. Chapter 3 deals, in the main, with 'The Principle of Effective Demand', but on pages 25 and 26 Keynes briefly returns to the issue of Say's Law. It is the only stage where Say's Law is specifically named.

Chapter 3 begins with a number of definitions, after which Keynes commences an overview of the theory of effective demand. He states (ibid.: 24) that entrepreneurs have an expectation of the revenue they will receive from the sale of their production. This expectation will determine the amount of employment that will be offered, both at the level of the firm and in aggregate. Employment will be at the level that will produce the greatest expected excess of revenue over factor costs. Keynes discusses the concept of the 'aggregate supply price' (Z) and the 'aggregate demand price' (D) (ibid.: 25). The aggregate supply price is a schedule representing the total costs of production from employing various numbers of employees. The aggregate demand price is a schedule representing the expectations of the revenue that will be received from employing various numbers of employees. Where the expected proceeds from the sale of production exceed the costs of production, there will be a tendency to increase the number of employees. Costs of production will tend to rise as producers compete with each other for factors of production. This will occur up to the point where the value of Z becomes equal to D. The point of equilibrium is where the aggregate demand and the aggregate supply curves intersect. At this point the expectation of profit is at a maximum. The value at the point at which the aggregate demand function is met by the aggregate supply function is termed 'the effective demand' (ibid.).

Having explained the generation of effective demand, Keynes then returns briefly, and for the last time in the *General Theory*, to Say's Law. As interpreted by Keynes, Say's Law means that total revenue must cover the total costs of production irrespective of the level of employment. Keynes argues that, according to classical economic theory, an increase in total costs of production, Z, associated with increased employment, will lead to an identical increase in total revenue, D. Keynes's argument is put as follows:

> The classical doctrine...which used to be expressed categorically in the statement that 'Supply creates its own Demand' and continues to underlie all orthodox economic theory, involves a special assumption as to the relationship between these two functions. For 'Supply creates its own Demand' must mean that f(N) and ϕ(N) are equal for *all* values of N, i.e. for all levels of output and employment; and that when

there is an increase in $Z(=\phi(N))$ corresponding to an increase in N, $D(=f(N))$ necessarily increases by the same amount as Z. (Ibid.: 25–6)

Keynes argues that the assumption held by classical economists was that the aggregate revenue accruing to producers would always accommodate itself to the aggregate costs of production. Irrespective of the level of employment, the total revenues earned by the sale of goods and services would equal the total factor costs of production. This would mean that the level of effective demand would not have some unique equilibrium value determined by all of the conditions of the economy, but could be at any level whatsoever. Moreover, the level of employment would be indeterminate except for an upper limit set by the marginal disutility of labour. If this were so, Keynes concluded, competition would lead to an expansion of employment right up to the point where the supply of output becomes completely inelastic; that is, employment would expand to a point where increases in nominal spending, which is described as 'a further increase in the value of effective demand' (ibid.: 26), would not lead to any further increase in output.

Keynes now uses this analysis to refer back to his definition of full employment in the previous chapter. This was that full employment existed when there was no involuntary unemployment as he defined it. He then enunciates a second definition of involuntary unemployment which, he states, is equivalent to his original one. That is, full employment occurs where an increase in the money demand for output (an upwards shift of the entire aggregate demand curve) does not lead to an increase in the level of employment.

And this brings Keynes back to Say's Law. He concludes that Say's Law, as he defines it, is the same thing as there being nothing in the way of full employment:

> Thus Say's Law, that the aggregate demand price of output as a whole is equal to its aggregate supply price for all volumes of output, is equivalent to the proposition that there is no obstacle to full employment. (Ibid.)

That is, someone who accepts Say's Law must conclude that there are no impediments to full employment. Because if one believes in the validity of Say's Law, one believes that all of the incomes earned during the production process will be spent on buying everything that has been produced. Therefore, unsold goods and services are a theoretical impossibility, and recessions and unemployment are themselves a theoretical impossibility.

Appendix B: The Classical Definition of Say's Law

To understand the difference between classical business cycle theory and the theory which replaced it following the publication of the *General Theory*, it is important to recognise the critical importance of Say's Law in classical economic theory. Since the publication of the *General Theory*, Say's Law has generally been taken to mean that 'supply creates its own demand', that is, that everything produced will find a market and that therefore recessions and involuntary unemployment are in theory impossible. Keynes's clearest statement on this point is found in the introduction to the French edition:

> I believe that economics everywhere up to recent times has been dominated, much more than has been understood, by the doctrines associated with the name of J.-B. Say. It is true that his 'law of markets' has been long abandoned by most economists; but they have not extricated themselves from his basic assumptions and particularly from his fallacy that demand is created by supply. Say was implicitly assuming that the economic system was always operating up to its full capacity, so that a new activity was always in substitution for, and never in addition to, some other activity. Nearly all subsequent economic theory has depended on, in the sense that it has required, this same assumption. Yet a theory so based is clearly incompetent to tackle the problems of unemployment and of the trade cycle. (*CW* VII, xxxv)

This is in fact a gross distortion of the meaning that Say's Law held in classical theory. The importance of Say's Law was that it ruled out one particular explanation for recession, namely demand deficiency. In classical theory, this was generally stated either as the proposition that general gluts were impossible or as the denial of the possibility of over-production. The point being made was that, whatever else might have caused a recession, the correct explanation would never be found in terms of producers having produced more in aggregate than demanders were willing to buy. Failure of effective demand was thus not a legitimate explanation for recession so that remedies for recession were not to be found in stimulating demand.

What then did cause recession? The classical answer was that recessions were due to miscalculation on the part of producers (or in modern terminology, co-ordination failure). In simplest terms, decisions by producers on what to produce did not mesh with decisions by buyers on what to buy. Errors made by producers meant that orders and sales were lower than expected, and often lower than would cover costs of production. The result was a downturn in activity, a reduction in employment and a period of recession until a subsequent revival commenced. Only when confidence was again restored would there be a gradual improvement in activity, employment and real incomes.

The classical statement of Say's Law was that general gluts were impossible, by which was meant explanations of recession based on the assumption that more was being produced than would be bought were invalid. Or, to put this in a positive way rather than in the negative, Say's Law declared that demand would never fall short of properly proportioned supply.

To cite but one twentieth-century example of this position, Taussig, in his *Principles of Economics*, denied the possibility of over-production in the sense of demand deficiency in a way which perfectly captured classical reasoning:

> Some of the phenomena connected with crises, and especially the course of events during a period of depression, have been ascribed to overproduction. During times of depression, it would seem, more is produced than can be readily sold or than can be sold at a profit: is there not general overproduction?
>
> These phenomena, however, result from the breakdown of the machinery of exchange. They are not due to permanent or deep-seated difficulties of finding an extensible or profitable market. They are due to the fact that confidence has been shaken, credit disturbed, the usual course of production and sale subjected to shock.... *They are little related to those supposed limitations of demand* and those possibilities of permanent overinvestment, which are urged by the persons who maintain that there is danger of general overproduction.... These things correct themselves in time. The mechanism of exchange is restored to its normal working, and the maladjustment in production is set right. (Taussig 1927: II. 60–61, italics added)

That is, demand deficiency is not the cause of recession. Demand would never fall short of properly proportioned supply. This is a line of argument which can be traced back to the earliest classical writers.

Given the way in which the process underlying Say's Law was stated, it should be clear that it was a principle which was in continuous operation, not one which only operated in the long run. The process of Say's Law was that demand was constituted by supply. That is, one made purchases with the receipts from one's own sales. The process focused on the creation of value. Given the assumption that everyone seeks to improve their standard of living, so long as everyone is able to create value, the processes of an exchange economy will ensure that demand keeps pace with supply. If, however, the economy moves out of phase, where the array of goods and services produced does not coincide with the array of goods and services demanded, the result is unsold goods and services. But this is not due to a failure of demand but to production miscalculation. The economy may then go into recession and involuntary unemployment may rise to extreme levels. Nevertheless, Say's Law remains in operation, in the sense that demand continues to be constituted by supply, and the recession, with its related high level of unemployment, is not properly attributable to demand deficiency.

It should also be noted that the criticism made by Keynes that classical economists ignored the destabilising role of money will not stand up to scrutiny. This criticism should rightfully have disappeared following the classic article by Becker and Baumol (1952) where they refuted the allegation that 'cash has no utility of its own' (ibid.: 363). In rejecting this criticism of the classics, they quote Say, Ricardo, Senior, Jevons, Wicksteed, Marshall, Walras, Pareto and John Stuart Mill. Nevertheless, it is a criticism of classical economics which continues to be levelled.

The essence of this critique is that pre-Keynesian economics conceived the business cycle in terms of real relationships and basically ignored the separation in time between purchase and sale permitted by the existence of money. This is what Keynes referred to as 'liquidity preference'. Yet this phenomenon is clearly described by Mill in his *Principles* in explaining the course of a commercial crisis:

> At such times there is really an excess of all commodities above the money demand: in other words, there is an under-supply of money. From the sudden annihilation of a great mass of credit, every one dislikes to part with ready money, and many are anxious to procure it at any sacrifice. Almost everybody therefore is a seller, and there are scarcely any buyers; so that there may really be, though only while the crisis lasts, an extreme depression of general prices, from what may be indiscriminately called a glut of commodities or a dearth of money. But it is a great error to suppose, with Sismondi, that a commercial crisis is the effect of a general excess of production. (Mill [1871] 1921: 561)

Pre-Keynesian economists understood perfectly well that the separation in time between buying and selling permitted by the existence of money could deepen a recession but, as Mill specifically pointed out, that the resulting failure of goods to sell had nothing to do with over-production. To think so would allow the superficial to cloud the deeper underlying reality.

Bibliography

Adams, Arthur B. 1925. *Economics of business cycles*. New York: McGraw-Hill.

Aftalion, A. 1913. *Les crises périodiques de surproduction*. 2 vols. Paris: M. Rivière.

Ambirajan, S. 1959. *Malthus and classical economics*. Bombay: Popular Book Depot.

Anderson, Benjamin M. [1949] 1979. *Economics and the public welfare: a financial and economic history of the United States, 1914–1946*. Indianapolis: Liberty Press.

Bagehot, Walter [1873] 1919. *Lombard Street: a description of the money market*. London: John Murray.

Bagehot, Walter 1888. *Economic studies*, 2nd edn. Ed. Richard Holt Hutton. London: Longmans, Green.

Balassa, Bela A. 1959. 'John Stuart Mill and the law of markets.' *Quarterly Journal of Economics*, vol. 73, pp. 263–74.

Baumol, William J. 1959. *Business behaviour, value and growth*. New York: The Macmillan Company.

Baumol, William J. 1972. *Economic theory and operations analysis*, 3rd edn. London: Prentice-Hall International.

Baumol, William J. 1976. *Selected economic writings of William J. Baumol*. Ed. Elizabeth E. Bailey. New York: New York University Press.

Baumol, William J. 1977. 'Say's (at least) eight laws, or what Say and James Mill may really have meant.' *Economica*, vol. 44, pp. 145–62.

Baumol, William J. 1997. 'J.-B. Say on unemployment and public works.' *Eastern Economic Journal*, vol. 23, pp. 219–30.

Becker, Gary and Baumol, William J. 1952. 'The classical economic theory: the outcome of the discussion.' *Economica*, vol. 19, pp. 355–76.

Becker, Gary and Baumol, William J. 1976. 'The classical economic theory: the outcome of the discussion.' In Baumol, William J. *Selected economic writings of William J. Baumol*. Ed. Elizabeth E. Bailey. New York: New York University Press.

Beveridge, W.H. 1914. Review of Pigou, A.C. *Unemployment. Economic Journal*, vol. 24, pp. 250–52.

Beveridge, W.H. 1931. *Unemployment: a problem of industry (1909 and 1930)*. London: Longmans, Green.

Beveridge, W.H. 1944. *Full employment in a free society*. London: George Allen & Unwin.

Bigg, Robert J. 1990. *Cambridge and the monetary theory of production: the collapse of Marshallian macroeconomics*. Basingstoke: Macmillan.

Black, R.D. Collison 1967. 'Parson Malthus, the General and the Captain.' *Economic Journal*, vol. 77, pp. 59–74.

Black, R.D. Collison 1983. 'W.S. Jevons, 1835–82.' In O'Brien, D.P. and Presley, John R. *Pioneers of modern economics in Britain*. London: The Macmillan Press.

Bladen, V.W. 1974. *From Adam Smith to Maynard Keynes: the heritage of political economy*. Toronto: University of Toronto Press.

Blanqui, Jerome Adolphe [1880] 1968. *History of political economy in Europe*. New York: Augustus M. Kelley.

Blaug, Mark 1958. *Ricardian economics: a historical study*. New Haven, Conn.: Yale University Press.

Blaug, Mark 1985. *Economic theory in retrospect*. Cambridge: Cambridge University Press.

Blaug, Mark (ed.) 1991a. *Jean-Baptiste Say (1776–1832)*. Aldershot, Hants.: Edward Elgar.

Blaug, Mark 1991b. 'Second thoughts on the Keynesian revolution.' *History of Political Economy*, vol. 23, pp. 171–92.

Blaug, Mark 1994. 'Recent biographies of Keynes.' *Journal of Economic Literature*, vol. 32, pp. 1204–15.

Blaug, Mark 1997. 'Say's Law of markets: what did it mean and why should we care?' *Eastern Economic Journal*, vol. 23, pp. 231–5.

Blaug, Mark and Sturges, Paul (eds) 1983. *Who's who in economics: a biographical dictionary of major economists, 1700–1981*. Brighton, Sussex: Wheatsheaf Books.

Bonar, James [1924] 1966. *Malthus and his work*, 2nd edn. London: Frank Cass.

Brandis, Royall 1985. 'Marx *and* Keynes? Marx *or* Keynes?' *Journal of Economic Issues*, vol. 19, 643–59.

Bridel, Pascal 1979. 'On Keynes's quotations from Mill: a note.' *Economic Journal*, vol. 89, pp. 660–62.

Bridel, Pascal 1987. *Cambridge monetary thought: the development of saving–investment analysis from Marshall to Keynes*. Basingstoke: Macmillan Press.

Brown, Arthur 1988. 'A worm's eye view of the Keynesian Revolution.' In Hillard, John (ed.) *J.M. Keynes in retrospect: the legacy of the Keynesian Revolution*. Aldershot, Hants.: Edward Elgar.

Brunner, Karl 1951. 'Inconsistency and indeterminacy in classical economics.' *Econometrica*, vol. 19, pp. 152–73.

Cairnes, J.E. 1874. *Some leading principles of political economy newly expounded*. London: Macmillan.

Cannan, Edwin 1916. Review of Robertson, D.H. *A study of industrial fluctuation: an enquiry into the character and causes of the so-called cyclical movements of trade. Economic Journal*, vol. 26, pp. 228–9.

Cannan, Edwin 1932. Review of Hawtrey, R.G. *Trade depression and the way out. Economic Journal*, vol. 36, pp. 70–72.

Chalmers, Thomas [1832] 1968. *On political economy, in connexion with the moral state and moral prospects of society*. New York: Augustus M. Kelley.

Chick, Victoria 1983. *Macroeconomic theory after Keynes: a reconsideration of the General Theory*. Oxford: Philip Allan.

Chipman, John S. 1965. 'A survey of the theory of international trade. Part 2: the neo-classical theory.' *Econometrica*, vol. 33, pp. 685–760.

Clark, J.M. 1917. 'Business acceleration and the law of demand.' *Journal of Political Economy*, vol. 25, pp. 217–35.

Clarke, Peter 1988. *The Keynesian revolution in the making, 1924–1936*. Oxford: Clarendon Press.

Clay, Henry [1916] 1924. *Economics: an introduction for the general reader*. London: Macmillan.

Clay, Henry 1928. 'Unemployment and wage rates.' *Economic Journal*, vol. 38, pp. 1–15.

Clay, Henry 1942. *Economics: an introduction for the general reader*, 2nd edn. London: Macmillan.

Clower, Robert W. [1962] 1984a. 'The Keynesian counter-revolution: a theoretical appraisal.' In Walker, Donald A. (ed.) *Money and markets: essays by Robert W. Clower*. Cambridge: Cambridge University Press.

Clower, Robert W. [1967] 1984b. 'A reconsideration of the microfoundations of monetary theory.' In Walker, Donald A. (ed.) *Money and markets: essays by Robert W. Clower*. Cambridge: Cambridge University Press.

Clower, Robert W. (ed.) 1971. *Monetary theory: selected readings*. Harmondsworth, Middx.: Penguin Books.

Clower, Robert W. [1973] 1984c. 'Say's Principle, what it means and doesn't mean.' In Walker, Donald A. (ed.) *Money and markets: essays by Robert W. Clower*. Cambridge: Cambridge University Press.

Clower, Robert W. 1989. 'The state of economics: hopeless but not serious.' In Colander, David C. and Coats, A.W. (eds) *The spread of economic ideas*. Cambridge: Cambridge University Press.

Clower, Robert and Leijonhufvud, Axel 1973. 'Say's Principle, what it means and doesn't mean.' *Intermountain Economic Review*, vol. 4, pp. 1–16.

Coddington, Alan 1983. *Keynesian economics: the search for first principles*. London: George Allen & Unwin.

Collard, David A. 1983. 'A.C. Pigou, 1877–1959.' In O'Brien, D.P. and Presley, John R. (eds) *Pioneers of modern economics in Britain*. London: Macmillan Press, pp. 105–39.

Collard, David A. 1996. 'Pigou and modern business cycle theory.' *Economic Journal*, vol. 106, pp. 912–24.

Corry, B.A. 1959. 'Malthus and Keynes: a reconsideration.' *Economic Journal*, vol. 69, pp. 717–24.

Corry, B.A. 1962. *Money, saving and investment in English economics 1800–1850*. London: Macmillan.

Corry, B.A. 1978. 'Keynes in the history of economic thought: some reflections.' In Thirlwall, A.P. (ed.) *Keynes and laissez-faire: the third Keynes seminar held at the University of Kent at Canterbury 1976*. London: Macmillan, pp. 3–34.

Cowan, Tyler 1982. 'Say's Law and Keynesian economics.' In Fink, Richard H. (ed.) *Supply-side economics: a critical appraisal*. Frederick, Md: Aletheia Books, University Publications of America, pp. 160–84.

Davidson, Paul 1972. *Money and the real world*. London: Macmillan.

Davidson, Paul 1991. *Controversies in post-Keynesian economics*. Aldershot, Hants.: Edward Elgar.

Davidson, Paul 1994. *Post-Keynesian macroeconomic theory*. Aldershot: Edward Elgar.

Davis, J. Ronnie 1979. 'Keynes's misquotation of Mill: further comment.' *Economic Journal*, vol. 89, pp. 658–9.

Davis, J. Ronnie and Casey, Francis J. Jr 1977. 'Keynes's misquotation of Mill.' *Economic Journal*, vol. 87, pp. 329–30.

Deutscher, Patrick 1990. *R.G. Hawtrey and the development of macroeconomics*. Basingstoke, Hants.: Macmillan.

Dillard, Dudley [1948] 1960. *The economics of John Maynard Keynes: the theory of a monetary economy*. London: Crosby Lockwood.

Dimand, Robert W. 1988. *The origins of the Keynesian revolution: the development of Keynes' theory of employment and output*. Aldershot, Hants.: Edward Elgar.

Dobb, Maurice [1940] 1980. *Political economy and capitalism: some essays in economic tradition*, 2nd edn. London: Routledge & Kegan Paul.

Eatwell, John, Milgate, Murray and Newman, Peter 1987. *The new Palgrave: a dictionary of economics*, 4 vols. London: Macmillan Press.

Edgeworth, F.Y. 1890. Review of Hobson J.A. and Mummery A.F. *The physiology of industry: being an exposure of certain existing theories of economics. Journal of Education*, vol. XII (new series), p. 194.

Edgeworth, F.Y. 1926. 'Over-production.' In Higgs, Henry (ed.) *Palgrave's Dictionary of Political Economy*. London: Macmillan, vol. 3, pp. 45–6.

Ellis, Howard S. 1936. Review of Wilhem Röpke *Crises and cycles. American Economic Review*, vol. 26, pp. 762-764.

Eshag, Eprime 1964. *From Marshall to Keynes: an essay on the monetary theory of the Cambridge school*. Oxford: Basil Blackwell.

Fawcett, Henry 1888. *Manual of political economy*, 7th edn. London: Macmillan.

Fitzgerald, F. Scott [1926] 1990. *The great Gatsby*. Harmondsworth, Middx.: Penguin.

Furniss, H. Sanderson 1916. Review of Henry Clay, *Economics: an introduction for the general reader. Economic Journal*, vol. 26, pp. 350–51.

Gide, Charles 1926. 'Jean-Baptiste Say.' In Higgs, Henry (ed.) *Palgrave's Dictionary of Political Economy*. London: Macmillan.

Gide, Charles and Rist, Charles [1915] 1925. *A history of economic doctrines: from the time of the physiocrats to the present day*, trans. from the 2nd French edn of 1913 by R. Richards. London: George C. Harrap.

Gray, Alexander 1929. Review of Teilhac, E. *L'Oeuvre économique de Jean Baptiste Say. Economic Journal*, vol. 39, pp. 453–6.

Gray, Alexander [1931] 1944. *The development of economic doctrine: an introductory survey*. London: Longmans, Green.

Groenewegen, P.D. (ed.) 1984. *Robert Torrens: the economists refuted, 1808, and other early economic writings*. Sydney: Department of Economics, University of Sydney.

Haberler, Gottfried 1937. *Prosperity and depression: a theoretical analysis of cyclical movements*. Geneva: League of Nations.

Haberler, Gottfried 1941. *Prosperity and depression: a theoretical analysis of cyclical movements*, 3rd edn. Geneva: League of Nations.

Haberler, Gottfried [1947] 1960. 'The *General Theory*.' In Harris, Seymour E. (ed.) *The new economics: Keynes' influence on theory and public policy*. London: Dennis Dobson, pp. 161–80.

Hansen, Alvin Harvey 1927. *Business-cycle theory: its development and present status*. Boston: Ginn.

Hansen, Alvin Harvey [1932] 1971. *Economic stabilization in an unbalanced world*. New York: Augustus M. Kelley.

Hansen, Alvin Harvey 1936. 'Mr Keynes on underemployment equilibrium.' *Journal of Political Economy*, vol. 44, pp. 667–86.

Hansen, Alvin Harvey 1938. *Full recovery or stagnation?* London: Adam & Charles Black.

Hansen, Alvin Harvey 1953. *A guide to Keynes*. London: McGraw-Hill.

Harris, Seymour E. (ed.) [1947] 1960. *The new economics: Keynes' influence on theory and public policy*. London: Dennis Dobson.

Harrod, R.F. 1934a. 'Professor Pigou's theory of unemployment.' Review of Pigou, A.C. *Theory of unemployment. Economic Journal*, vol. 44, pp. 19–32.

Harrod, R.F. 1934b. Review of Hawtrey, Ralph. *Trade depression and the way out. Economic Journal*, vol. 44, pp. 279–82.

Harrod, R.F. [1951] 1972. *The life of John Maynard Keynes*. Harmondsworth, Middx.: Penguin Books.

Hawtrey, R.G. [1926] 1954. 'The trade cycle.' In Haberler, Gottfried (ed.) *Readings in business cycle theory: selected by a committee of the American Economics Association*. London: George Allen & Unwin, pp. 330–49.

Hawtrey, R.G. 1933. *Trade depression and the way out*. London: Longmans, Green.

Hawtrey, R.G. 1937. *Capital and employment*. London: Longmans, Green.

Hawtrey, R.G. 1938. 'Professor Haberler on the trade cycle.' *Economica*, vol. 5 (new series), pp. 93–7.

Hazlitt, Henry 1959. *The failure of the 'new economics': an analysis of the Keynesian fallacies*. New Rochelle, N.Y.: Arlington House.

Hazlitt, Henry (ed.) 1960. *The critics of Keynesian economics*. Princeton, N.J.: Van Nostrand.

Heckscher, Eli F. 1955. *Mercantilism*, 2nd edn. London: George Allen & Unwin.

Hickman, W. Braddock 1950. 'The determinacy of absolute prices in classical economic theory.' *Econometrica*, vol. 18, pp. 9–20.

Higgs, Henry 1926a. '*Théorie de débouchés.*' In Higgs, Henry (ed.) *Palgrave's dictionary of political economy.* London: Macmillan.

Higgs, Henry (ed.) 1926b. *Palgrave's dictionary of political economy*, 3 vols. London: Macmillan.

Hobson, J.A. [1938] 1976. *Confessions of an economic heretic.* Brighton, Sussex: Harvester.

Hobson, J.A. and Mummery, A.F. 1889. *The physiology of industry: being an exposition of certain fallacies in existing theories of economics.* London: John Murray.

Hollander, Samuel 1962. 'Malthus and Keynes: a note.' *Economic Journal*, vol. 72, pp. 355–9.

Hollander, Samuel 1973. *The economics of Adam Smith.* London: Heinemann Educational Books.

Hollander, Samuel 1979. *The economics of David Ricardo.* Toronto and Buffalo: University of Toronto Press.

Hollander, Samuel 1985. *The economics of John Stuart Mill*, vol. I: *Theory and method*; Vol. II: *Political economy.* Oxford: Basil Blackwell.

Hollander, Samuel 1987. *Classical economics.* Oxford: Basil Blackwell.

Hollander, Samuel 1997. *The economics of Thomas Robert Malthus.* Toronto: University of Toronto Press.

Horwood, O.P.F. 1990. 'William Harold Hutt: a personal memoir.' *South African Journal of Economics*, vol. 58, pp. 270–78.

Hutchison, T.W. [1953] 1962. *A review of economic doctrines: 1870–1929.* Oxford: Clarendon Press.

Hutchison, T.W. 1978. *On revolutions and progress in economic knowledge.* Cambridge: Cambridge University Press.

Hutt, W.H. [1936] 1990. *Economists and the public: a study of competition and opinion.* London: Transaction Publishers.

Hutt, W.H. 1960. 'The significance of price flexibility.' In Hazlitt, Henry (ed.) *The critics of Keynesian economics.* Princeton: Van Nostrand, pp. 386–403.

Hutt, W.H. 1963. *Keynesianism: retrospect and prospect. A critical restatement of basic economic principles.* Chicago: Henry Regnery.

Hutt, W.H. 1974. *A rehabilitation of Say's Law.* Athens, Ohio: Ohio University Press.

Hutt, W.H. 1979. *The Keynesian episode: a reassessment.* Indianapolis: Liberty Press.

Jevons, William Stanley [1871] 1970. *The theory of political economy.* Harmondsworth, Middx: Penguin Books.

Jonsson, Petur O. 1995. 'On the economics of Say and Keynes' interpretation of Say's Law.' *Eastern Economic Journal*, vol. 21, pp. 147–55.

Jonsson, Petur O. 1997. 'On gluts, effective demand, and the true meaning of Say's Law.' *Eastern Economic Journal*, vol. 23, pp. 203–18.

Kahn, R.F. 1984. *The making of Keynes' general theory.* Cambridge: Cambridge University Press.

Kaldor, Nicholas 1989. *Further essays on economic theory and policy.* Ed. Targetti, F. and Thirwall, A.P. London: Duckworth.

Kates, Steven 1994. 'The Malthusian origins of the *General Theory*: or how Keynes came to write a book about Say's law and effective demand.' *History of Economics Review*, vol. 21, pp. 10–20.

Kates, Steven 1995. 'Crucial influences on Keynes's understanding of Say's Law.' *History of Economics Review*, vol. 23, pp. 74–82.

Kates, Steven 1996. 'Keynes, Say's Law and the theory of the business cycle.' *History of Economics Review*, vol. 25, pp. 119–26.

Kates, Steven 1997a. 'A discussion of Say's Law: the outcome of the symposium.' *Eastern Economic Journal*, vol. 23, pp. 237–9.

Kates, Steven 1997b. 'On the true meaning of Say's Law.' *Eastern Economic Journal*, vol. 23, pp. 191–202.

Keynes, John Maynard. *The collected writings of John Maynard Keynes*. Edited by Donald Moggridge. London: The Macmillan Press Ltd.

Vol. V:　　*A treatise on money, 1: the pure theory of money*. [1930]

Vol. VI:　　*A treatise on money, 2: the applied theory of money*. [1930]

Vol. VII:　　*The general theory of employment, interest and money*. [1936]

Vol. IX:　　*Essays in persuasion* (full text with additional essays). [1931]

Vol. X　　*Essays in biography* (full text with additional biographical writings). [1933]

Vol. XI:　　*Economic articles and correspondence* (various).

Vol. XII:　　*Economic articles and correspondence* (various/academic).

Vol. XIII:　　*The general theory and after, Part I: preparation*.

Vol. XIV:　　*The general theory and after, Part II: defence and development*.

Vol. XXI:　　*Activities 1931–1939: world crises and policies in Britain and America*.

Vol. XXIX: *The general theory and after: a supplement* [to Vols XIII and XIV].

Klein, Lawrence R. 1968. *The Keynesian revolution*, 2nd edn. London: Macmillan.

Kohn, Meir 1986. 'Monetary analysis, the equilibrium method, and Keynes's "general theory".' *Journal of Political Economy*, vol. 94, pp. 1191–1224.

Lambert, Paul 1956. 'The law of markets prior to J.-B. Say and the Say–Malthus debate.' *International Economic Papers*, number 6.

Lange, Oskar [1942] 1970. 'Say's Law: a restatement and criticism.' In Lange, Oskar (ed.). *Papers in economics and sociology*. Oxford: Pergamon Press.

Lange, Oskar and Taylor, F.M. [1938] 1964. *On the economic theory of socialism*. New York: McGraw-Hill.

Lavington, F. 1912. 'Uncertainty in its relation to the net rate of interest.' *Economic Journal*, vol. 22, pp. 398–409.

Lavington, F. [1922] 1938. *The trade cycle: an account of the causes producing rhythmical changes in the activity of business*. London: P.S. King.

Lavington, F. 1925. 'An approach to the theory of business risks. Part I.' *Economic Journal*, vol. 35, pp. 186–99.

Lavington, F. 1926. 'An approach to the theory of business risks. Part II.' *Economic Journal*, vol. 36, pp. 192–203.

Leijonhufvud, Axel 1968. *On Keynesian economics and the economics of Keynes: a study in monetary theory.* New York: Oxford University Press.

Leijonhufvud, Axel 1969. *Keynes and the classics: two lectures on Keynes's contribution to economic theory.* London: Institute of Economic Affairs.

Leijonhufvud, Axel 1986. 'What would Keynes have thought of rational expectations?' In Butkiewicz, James L., Koford, Kenneth L. and Miller, Jeffery B. (eds) *Keynes' economic legacy: contemporary economic theories.* New York: Praeger.

Lekachman, Robert 1967. *The age of Keynes.* London: Allen Lane, The Penguin Press.

Leontief, W.W. 1950. 'The consistency of the classical theory of money and prices.' *Econometrica*, vol. 18, pp. 21–4.

Lerner, A.P. 1936. 'Mr Keynes' "general theory of employment, interest and money".' *International Labour Review*, vol. 34, pp. 435–54.

Lerner, A.P. [1939] 1951. 'The relation of wage policies and price policies.' In Fellner, William and Haley, Bernard F. (eds) *Readings in the theory of income distribution.* Homewood, Ill.: Richard D. Irwin, pp. 314–29.

Littleboy, Bruce 1990. *On interpreting Keynes: a study in reconciliation.* London: Routledge.

Macgregor, D.H. 1949. *Economic thought and policy.* London: Oxford University Press.

Maitland, James, 8th Earl of Lauderdale 1962. *An inquiry into the nature and origin of public wealth and into the means and causes of its increase (1804),* ed. with an introduction and revisions appearing in the 2nd edn (1819) by Morton Paglin. New York: Augustus M. Kelley.

Malthus, Thomas Robert 1827. *Definitions in political economy.* London: John Murray.

Malthus, Thomas Robert 1986. *The works of Thomas Robert Malthus.* Ed. E.A. Wrigley and David Souden. London: William Pickering.

Vol. 6: *Principles of political economy: the second edition (1836) with variant readings from the first edition (1820).* Part II

Vol. 8: *Definitions in political economy (1827).*

Malthus, Thomas Robert 1989. *Principles of political economy,* variorum edn. Ed. John Pullen, 2 vols. Cambridge: Cambridge University Press.

Mantoux, Étienne [1937] 1960. 'Mr Keynes' "general theory".' In Hazlitt, Henry (ed.) *The critics of Keynesian economics.* Princeton, N.J.: Van Nostrand, pp. 97–124.

Marget, Arthur W. [1938] 1966a. *The theory of prices: a re-examination of the central problems of monetary theory,* vol. I. New York: Augustus M. Kelley.

Marget, Arthur W. [1942] 1966b. *The theory of prices: a re-examination of the central problems of monetary theory,* vol. II. New York: Augustus M. Kelley.

Marshall, Alfred 1876. 'On Mr. Mill's theory of value.' *Fortnighly Review*, vol. XIX new series (vol. XXV old series), pp. 591–602.

Marshall, Alfred [1920] 1947. *Principles of economics: an introductory volume,* 8th edn. London: Macmillan.

Marshall, Alfred 1961. *Principles of economics*, 2 vols. 9th (variorum) edn, with annotations by C.W. Guillebaud. London: Macmillan, for the Royal Economic Society.

Marshall, Alfred and Marshall, Mary Paley [1879] 1881. *The economics of industry*, 2nd edn. London: Macmillan.

McCracken, Harlan Linneus 1933. *Value theory and business cycles*. Binghampton, N.Y.: Falcon Press.

McCracken, Harlan Linneus 1961. *Keynesian economics in the stream of economic thought*. Kingsport, Tenn.: Louisiana State University Press.

McCulloch, J.R. [1864] 1965. *The principles of political economy, with some inquiries respecting their application*, 5th edn. New York: Augustus M. Kelley.

Meade, J.E. 1936. Review of Wilhelm Röpke. *Crises and cycles*. *Economic Journal*, vol. 46, pp. 694–5.

Meade, J.E. 1937. Review of McCracken, H.L. *Value theory and business cycles*. *Economic Journal*, vol. 49, pp. 52–65.

Meek, Ronald L. [1951] 1967a. 'The place of Keynes in the history of economic thought.' In Meek, Ronald L. (ed.) *Economics and ideology and other essays: studies in the development of economic thought*. London: Chapman & Hall, pp. 179–95.

Meek, Ronald L. 1967b. 'The decline of Ricardian economics in England.' In Meek, Ronald L. (ed.) *Economics and ideology and other essays: studies in the development of economic thought*. London: Chapman & Hall, pp. 51–74.

Meek, Ronald L. 1967c. *Economics and ideology and other essays: studies in the development of economic thought*. London: Chapman & Hall.

Mehta, Ghanshyam 1978. *The structure of the Keynesian revolution*. New York: St Martin's Press.

Metzler, Lloyd A. [1947] 1960. 'Keynes and the theory of business cycles.' In Harris, Seymour E. (ed.) *The new economics: Keynes' influence on theory and public policy*. London: Dennis Dobson, pp. 436–49.

Milgate, Murray 1982. *Capital and employment: a study of Keynes's economics*. London: Academic Press.

Mill, James [1808] 1966a. *Commerce defended*, 2nd edn. In Winch, Donald (ed.) *James Mill: selected economic writings*. Edinburgh: Oliver & Boyd, pp. 85–159.

Mill, James [1826] 1966b. *Elements of political economy*, 3rd edn. In Winch, Donald (ed.) *James Mill: selected economic writings*. Edinburgh: Oliver & Boyd, pp. 203–366.

Mill, John Stuart [1871] 1921. *Principles of political economy with some of their applications to social philosophy*, 7th edn, ed. with an introduction by Sir W.J. Ashley. London: Longmans, Green.

Mill, John Stuart [1874] 1974a. *Essays on some unsettled questions in economics*, 2nd edn. Clifton, N.J.: Augustus M. Kelley.

Mill, John Stuart [1874] 1974b. 'Of the influence of consumption on production.' In *Essays on Some Unsettled Questions of Political Economy*, 2nd edn. Clifton, N.J.: Augustus M. Kelley, pp. 47–74.

Mills, Herbert E. 1916. Review of Clay, Henry *Economics for the general reader*. *American Economic Review*, vol. 6., pp. 878–80.

Mises, Ludwig von [1950] 1980a. 'Lord Keynes and Say's Law.' In *Planning for freedom: and sixteen other essays and addresses*, 4th edn. South Holland, Ill.: Libertarian Press, pp. 64–71.

Mises, Ludwig von [1950] 1980b. 'Benjamin M. Anderson challenges the philosophy of the pseudo-progressives.' In *Planning for freedom: and sixteen other essays and addresses*, 4th edn. South Holland, Ill.: Libertarian Press, pp. 94–107.

Mitchell, Wesley C. 1916. Review of Robertson, D.H. *A study of industrial fluctuation: a study into the character and causes of the so-called cyclical movements of trade*. *American Economic Review*, vol. 6, pp. 638–9.

Mitchell, Wesley C. 1927. *Business cycles: the problem and its setting*. New York: National Bureau of Economic Research.

Modigliani, Franco [1944] 1960. 'Liquidity preference and the theory of interest and money.' In Hazlitt, Henry (ed.) *The critics of Keynesian economics*. Princeton, N.J.: Van Nostrand, pp. 132–84.

Moggridge, D.E. 1973. 'From the *Treatise* to the *General Theory*: an exercise in chronology.' *History of Political Economy*, vol. 5, pp. 249–71.

Moggridge, D.E. 1980. *Keynes*, 2nd edn. London: Macmillan (Fontana Papermac).

Moggridge, D.E. 1992. *Maynard Keynes: an economist's biography*. London: Routledge.

Neisser, Hans 1934. 'General overproduction: a study of Say's Law of Markets.' *Journal of Political Economy*, vol. 42, pp. 433–65.

Neisser, Hans 1936. 'Commentary on Keynes.' *Social Research*, vol. 3, pp. 459–78.

Niehans, J. 1990. *A history of economic theory: classic contributions, 1720–1980*. Baltimore, Md.: Johns Hopkins University Press.

O'Brien, D.P. 1970. *J.R. McCulloch: a study in classical economics*. London: George Allen & Unwin.

O'Brien, D.P. 1975. *The classical economists*. Oxford: Clarendon Press.

O'Brien, D.P. 1988. 'Classical reassessments.' In Thweatt, William O. (ed.) *Classical political economy: a survey of recent literature*. Boston, Mass.: Kluwer Academic Publishers, pp. 179–220.

O'Brien, D.P. 1990. 'Marshall's work in relation to classical economics.' In Whitaker, John K. (ed.) *Centenary essays on Alfred Marshall*. Cambridge: Cambridge University Press, pp. 127–63.

O'Brien, D.P. and Darnell, A.C. 1980. 'A rejoinder' to Thweatt, William O. 'Torrens, McCulloch, and the "digression on Sismondi": whose digression? a reply.' *History of Political Economy*, vol. 12, pp. 411–19.

O'Brien, D.P. and Presley, John R. 1983. *Pioneers of modern economics in Britain*. London: Macmillan Press.

O'Leary, James J. 1942. 'Malthus and Keynes.' *Journal of Political Economy*, vol. 50, pp. 901–19.

Patinkin, Don 1948. 'Relative prices, Say's Law, and the demand for money.' *Econometrica*, vol. 16, pp. 135–54.

Patinkin, Don 1949. 'The indeterminancy of absolute prices in classical economic theory.' *Econometrica*, vol. 17, pp. 1–27.

Patinkin, Don 1951. 'The invalidity of classical monetary theory.' *Econometrica*, vol. 19, pp. 134–51.

Patinkin, Don 1965. *Money, interest and prices: an integration of monetary and value theory*, 2nd edn. New York: Harper & Row.

Patinkin, Don 1976. *Keynes' monetary thought: a study of its development*. Durham, N.C.: Duke University Press.

Patinkin, Don 1978. 'Keynes's misquotation of Mill: comment.' *Economic Journal*, vol. 88, pp. 341–2.

Patinkin, Don 1982. *Anticipations of the 'General Theory'? and other essays on Keynes*. Oxford: Basil Blackwell.

Patinkin, Don 1993. 'On the chronology of the *General Theory.*' *Economic Journal*, vol. 103, pp. 647–63.

Peach, Terry 1988. 'David Ricardo: a review of some interpretive issues.' In Thweatt, William O. (ed.) *Classical political economy: a survey of recent literature*. Boston, Mass.: Kluwer Academic Publishers, pp. 103–36.

Peach, Terry 1993. *Interpreting Ricardo*. Cambridge: Cambridge University Press.

Phipps, Cecil G. 1950. 'A note on Patinkin's "relative prices".' *Econometrica*, vol. 18, pp. 25–6.

Pigou, A.C. 1914. *Unemployment*. London: Williams & Norgate.

Pigou, A.C. [1921] 1923. 'Unemployment and the great slump.' In Pigou, A.C. *Essays in applied economics*. London: P.S. King.

Pigou, A.C. (ed.) 1925. *Memorials of Alfred Marshall*. London: Macmillan.

Pigou, A.C. 1929. *Industrial fluctuations*, 2nd ed. London: Macmillan.

Pigou, A.C. 1933. *The theory of unemployment*. London: Macmillan.

Pigou, A.C. 1936. 'Mr J.M. Keynes' general theory of employment, interest and money.' *Economica*, vol. 3 (new series), pp.115–32.

Pigou, A.C. 1951. *Keynes's 'General Theory': a retrospective view*. London: Macmillan.

Presley, John R. 1979. *Robertsonian economics: an examination of the work of Sir D.H. Robertson on industrial fluctuations*. London: Macmillan.

Presley, John R. 1983. 'D.H. Robertson, 1890–1963.' In O'Brien, D.P. and Presley, John R. (eds) *Pioneers of modern economics in Britain*. London: Macmillan, pp. 175–202.

Presley, John R. (ed.) 1992. *Essays on Robertsonian economics*. New York: St Martin's Press.

Rashid, Salim [1977] 1986. 'Malthus' model of general gluts.' In Wood, John Cunningham (ed.) *Thomas Robert Malthus: critical assessments*, 4 vols. London: Croom Helm, vol. 3, pp. 224–38.

Reddaway, W.B. [1936] 1964. 'The general theory of employment, interest and money.' In Lekachman, Robert (ed.) *Keynes' general theory: reports of three decades*. New York: St Martin's Press, pp. 99–108.

Ricardo, David 1951–73. *The works and correspondence of David Ricardo*, 11 vols. Ed. by P. Sraffa with M.H. Dobb. Cambridge: Cambridge University Press.
Vol. I: *Principles of political economy and taxation.*
Vol. II: *Notes on Malthus's principles of political economy.*
Vol. VI: *Letters, 1810–1815.*
Vol. VII: *Letters, 1816–1818.*
Vol. VIII: *Letters, 1819–June 1821.*
Vol. IX: *Letters, July 1821–1823.*
Robbins, Lionel 1958. *Robert Torrens and the evolution of classical economics.* London: Macmillan.
Robertson, D.H. 1914. Review of Tugan-Baranowsky, M. *Les crises industrielles en Angleterre*, and Aftalion, A. *Les crises périodiques de surproduction. Economic Journal*, vol. 24, pp. 81–9.
Robertson, D.H. 1915. *A study of industrial fluctuation: an enquiry into the character and causes of the so-called cyclical movements of trade.* London: P.S. King.
Robertson, D.H. 1926. *Banking policy and the price level.* London: P.S. King.
Robertson, D.H. 1931a. Review of Beveridge, W.B. *Unemployment: a problem of industry (1909 and 1930). Economic Journal*, vol. 41, pp. 74–7.
Robertson, D.H. [1930] 1931b. 'The world slump.' In Pigou, A.C. and Robertson, D.H. (eds) *Economic essays and addresses.* London: P.S. King.
Robertson, D.H. [1929] 1931c. 'The monetary doctrines of Messrs. Foster and Catchings.' In Pigou, A.C. and Robertson, D.H. (eds) *Economic essays and addresses.* London: P.S. King.
Robertson, D.H. 1933a. 'Saving and hoarding.' *Economic Journal*, vol. 43, pp. 399–413.
Robertson, D.H. 1933b. Review of Durbin, E.F.M. *Purchasing power and the trade depression: a critique of underconsumption theories. Economic Journal*, vol. 43, pp. 281–3.
Robertson, D.H. [1936] 1983. 'Some notes on Mr Keynes' general theory of employment.' Reprinted in Wood, John Cunningham (ed.) *John Maynard Keynes: critical assessments*, vol. 2. London: Croom Helm, pp. 99–114.
Robinson, Joan 1976. 'The age of growth.' In Robinson, Joan. (ed.) *Collected economic papers*, vol. 5. Oxford: Basil Blackwell, pp. 120–29.
Roll, Erich 1939. *A history of economic thought.* New York: Prentice-Hall.
Röpke, Wilhelm 1933. 'Trends in German business cycle policy'. *Economic Journal*, vol. 43, pp. 427–41.
Röpke, Wilhelm 1936. *Crises and cycles*, adapted from the German and rev. Vera C. Smith. London: William Hodge.
Rothbard, Murray N. 1992. 'Keynes, the man.' In Skousen, Mark (ed.) *Dissent on Keynes: a critical appraisal of Keynesian economics.* New York: Praeger, pp. 171–98.
Rutkoff, Peter M. and Scott, William B. 1986. *New school: a history of the New School for Social Research.* New York: The Free Press.

Rymes, Thomas K. (ed.) 1988. *Keynes's lectures, 1932–35: notes of students.* Carleton Economic Papers. Ottawa: Department of Economics, Carleton University. [These are the full transcriptions of the surviving student notes of Keynes's Michaelmas lectures given between 1932 and 1935.]

Rymes, Thomas K. (ed.) 1989. *Keynes's lectures, 1932–35: notes of a representative student.* London: Macmillan.

Samuels, Warren J. 1990. Introduction to Hutt, W.H. [1936] 1990. *Economists and the public: a study of competition and opinion.* London: Transaction Publishers.

Samuelson, Paul A. [1947] 1960. 'The *General Theory.*' In Harris, Seymour E. (ed.) *The new economics: Keynes' influence on theory and public policy.* London: Dennis Dobson, pp.145–60.

Say, Jean-Baptiste 1821. *A treatise on political economy; or the production, distribution, and consumption of wealth,* trans. from the 4th edn of the French by C.R. Prinsep, MA with notes by the translator, 2 vols. London: Longman, Hurst, Rees, Orme, and Brown.

Say, Jean-Baptiste [1821] 1967. *Letters to Mr Malthus on several subjects of political economy and on the cause of the stagnation of commerce to which is added a catechism of political economy or familiar conversations on the manner in which wealth is produced, distributed and consumed in society,* trans. John Richter. New York: Augustus M. Kelley.

Schumpeter, Joseph A. [1912] 1954. *Economic doctrine and method: an historical sketch.* London: George Allen & Unwin.

Schumpeter, Joseph A. 1933. Review of Keynes, J.M. *Essays in biography. Economic Journal,* vol. 43, pp. 652-657.

Schumpeter, Joseph A. [1954] 1986. *History of economic analysis.* London: Allen & Unwin.

Schwartz, Pedro 1972. *The new political economy of J.S. Mill.* London: Weidenfeld & Nicolson.

Senior, Nassau W. 1854. *Political economy.* London: Richard Griffin.

Sidgwick, Henry 1883. *The principles of political economy.* London: Macmillan.

Simonde de Sismondi, J.C.L. [1815] 1966. *Political economy.* New York: Augustus M. Kelley.

Simonde de Sismondi, J.C.L. 1991. *New principles of political economy.* Trans. Richard Hyse. London: Transaction.

Skidelsky, Robert 1983. *John Maynard Keynes,* vol. I: *Hopes betrayed, 1883–1920.* London: Macmillan.

Skidelsky, Robert 1992. *John Maynard Keynes,* vol. II: *The economist as saviour, 1920–1937.* London: Macmillan.

Skinner, A.S. 1967. 'Say's Law: origins and content.' *Economica,* vol. 34, pp. 153–66.

Skinner, A.S. 1969. 'Of Malthus, Lauderdale and Say's Law.' *Scottish Journal of Political Economy,* vol. 16, pp. 177–95.

Skousen, Mark 1992. 'This trumpet gives an uncertain sound: the free-market response to Keynesian economics.' In Skousen, Mark. (ed.) *Dissent on Keynes: a critical appraisal of Keynesian economics.* New York: Praeger, pp. 9–34.

Smith, Adam [1776] 1976. *An inquiry into the nature and causes of the wealth of nations*. Ed. Edwin Cannan. Chicago: University of Chicago Press.

Sowell, Thomas 1972. *Say's Law: an historical analysis*. Princeton N.J.: Princeton University Press.

Sowell, Thomas 1987. 'Say's Law.' In Eatwell, John, Milgate, Murray and Newman, Peter. (eds) *The new Palgrave: a dictionary of economics*. London: Macmillan, vol. 4, pp. 249–51.

Sowell, Thomas [1974] 1994. *Classical economics reconsidered*, with a new preface by the author. Princeton, N.J.: Princeton University Press.

Spence, William 1807. *Britain independent of commerce; or, proofs, deduced from an investigation into the true causes of the wealth of nations, that our riches, prosperity, and power, are derived from resources inherent in ourselves, and would not be affected, even though our commerce were annihilated*, 2nd edn. London: W. Savage, Bedford Bury for T. Cadell and W. Davies.

Spengler, Joseph J. 1945a. 'The physiocrats and Say's Law of Markets. I.' *Journal of Political Economy*, vol. 53, pp. 193–211.

Spengler, Joseph J. 1945b. 'The physiocrats and Say's Law of Markets. II.' *Journal of Political Economy*, vol. 53, pp. 317–47.

Spiegel, Henry William 1991. *The growth of economic thought*, 3rd edn. Durham N.C.: Duke University Press.

St Clair, Oswald [1957] 1965. *A key to Ricardo*. New York: Augustus M. Kelley.

Stamp, Josiah 1931. Review of Keynes, J.M. *A Treatise on money*. *Economic Journal*, vol. 41, pp. 241–9.

Stewart, Michael 1972. *Keynes and after*, 2nd edn. Harmondsworth, Middx: Penguin Books.

Stigler, George J. 1965. *Essays in the history of economics*. Chicago: University of Chicago Press.

Sweezy, Paul M. [1947] 1960. 'Keynes, the economist.' In Harris, Seymour E. (ed.) *The new economics: Keynes' influence on theory and public policy*. London: Dennis Dobson, pp. 102–9.

Taussig, F.W. 1927. *Principles of economics*, 3rd edn, 2 vols. New York: Macmillan.

Taylor, F.M. 1909. 'Methods of teaching elementary economics at the University of Michigan.' *Journal of Political Economy*, vol. 17, pp. 688–701. [This is part of the Proceedings of a Conference on the Teaching of Elementary Economics, *Journal of Political Economy*, vol. 17, pp. 673–727.]

Taylor, F.M. [1921] 1925. *Principles of economics*, 9th edn. New York: Ronald Press.

Thompson, J.H. 1975. 'Mill's fourth fundamental proposition: a paradox revisited.' *History of Political Economy*, vol. 7, pp. 174–92.

Thweatt, William O. 1974. 'The digression on Sismondi: by Torrens or McCulloch?' *History of Political Economy*, vol. 6, pp. 435–53.

Thweatt, William O. 1979. 'Early formulators of Say's Law.' *Quarterly Review of Economics and Business*, vol. 19, pp. 79–96.

Thweatt, William O. 1980. 'Baumol and James Mill on "Say's" Law of Markets.' *Economica*, vol. 47, pp. 467–9.

Torrens, Robert [1808] 1984a. 'The economists refuted.' In Groenewegen, P.D. (ed.) *Robert Torrens, 'The economists refuted' 1808, and other early economic writings*. Sydney: Department of Economics, University of Sydney, pp. 1–55.

Torrens, Robert [1818] 1984b. 'Strictures on Mr Ricardo's doctrine respecting exchangeable value.' In Groenewegen, P.D. (ed.) *Robert Torrens. 'The economists refuted, 1808, and other early economic writings.'* Sydney: Department of Economics, University of Sydney, pp. 56–60.

Torrens, Robert [1819] 1984c. 'Mr Owen's plans for relieving national distress.' In Groenewegen, P.D. (ed.) *Robert Torrens. 'The economists refuted, 1808, and other early economic writings.'* Sydney: Department of Economics, University of Sydney, pp. 61–79.

Torrens, Robert [1821] 1965. *An essay on the production of wealth*. New York: Augustus M. Kelley.

Viner, Jacob 1936. 'Mr Keynes on the causes of unemployment.' *Quarterly Journal of Economics*, vol. 51, pp. 147–67.

Whittaker, Edmund 1940. *A history of economic ideas*. New York: Longmans, Green.

Wicksell, Knut [1935] 1967 *Lectures on political economy. Volume II: Money*. ed. with an introduction by Lionel Robbins. London: Routledge & Kegan Paul.

Wicksteed, Philip H. [1910] 1950. *The common sense of political economy and selected papers and reviews on economic theory*, ed. with an introduction by Lionel Robbins, 2 vols. London: Routledge & Kegan Paul.

Williams, John H. [1941] 1954. 'Deficit spending.' In Haberler, Gottfried (ed.) *Readings in business cycle theory: selected by a committee of the American Economics Association*. London: George Allen & Unwin, pp. 270–90.

Winch, Donald (ed.) 1966. *James Mill: selected economic writings*. Edinburgh: Oliver & Boyd.

Winch, Donald 1987a. 'James Mill.' In Eatwell, John, Milgate, Murray and Newman, Peter. (eds) *The new Palgrave: a dictionary of economics*. London: Macmillan, vol. 3, pp. 465–6.

Winch, Donald. 1987b. *Malthus*. Oxford: Oxford University Press.

Wolfe, J.N. [1956] 1982. 'Marshall and the trade cycle.' In Wood, John Cunningham (ed.) *Alfred Marshall: critical assessments*. London: Croom Helm, vol. 4, pp. 82–94.

Wood, John Cunningham (ed.) 1983. *John Maynard Keynes: critical assessments*, 4 vols. London: Croom Helm.

Index

Printed and bound by CPI Group (UK) Ltd, Croydon, CR0 4YY

16/04/2025

14658484-0001